❖ ❖ ❖ ❖ ❖ ❖ ❖ ❖ ❖ ❖ ❖ ❖ ❖

RECOGNITION FOR
BUTCH CASSIDY, MY UNCLE

❖ ❖

WINNER, BOOK AWARD 2013 — BIOGRAPHY
presented by
Wyoming State Historical Society

BEST OF THE WEST LIST 2012 — BIOGRAPHY
presented by
True West *magazine*

FINALIST, BEN FRANKLIN AWARD 2013 — BIOGRAPHY
presented by
Independent Book Publishers' Association

"Betenson meticulously dispels myths and misinformation about Parker. All kinds of details are included that bring the stories home for 'fans' of the infamous outlaw. He tells an honest, enlightening story about his uncle."   •• *Deseret News (Sharon Haddock)*

"[This book] should be read by all who have an interest in Cassidy's life and an open mind regarding his death."   •• *True West (Mike Bell)*

"Of all of these accounts (Butch and Sundance accounts), this biographical 'portrait' is one of the most readable."
•• *Glenwood Gazette (Dave Remley)*

"This book is an enjoyable read and the new information that has been brought out on Butch Cassidy from the research that Betenson has done through the past years is appreciated. "
•• *Wild West History Association (Jim Miller)*

"Betenson has learned more than a few things about the outlaw's life from family, friends, his own research and the research of others, and sharing the story of his 'uncle' was clearly a labor of love." •• *Wild West*

❖ ❖ ❖ ❖ ❖ ❖ ❖ *Revised and Updated Printing* ❖ ❖ ❖ ❖ ❖ ❖ ❖

Butch Cassidy, My Uncle

A Family Portrait

W. J. "Bill" Betenson

HIGH PLAINS PRESS

*The Wyoming bucking horse and rider trademark in our logo is federally registered by the
State of Wyoming and is licensed for restricted use through the Secretary of State.*

COVER AND TITLE PAGE PHOTOGRAPH: Cropped from the photograph "Butch
Cassidy and friends in Fort Worth, Texas" taken in November 1900 by John
Swartz. (Courtesy Bob McCubbin Collection)

Library of Congress Cataloging-in-Publication Data

Betenson, W. J. (William James), 1965-
  Butch Cassidy, my uncle : a family portrait / W.J. "Bill" Betenson.
    p. cm.
  Includes bibliographical references and index.
  ISBN 978-1-937147-02-0 (cloth : alk. paper) --
  ISBN 978-1-937147-03-7 (trade paper : alk. paper)
1. Cassidy, Butch, b. 1866. 2. Outlaws--West (U.S.)--Biography.
3. Betenson, W. J. (William James), 1965---Family. I. Title.
  F595.C362B48 2012
  364.15'5092--dc23
  [B]
                                    2012004822

HIGH PLAINS PRESS
403 CASSA ROAD
GLENDO, WYOMING 82213
CATALOG AVAILABLE
www.highplainspress.com

In memory of Nana
For Liz, Chelsea, Will, Hayley, and Katie

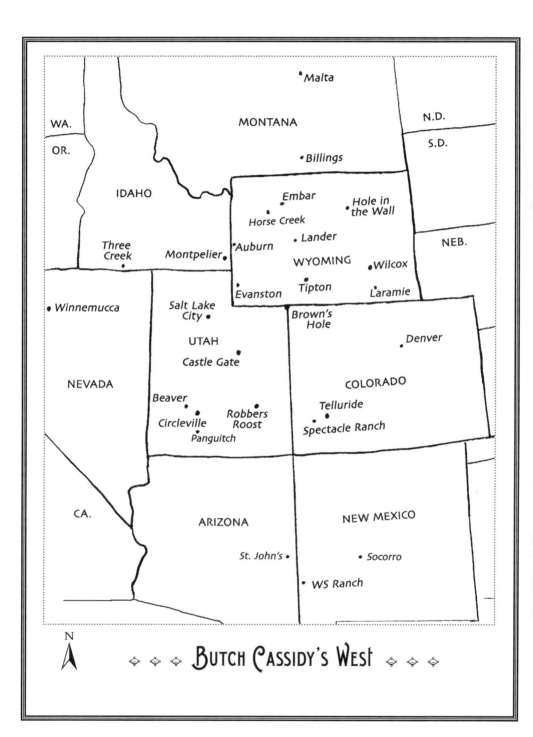

N

◇ ◇ ◇ BUTCH CASSIDY'S WEST ◇ ◇ ◇

Contents

(continued)

Foreword: Agree to Disagree

A ROBBERY IS REPORTED in the wilds of Bolivia. Two men are arrested. A short time later two other men are surprised in an isolated village some distance away. A gunfight erupts there, and those men die in the aftermath. Their bodies are buried in the little country cemetery as two "John Does." Meanwhile, the first two suspects are released into anonymity.

Can we, a century hence, say whose blood was spilled in that far off Bolivian village?

A prodigal son returns to stand over his mother's grave, to share his remorse with a Utah family he had left behind in his wayward youth. None of those present now remain to verify their bittersweet reunion.

Did it not happen?

For years there had been confusion and conflict about what actually became of the man known to the world as Butch Cassidy, Robin Hood of the American West. The now-cult cinema *Butch Cassidy and the Sundance Kid* opened in 1969 with these words on the screen: "Not that it matters, but most of what follows is true." Not all is as it appears to be. Distance, the passage of time, and the often fallible filters of human perception darken our rearward view. Chronicle leads to commentary, report to editorial. Egos engage. Opinions leap in conjecture up a ladder of abstraction, rising far above what plain facts remain. Debates are buffeted in clever turns of phrase.

Truth is not argument. Where can we turn to review the record, to assess the gaps, to expand our understanding. Who can help us sort fact from conjecture?

Bill Betenson is the great-grandson of Butch Cassidy's younger sister, Lula Parker Betenson. His own quest for answers has been a lifelong pursuit. His writing reveals a comprehensive, objective, and balanced approach, an open discourse of reason. He equally covers the various and at times conflicting accounts, fairly reconsiders the patchwork evidence of record. If he errs, it is in his reticence to forcefully state a position, respectfully deferring to the reader's conclusions. There is no "spin," no argument to defend, no pronouncements of omnipotent authority in the realm of investigation. There are no purposeful omissions of embarrassing information which conflicts with a predisposed position.

"We can agree to disagree," he often has said to proponents of varied theories, "and still be friends."

✧ ✧ ✧

BILL BETENSON IS A refreshing light of reason in an area of historical investigation astutely assessed by the dean of Western historians Ramon Adams: "Nowhere has research been so inadequate or writing so careless as in the accounts of western outlaws and gunmen."

The reader will come away with a heightened respect for the integrity of a great-grandmother who nurtured this fair and thoughtful man, and with insight in no little measure into what constituted the character and intelligence of that other scion of the family tree, Robert LeRoy Parker, alias Butch Cassidy.

LARRY POINTER
author of *In Search of Butch Cassidy*
Billings, Montana

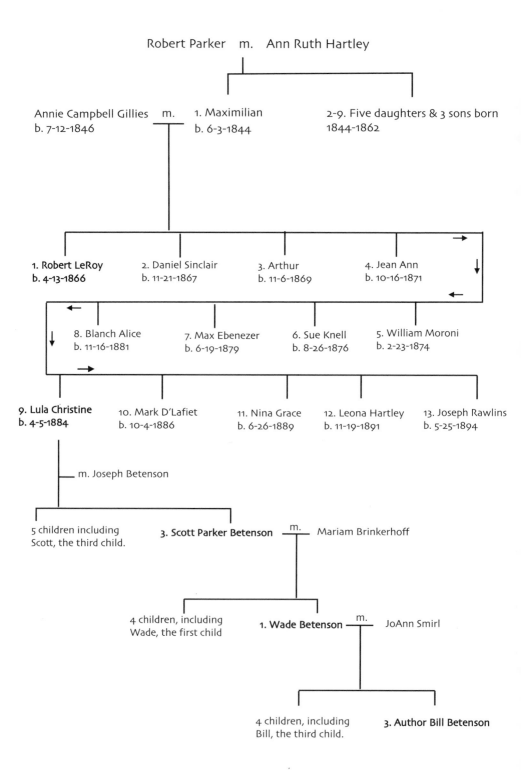

Robert Parker　m.　Ann Ruth Hartley

Annie Campbell Gillies　m.
b. 7-12-1846

1. Maximilian
b. 6-3-1844

2-9. Five daughters & 3 sons born
1844-1862

1. Robert LeRoy
b. 4-13-1866

2. Daniel Sinclair
b. 11-21-1867

3. Arthur
b. 11-6-1869

4. Jean Ann
b. 10-16-1871

8. Blanch Alice
b. 11-16-1881

7. Max Ebenezer
b. 6-19-1879

6. Sue Knell
b. 8-26-1876

5. William Moroni
b. 2-23-1874

9. Lula Christine
b. 4-5-1884

10. Mark D'Lafiet
b. 10-4-1886

11. Nina Grace
b. 6-26-1889

12. Leona Hartley
b. 11-19-1891

13. Joseph Rawlins
b. 5-25-1894

m. Joseph Betenson

5 children including
Scott, the third child.

3. Scott Parker Betenson　m.　Mariam Brinkerhoff

4 children, including
Wade, the first child

1. Wade Betenson　m.　JoAnn Smirl

4 children, including
Bill, the third child.

3. Author Bill Betenson

1. Butch and Me

I WAS FOUR YEARS old at the time, yet I distinctly remember going with my family to a small theater in Utah for a private showing of the movie *Butch Cassidy and the Sundance Kid*. My mother later told me she and my father couldn't find a babysitter that night, so they had to take me along. I am grateful that all of the babysitters were busy because I will never forget that evening. I loved Western movies, and here I was watching one about my own relative—Butch Cassidy. And to make matters more impressive, parts of the movie were filmed right here in my home state of Utah—Butch Cassidy's home state too. Places I had seen in real life were on the screen. People I had heard my family discuss so often were on the screen. Amusingly, as a four-year-old, the part that left me the most wide-eyed was not the daring exploits of Butch and Sundance but the risqué scene when Etta Place undresses for the Sundance Kid.

A few weeks later, I watched my great-grandmother, Lula Betenson, on a national talk show, *The Mike Douglas Show*, discussing her brother Butch Cassidy, while a clip from the newly-released movie showed Butch and Sundance jumping off a cliff. A few days later, she was on the *Today Show* in New York.

Lula was unflappable in the face of all the publicity surrounding the movie. She loved to tell the story of meeting Paul Newman on the set of the movie. Paul jokingly greeted Lula with a smile and said, "Hi, I'm Butch." The eighty-five-year-old Lula grinned and replied without missing a beat, "Hi, I'm your sister."

It was an exciting time for me and my whole family. I spent nights dreaming of riding hell for leather with Uncle Butch and the gang.

✧ ✧ ✧

BUTCH CASSIDY'S REAL name was Robert LeRoy Parker. He was the oldest of thirteen children. My great-grandmother, Lula Parker, was his younger sister, born eighteen years after he was. Three more children were born into the family after her.

Just before I was born my parents moved from their hometown of Kanab, Utah, so as I was growing up we made regular trips "back home." We usually stopped at Lula's house on the way. Lula always had treats waiting for us kids.

I could never seem to get enough of the stories of Uncle Butch and the Parker family. I wish I had asked my great-grandmother more questions.

As a child I thought Lula, or "Nana" as we affectionately called her, was really old and wrinkled, but she always made me feel important and I loved to go to her house. She was working on a book about her famous brother. It seemed to take forever before it was published as *Butch Cassidy, My Brother*. I naively believed it would clear up all controversy about Butch. I have since come to realize that no book will ever do that.

I remember during the early 1970s my great-uncle and -aunt, Mark and Viv Betenson, worked hard to restore the old Parker homestead cabin in Circleville that has become known as the "Butch Cassidy Boyhood Home." Mark and Viv treated me like one of their own grandchildren, and I loved to stay with them.

The Butch Cassidy Boyhood Home was opened to the public for tours with two tiny rooms filled with Parker family heirlooms. I was excited to help Aunt Viv wait on customers and met numerous tourists. I saved my money and bought a copy of the small book, *Butch Cassidy and His Home,* that they sold at the cabin for fifty cents. I was eager to ask Nana to autograph it. She wrote, "To my Billie Boy—Love great-grandmother Betenson." Aunt Viv gave me a t-shirt that I proudly wore with Butch's famous mug shot on it. Unfortunately, a short time later, thieves broke into the cabin and stole all the family heirlooms. They've never come up for auction that I know of, and it bothers me to think they were taken away so the family and the public can no longer enjoy them.

My favorite time to visit Uncle Mark and Aunt Viv was in the fall when my dad, brother, and I went up on the mountain west of Circleville to a place called Dog Valley on the old Parker homestead to hunt for deer. Uncle Mark often stopped by on his horse. We stayed in an old cabin Mark had built and playfully called the "New Lennox Hotel." It was full of mice and I heard them scampering about when the light was turned off at night. Dog Valley held special significance to me because Uncle Butch had been there. Often, in the evenings, conversations turned to the old days and Butch.

When discussion of outlaws in the family came up, the focus was always on Butch Cassidy. I didn't learn about the outlaw days of Dan Parker, the brother of Butch and Lula, until much later.

Lula passed away in May of 1980 at the age of ninety-six. She'd had good health, and if I live to be that old, I want to enjoy life like Lula did. I visited her in the hospital shortly before she passed. She had suffered a stroke a few days before. She looked at me and tried to talk, but said nothing I could understand. I just wanted to pick her up and hold and comfort her. I was proud to help carry her casket at her funeral as a pallbearer.

✧ ✧ ✧

As I GREW OLDER, I started to read more about Butch. During college, time was scarce as I married, we started our family, and I worked my way through engineering school. After I graduated, I rediscovered how much fun it is to read a book without having to derive an equation. I fell in love with books.

The more I read about Butch, the more I decided that I was going to have to do my own research. Nearly every book or article seemed to contradict another. I learned more about Dan Parker and his troubles as an outlaw and knew I had to find out more about Butch, Dan, and the rest of Parker family. I had a unique opportunity to talk with family members in a way no other researcher or writer could. And the more questions I asked, the more things I learned and the more questions I had.

At one point, I decided that something needed to be written about Dan Parker. Nana was close to the pain and embarrassment of having outlaws in the family; as a result she was extremely cautious about what she said and wrote. For instance, she mentioned little about Dan in her book because she was concerned about protecting his children. But enough time has passed that Dan's descendants now have decided that his life story needs to be told because it illustrates that people can overcome the troubles of their youth, even the nightmare of a life sentence in prison. By February 2007, I had compiled much research, but I knew it would not be really complete until I traveled to Argentina to see Butch's ranch there. Nothing will ever compare to that grand and informative trip and the wonderful people I got to know there.

The opportunity to meet warm people who have shared personal family stories of Butch is the best part of researching Butch Cassidy. He was certainly well-liked and helped many people along the way.

Butch wasn't the typical outlaw of the old west. He wasn't the killer that many outlaws were. He stood out as one of the "good guy" outlaws. His up-bringing in a warm loving family probably had a lot to do with that. I have always thought if I had to pick an outlaw to be related to, I would pick Butch. As author and historian Charles Kelly said, based on his research and inter-views with many old timers, Butch "was considered a gentleman outlaw. He never drank to excess, was always courteous to women, was free with money when he had it, and extremely loyal to his friends." Good traits for anyone.

I've delayed writing this book for too long; the story is no longer a huge family embarrassment like it was for great-grandma Lula's generation. It's time I put on paper what I know.

2. Butch's Heritage

THE STORY OF Robert LeRoy Parker (later known as Butch Cassidy) begins with his namesake and grandfather, Robert Parker, who was born March 29, 1820, in Burnley, Lancashire, England.[1] Lancashire was a textile district; as a result Robert worked in a local textile factory where he became an excellent weaver.[2] Robert also formally studied art and music and was well-versed in the humanities. He developed a love and talent for singing.

He met his future wife, Ann Hartley, in the textile factory. Ann was also born in Burnley, on March 22, 1819.[3]

Starting in the late 1830s, the Church of Jesus Christ of Latter-Day Saints (Mormons) sent missionaries to England to teach, convert, and encourage the new members to migrate to the Salt Lake Valley in Utah Territory. The Parker and the Hartley families had traditionally been strict members of the Church of England. Robert's family disowned him when he joined the Mormon church on November 7, 1840. No longer having a place to stay, he went to live with the missionaries at the mission home. He helped the missionaries in their proselytizing efforts by singing hymns, which drew large crowds to street corners where the missionaries could then begin their teaching.

Robert invited Ann to a meeting where the missionaries were speaking; in time she joined the Mormon church.

Robert and Ann were married on May 25, 1843. They were appointed to preside over the mission home together. She used her excellent cooking and homemaking skills to care for the missionaries. The young couple soon moved to Accrington, Lancashire, where Robert once again found a job in a textile mill. While the Parkers lived in Accrington five children were born to them: Maximilian born on June 8, 1844,[4] Martha Alice, Margaret Ann, Arthur, and Emily. In 1853, the Parkers moved to Preston where another daughter, Ada, was born. In Preston, they prepared to emigrate to

Maximilian Parker
B.   8 June 1844
D. 28 July   1938

Robert Parker
B. 29 March 1820
D. 24 Feb.   1901

Ann Ruth Hartley
B. 22 March 1819
D. 25 Jan.   1899

Robert LeRoy Parker
aka Butch Cassidy
B. 13 April   1866

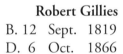

Robert Gillies
B. 12 Sept. 1819
D. 6   Oct.   1866

Annie Gillies
B.   12 July 1846
D.   1 May 1905

Jane Sinclair
B.   5 May 1819
D. 25 Aug. 1899

America. Two of their children, Margaret Ann and Emily, died before they left England.[5]

While in Preston, the Parkers assisted the Mormon missionaries and often invited them stay in their home. Young Maximilian, or "Maxi" as he was known, was given the task of shining the shoes of the missionaries, a job he did not relish.[6]

Robert arranged for Maxi to apprentice at the age of only nine or ten in the textile mill where Robert worked. Maxi was unhappy, and, to his family's disgrace, he ran away from the mill one day. Robert severely punished the boy, however Maxi would still not return to the mill. As a result, the Parkers sped up the process by selling their home and possessions in preparation for the journey to America. All was sold at a loss.[7]

The Mormon church, under the direction of President Brigham Young, instituted a handcart program in 1856 as a means for members to make the trek to the Salt Lake Valley with a smaller investment in travel. The Parkers packed their remaining possessions accordingly[8] and left much behind. Ann, however, could not leave behind her precious silverware and paintings, including a painting done by Robert.

On March 22, 1856, the Parkers boarded the ship *Enoch Train* at Liverpool and set sail the next day.[9] The ship had a total of 534 Mormons, most from England.

The ship arrived at Constitution Wharf in Boston on May 1 of that year. The Parkers boarded a train in New York City destined for Iowa City.

Eleven days later, the train arrived in Iowa City where the emigrants waited nearly a month while workers finished the construction of the handcarts. They finally departed on June 11, 1856, with the second handcart company, the Daniel D. MacArthur Company. The company was made up of 221 persons.

Robert pulled the handcart, while Maxi, who by then was twelve years old, helped his mother push. Ten-year-old Martha Alice was assigned to look after Arthur, who was six, and baby Ada rode in the handcart.

Less than a month into the trek near present day Anita, Iowa, Arthur became lost.[10] Journals recorded the event differently. Late in the afternoon of July 1, the handcart company stopped for the day. One diary states that both Robert and his youngest son, Arthur, had been ill with a fever. Arthur sat down to rest early in the day and became separated from the travelers.[11]

Arthur Parker, brother of
Maxi Parker, uncle of
Butch. (*Author's collection*)

Another journal states that after stopping for the day, the children were playing a short distance away while the parents made preparations for the evening
meal. Suddenly, a rainstorm sent the children running back to camp, but without Arthur.[12] Another pioneer journal simply recorded, "Brother Parker's little boy, age six, was lost."[13]

The youngsters did not know Arthur's whereabouts. Ann began calling
and searching, trying not to panic. Soon others in the company joined in the
search for little Arthur. The hunt continued throughout the night and into
the next day without any success.

The head of the company, Elder MacArthur, insisted that the company
continue onward because food was in limited supply, and they could not be
delayed indefinitely. Robert decided that he would walk back, retracing their
steps, and look for Arthur. He'd catch up with the company later. Ann pinned
a red shawl on his shoulders and told him to wave the shawl as he approached
the camp on his return as a sign that Arthur was all right, or, if he found the
boy too late and he had died, to wrap him in the shawl to bury him. Robert
assured Ann that he would find the boy and catch up with the company.[14]

Ann watched as Robert's image disappeared into the distance and then
pulled the handcart on, trying to hide her despair from the children. At the

end of each day, she found the highest point to look into the distance for her husband and son. Ann prayed and tried to sleep. She worried that Indians or wild animals had killed them both. Ann persuaded the company to travel as slowly as possible. She and her family took the last position in the company so she could watch for their return, and, by the end of the each day, the Parker family was caked with dust.

By July 5 Ann had almost given up hope. At the end of the day she found a high place to search the horizon. Suddenly, Ann thought she saw something in the distance. When she looked closer, it had disappeared. Her heart sank, and she knelt down in sorrow and prayed. Finally she knew she must return to camp. Taking one last look, she again saw a man in the distance. As the image got closer, she could see that he held the red shawl in his arms. She started to scream, and, as others from the handcart company came running, Ann saw that Robert was carrying Arthur in his arms. Ann's heart filled with joy and gratitude.

A pioneer journal recorded: "Robert Parker came into camp with his little boy that had been lost. Great joy throughout the camp. The mother's joy, I cannot describe."[15]

Robert recounted that on the second day of his search he had come to a trading post where he learned that a woodcutter had found a little boy suffering from hunger and exposure. The woodcutter and his wife had cared for the boy with much tenderness. Arthur told how big dogs had barked at him in the dark. The dogs had most likely been wolves or coyotes.

The Parkers continued on their journey, reaching Florence (Winter Quarters), Nebraska, on July 17, 1856. Travel became much more difficult after Florence. Vegetation and wildlife were scarce, and the route led through sand and numerous streams. As the company neared Fort Laramie, Robert experienced trouble walking due to his sore and infected feet.[16] Ann traded her precious silverware and valuables for food at the fort.[17]

Robert's feet continued to worsen until he was forced to ride in one of the wagons. Ann and the children were left to pull the handcart. Later Ann related to her grandchildren that the sun, the physical work, and poor diet changed her appearance so much that she didn't recognize her own reflection in the water one day. She continued to pull the handcart without her husband's assistance. In Echo Canyon, about fifty miles from the Salt Lake Valley, Ann told her children, "I can go no farther; we will wait here until someone comes for us." Another account says that Ann was so exhausted from pulling the handcart, that she pushed it off a cliff near the entrance to the Salt Lake Valley. Either way, it was an act of determination and courage. Later that evening, a carriage came by, and the driver stopped to see if he could help. He lifted Ann and her children into the carriage and brought them into the valley on September 27, 1856, one day after the main contingent of the handcart company had arrived.

The Parkers recovered from their ailments and infirmities by late fall of 1856 and were "called" by the church to move south to American Fork. Robert taught school for a short time before moving farther south to Beaver City, Utah. Robert worked in the woolen mill in Beaver, utilizing his skill as a weaver. Three more children were born to the Parkers in Beaver: Robert, Ellen, and Ruth Caroline. Little Robert only lived thirteen months.

The Parkers had arrived in Beaver late in the year and lived in a dugout the first winter. The next summer the family built a one-room cabin, and the following year added two more rooms. On July 24, 1865, Robert was "Orator" in the festivities commemorating the arrival of the 1847 pioneers to Utah.[18] The celebration included music and artillery firing at daylight along with a parade and 120 school children singing.

Later in the year of 1865, Robert and Ann moved south to Washington, Utah. Robert was asked to work in the newly opened cotton and silk mill. Early in 1878, Robert was called to a short home mission in St. George.[19] By mid-year he was appointed postmaster of the town of Washington.[20] In addition, he ran a store in town.[21]

Robert conducted the Washington choir, which was said to be well received, "particularly when Robert Parker conducted it."[22]

Robert was appointed Election Judge in Washington in both 1882 and 1885.[23] In 1883 he was appointed Deputy Registration Officer of the Washington Precinct.[24] He was excused from serving on a jury due to his age (sixty-one) in 1881.[25]

In spite of his respectability, Robert developed some legal problems of his own. He had at least one polygamist wife, Jensenie "Sena" Hansmire Madsen.[26] In October 1887, the U.S. Marshal came after him for cohabitation. As postmaster, he went outside to meet the buckboard wagon, thinking it was bringing the mail. Deputy Marshal Armstrong of Beaver surprised him and said, "I am here to place you under arrest, Mr. Parker: you will please

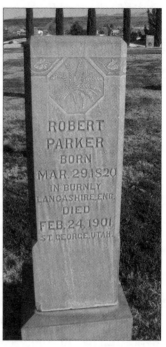

Robert Parker's grave in Washington, Utah.
(Author's photograph)

come with me?" Robert responded, "Do you mind if I get my coat and hat?" The marshal said, "No, but don't keep me waiting." Robert went in his house, grabbed his coat and hat, and ran out his back door. He was said to have gone through a "cockle-bur patch" and a few clung to him. He hid in a neighbor's cellar and avoided arrest, but received the nickname "Cockleberry Jim" afterwards. Sena Madsen, his plural wife, was also arrested, but later released when the authorities could not find Robert.[27] Sena was described as being "a very good looking young woman" and ironically was employed as a cook for U.S. Marshal Frank H. Dyer of Utah.[28]

Court records indicate that Robert was indicted for polygamy on December 9, 1887. The second wife named in the indictment was Sena Madsen.[29]

Robert was sent on a mission to his homeland of England to escape further prosecution, however law officials continued to keep tabs on his movements.[30] On March 2, 1888, he was released from laboring in Liverpool, England, and reassigned to Manchester, England.[31]

Robert returned home and was later indicted with two charges of postal fraud, once in 1888 and again in 1889, but went into hiding and may have returned to England.[32] Both Mrs. Parker and Sena Madsen (with the last name now listed as Gulbransen) were subpoenaed for the 1888 case. The 1889 case was dismissed later by the judge.[33] One wonders if the postal fraud cases were trumped up as an additional means to take him into custody.

✧ ✧ ✧

IN 1891, AT THE age of seventy-one, Robert was attending the April Mormon Conference in Salt Lake City at the tabernacle and was arrested upon his departure by two deputy marshals. The charge was unlawful cohabitation. He was taken to the penitentiary and held for three days until he paid a $1,000 bond with a promise to return to the next term of court.[34] His prison record states that he was 5 foot, 7 ½ inches tall with a dark complexion with blue eyes and brown hair. His weight was 155 lbs. His left hand was described as being deformed with the little finger missing at the first joint. He had a scar on his right wrist. His shoe size was No. 7.[35] Some authors, such as Charles Kelly, have written that Robert Parker died on the plains while crossing in early snows, but this is far from the truth as he lived the remainder of his days in Washington, Utah. Both Robert and Ann are buried in the Washington City Cemetery. Ann died on January 25, 1899, and Robert died on February 24, 1901.[36]

MEANWHILE, MAXIMILIAN, the father of Robert LeRoy Parker (Butch), had grown to manhood. At age eighteen, Maxi made two trips to St. Louis, Missouri, to assist Mormon emigrants making the trek to Utah.[37] When his parents moved to Washington, Maxi stayed in Beaver. He married a young lass of Scottish decent, Annie Campbell Gillies, on July 12, 1865, in Salt Lake City in the Temple endowment house.[38] Maxi later served in the Utah Indian Blackhawk War. When he was older he looked forward to reunions with his fellow veterans.[39] Maximilian received his United States citizenship on May 26, 1887.[40]

Arthur Parker, the child lost on the plains, as a teenager of seventeen, went to California with a friend for work. He was never heard from again. Part of their wagon was discovered burned, and it was assumed that they had been killed by Indians.[41]

Maximilian grew to be a quiet unassuming man. He wasn't the stern disciplinarian that his father had been and his children loved him. In his old age, he kept a large garden while a widower in Circleville and was known as the "silent giver." He quietly shared his garden with the widows in town. He was known to play marbles on the ground with the neighborhood boys in his nineties. In 1937 on his ninety-third birthday, the family had a large celebration for him, as Maxi was the oldest man living in Piute County.[42] Maxi reached his ninety-fourth birthday, still the oldest living man in the county.[43] He lived another month and passed away on July 28, 1938.[44]

Robert LeRoy Parker's mother was born as Ann Campbell Gillies on July 12, 1846.[45] The family had moved from Scotland to Newcastle upon Tyne[46] in Northern England shortly before her birth.[47]

When Ann was eight years old her family emigrated to America as Mormon converts. Ann traveled with her parents, Robert and Jane, along with her siblings, John Moroni, Daniel, and Christine, and her aged grandfather, John, who was nearly eighty-four years old at the time.

The family left Liverpool, England, on the ship *Samuel Curling* on April 19, 1856.[48] The ship carried 707 Mormons under the direction of Elder Dan Jones. The majority of the passengers were recent converts from Wales where Elder Jones had labored. The passengers were divided up into eleven wards and took turns cooking and eating their meals. During the voyage several severe storms were encountered and the "Saints" turned to prayer to calm the waters.

The *Samuel Curling*, a sailing vessel, was chartered by the Mormon Church to carry the Saints, as they were known. Faster steamships were available at the time, but due to the tight finances of the Mormon Church, sailing vessels were chartered. The journey across the Atlantic took four weeks and in some cases longer.[49] The emigrants endured sea sickness for days and often weeks due to high winds and waves. In times of low wind the journey seemed to pass extremely slowly. Some journals describe being passed by steamships at a "tearing pace."[50] During these calm periods, the travelers made tents for the coming journey across the plains. The pioneers danced to fiddles and tambourines for fun. The children played marbles and skipped rope.[51]

The ship arrived in Boston on May 23, 1856. The emigrants described joy at setting their feet on dry land once again after being on the ship for over a month. About four hundred of the Saints immediately traveled by rail to Iowa City within days of their arrival. In an eight-day journey they traveled through "Albany and Buffalo, New York; Cleveland and Toledo, Ohio; and Chicago and Rock Island, Illinois." Part of the journey was made in cattle cars and the emigrants used their luggage for seats.[52] The Gilles family arrived in Iowa City on June 1 which put them in Iowa City at the same time as the Parkers who left in the second handcart company on June 11. The Gillies, however, stayed in Iowa City for nearly two months and finally left with the Hodgett wagon train on July 30, 1856. The Hodgett Company was made up of 150 individuals and about thirty-three wagons pulled by oxen.

The Hodgett wagon train along with the Hunt wagon train traveled with the ill-fated Martin and Willie handcart companies which experienced bad weather and suffering in Wyoming due to their late departure and early winter storms. The wagon trains were made up of a combination of Church owned wagons plus wagons and teams purchased by families financially able to afford them. The Gillies family was among those who purchased their own team and wagon.

However, the Gillies group did not remain with the Hodgett wagon train. They turned around and returned to Iowa City at some point and decided to try again the following year.[53] That decision may have saved their lives as many from the Martin and Willie companies later perished. It is estimated that between 135 and 150 people[54] from the Martin, Hodgett, and Hunt companies lost their lives.

At what point the family turned back is not recorded, but today a visitor center at Martin's Cove, Wyoming, lists the Gillies family on a historical marker as survivors of the tragedy there: "Robert (35), Jane (35), Moroni (10), Ann (9), Daniel (7) and Christian (3)."[55] However, it is unlikely that they actually traveled that far west and then turned back, especially with the winter storms and Indian problems that faced travelers.

The following June the Gillies family joined the Jesse Bigler Martin wagon train company which departed Iowa City on June 1, 1857. The company was comprised of 192 individuals and thirty-four oxen-driven wagons.[56]

Around July 1, Robert's father John passed away at the age of eighty-five, while the company was camped one mile west of the Elk Horn River in present day Nebraska.[57]

On July 16, Captain J. B. Martin wrote in his journal that there was "grumbling and discontented spirit in camp" and named Robert Gillies as one of the perpetrators. The following day it was decided that those perpetrators would return while the rest of the company continued on to the Salt Lake Valley.[58] Apparently the company had lost a number of cattle, and the captain used this shortage of stock as an excuse to send discontented families back east.

It is not known when or how the Gilles family finally got to the Salt Lake Valley, but they were living in Beaver City, Utah Territory, when the 1860 census was taken. So after two unsuccessful starts Robert LeRoy Parker's ancestors somehow made it to Utah.

The journey across the plains served to strengthen the faith of the Gillies family, and Ann, who became the mother of Robert LeRoy Parker later known as Butch Cassidy, reflected upon the experience the remainder of her life.

✧ ✧ ✧

AFTER MAXI AND ANNIE were married on Annie's birthday in 1865, they remained active in plays and performances. Maxi was apparently quite a co-median. Annie was sociable and often had a song on her lips.[59]

Robert Gillies was a cabinetmaker and skilled carpenter. Some of his furniture still exists today. On a business trip back to Woods Cross, he died of pneumonia on October 6, 1866.[60] He was only forty-six years old. The location of Robert Gillies grave is unknown.

Jane Sinclair Gillies, Annie's mother, remained in Beaver the rest of her life. She lived to be eighty-six.[61] She was active in the Mormon church, serving as a youth leader.

One author mistakenly wrote that Annie lost part of her ear to frostbite on the trail. Photographs show her favoring one side of her head. However, Lula wrote that the Gillies "suffered no lasting ill effects from the journey."[62]

The *Southern Utonian* reported the true story on April 20, 1888:

Serious and Appalling Accident.
A Terrible Ending of a Night of Pleasure.
Mrs. Annie Parker Has Nearly One-Half Her Face Torn Off

Mr. Max Parker, who lives about one and half miles from the town of Circleville, east of Beaver, was returning home about 3 o'clock Tuesday morning from a social gathering held in Circleville. He had his wife and two year old child with him in his buggy. The night was dark and it seems that as the team was jogging along one wheel of the vehicle struck a rock, thus throwing Mrs. Parker, who also held the child, out of her seat, As she went out of the buggy she threw the little one, which, by the way, was not injured in the least.

From the injuries received it seems evident that as she fell she must have turned around, for the wheel seems to have struck her just by the eye and grazed the left temple. The skin was peeled off the whole side of the face and the cartilage of the ear so badly cut and mu-tilated that the organ had to be entirely cut away. As soon as possible Mr. Parker got his wife comfortably fixed in the wagon and came to Beaver, calling on Dr. Christian who made examinations and dressed the wound.

The home in Beaver, Utah, where Robert LeRoy Parker (Butch Cassidy) was born. The right hand side of the house was the original building where Butch was born. (*Author's photograph*)

> The doctor found the skin of the left side of the face peeled off and rolled around the ear, or what there was left of it. He also found three rents in the scalp extending nearly to the crown. These were sewed up and the rest of the mutilated skin was cut away. The doctor describes it as being the most appalling sight he [had] seen, and says that though the lady is so terribly injured she may survive.[63]

Annie fully recovered from the accident. The child in the newspaper article would have been Mark Parker who was born in 1886. Mark survived without any known lasting effects. One relative recently confirmed that her mother, a daughter of Annie, had told her about the incident but told her not to talk about it.[64]

Annie was devout to her Mormon religion and loved her family. She had thirteen children. It broke her heart to have sons who were outlaws. Lula said she walked the field of their ranch crying over her wayward sons.

Annie's brother, Daniel Sinclair Gillies lived in Circleville, but in 1900 he bought a ranch on the San Rafael River[65] not far from the Robbers Roost area and moved there. Dan Parker (Butch's brother) was named after his uncle. Some accounts report that Butch used the Gillies ranch as a hideout, but, by 1900, Butch had made himself scarce from the Robbers Roost area.

3. Growing Up, 1866~1884

MAXI AND ANNIE'S first child was born on Friday the 13th, April 1866, in Beaver, Utah. He was named Robert LeRoy Parker after his two grandfathers, Robert Parker and Robert Gillies.[1] His grandfather Robert Parker traveled from Washington, Utah, to Beaver to bless and name the new baby according to Mormon tradition.[2]

There has been some discrepancy about his proper name. The Pinkerton National Detective Agency said his correct name was "George LeRoy Parker."[3] George was an alias that he started using in Wyoming as a young man, when he went by George Cassidy. The error has been picked up and used by several authors until his sister Lula attempted to set the record straight in her book in 1975.

Robert was born in the home of his maternal grandmother Jane Sinclair Gillies. Robert Gillies likely built the stone home after arriving in Beaver years before. It still stands today, though of course, has been updated.

Only nine days after little Robert's birth, his father, Maximilian, was fighting an Indian battle in the Utah Blackhawk War. Maxi was only twenty-two when he enlisted into the command of Edward Dalton on March 21, 1866, in Beaver. The company marched to Fort Sanford on the other side of the Tushar Mountains approximately seven miles north of Panguitch, Utah.[4] Maximilian's periodic absence from home was a pattern that continued for many years.

The 1870 U.S. Census shows Robert LeRoy, four years of age, living with his mother and grandmother in Beaver City, Utah. By then, Annie Parker had three sons, Robert, Daniel, and Arthur, and resided with her mother, Jane Gillies, and younger brother Daniel Sinclair Gillies.[5] Maximilian was working and living out-of-town at the time of the July 1870 census.

Robert's first thirteen years were in Beaver City. When Robert was eleven, Beaver was brimming with excitement over the trials of John D. Lee in 1877. Lee led the killing of immigrants from Arkansas traveling by wagon train in the Mountain Meadows Massacre near Cedar City, Utah, in 1857. Lee was found guilty of murder on March 10, 1877. He was sentenced to be shot on March 23, 1877. A petition to the Governor was quickly passed around Beaver City pleading for Lee's pardon as he was "one of fifty men" who were "equally guilty of the crime" and because he was in poor health. The Parkers and Gillies signed the petition along with 270 others.[6] The signatures of the Parkers appear to have been signed by Max Parker. The Parker names included Max, Annie, Robert (11), Daniel (10) and Arthur (9). Another petition was signed in the town of Panguitch for a total of 514 signatures. The Governor agreed to pardon Lee if he gave a full confession and named the other participants, but Lee refused and was executed.[7]

Fort Cameron, a military fort, was on the outskirts of town adding a wild saloon element to the little Mormon community and giving young Robert the opportunity to witness the seamier side of life. Robert's father, Maxi, worked on the construction of Fort Cameron.[8]

Maximilian delivered mail by horseback over the Tushar Mountain from Beaver to Panguitch. He looked over Circle Valley and decided he wanted to move his family there. (Several friends and families had already relocated from Beaver to Circleville as Lula said they were among friends when they made the move in 1879.[9]) The Parkers may have lived for a short time in a cabin north of Circleville "under the hill to get feed for their cattle," before buying a ranch three miles south of Circleville.[10] Maxi bought the ranch from a man named James who had previously built a two-room log cabin on the property.[11]

The main room of the cabin served as a living room and kitchen and held a fireplace. The small room was Maxi and Annie's bedroom. Annie covered the rough log ceiling with large pieces of cheap white cloth known as "factory." The floor was covered with homemade rag carpets with straw underneath them. Lula said every spring the carpets were cleaned outside, the straw was replaced, and then the carpets were tacked back down to the floor. The beds were filled with cornhusks or straw. Annie hung lace curtains on the windows. Soon, Maxi built a separate kitchen on the east and two additional rooms on the south that were used as bedrooms for the girls. The boys slept in the attic. Young Robert carved his initials on a beam in the attic.[12] (I remember this beam on display at the cabin, but it was stolen with the other family heirlooms.) In the summer, the boys slept outside under the stars.

Maxi and Annie had a tough go on the new ranch. The first year Maxi planted wheat; the infamous wind which seems ever-present in Circleville, blew it "right out of the ground." The second time the wind destroyed the new sprouts and finally with the third planting Maxi was able to harvest the wheat.[13]

The first winter in Circle Valley (1879-80) "was perhaps the most severe recorded. The extreme cold wiped out the herd of cattle except for two cows, named Hutch and Sal. The family didn't recover financially from this setback for years."[14]

The Parkers homesteaded fifty acres of land adjoining their ranch to the north. Maxi built a small cabin on the land where they lived a short time to meet homestead requirements. Then they returned to the other cabin that still stands today.[15] Maxi worked hard to clear the land with a "grubbing hoe."

Later they lost the additional fifty acres in a dispute. Lula said that the dispute went to a "Church Court" and the Bishop ruled against them. Maxi likely would have left the Church if it had not been for his wife. Lula explained that the Circleville saloonkeeper James Whittaker told Annie that he wanted to lease the land for a mill and would pay her $40. Annie signed the papers as Maxi was out-of-town working, only to discover later, to her horror, that she had signed a deed turning the land over to the saloonkeeper.[16]

❧ ❧ ❧

ROBERT LEROY GREW up in a happy home. Bob, as he was called by his siblings, adored his mother. Lula stated, "When he was in a frolicsome mood, he waltzed her around the room, then picked her up and set her on the table. 'Come on, kids,' he announced, 'Bring the crown, Ma's the queen.'"

The Parker ranch was somewhat isolated from town, so the family had to furnish their own fun. Gathering together each night, Maximilian and Annie sang and told stories to the children. Music seemed to be an integral part of growing up in the Parker family.[17]

Bob loved his younger siblings who looked up to him. Bob's next youngest brother, Dan, was especially fond of Bob and wanted to mimic the things he did.[18] Bob and Dan grew to be about the same height. Bob was recorded as being 5 foot 9 inches in 1894 while Dan was recorded as being 5 foot 9 ½ inches tall in 1890. Dan grew to be thin and lanky like his father, while Bob grew to be stocky, weighing about twenty pounds more than Dan, and having the looks of his mother's family, the Gillies.[19]

Lula told of one incident when Bob tied strings to the legs of grasshoppers and raced them with his younger siblings for entertainment.[20] The kids swam in the Sevier River and made a dam just south of the ranch. This was a favorite swimming hole of locals and was known as "Parker Dam."

Lula shared, "The Parker youngsters got hold of some of the neighbor's (Jim Kittleman) wine and put it out in pans for the chickens. When Mother came home from town, all the chickens were reeling around and acting funny. She couldn't imagine what was wrong, she soon found out what the trouble was, and didn't know what it would do to the chickens, but it didn't hurt them."[21]

Big brother Bob loved children and always made a fuss over them, whether they were family or neighbors. Lula said, "there was always room on his horse for as many as could scramble up. If they were little, he'd put them all on and lead the horse."

The Parkers gave everyone a nickname. Pinkerton detective Charlie Siringo claimed that Robert's was "Sally which would lead any boy to be bad."[22] If in fact this was the case, it was probably rarely used as he was always known as "Bob" to his siblings and "LeRoy" or "Roy" to his parents. Dan's nickname was "Snip." Lula was known as "Cute" and "Hag," apparently depending on the situation.

Maxi and Annie tried to teach their children to uphold Christian values while still enjoying life. Bob developed a reputation as one who enjoyed helping others. Dan was described during his trial in Cheyenne as having "a smile on his face and [being] willing to laugh at anything amusing that came up."[23]

The Parkers were poor. Because of the growing Parker family, young Robert hired on at local ranches to earn money to help the family. Lula wrote that, "Bob worked wherever he could get a job when he wasn't needed at home."[24] Maxi worked cutting cord wood for the Frisco kilns. Likely young Robert went along and worked on the Pat Ryan ranch near Milford.[25] Ryan's ranch was on Hay Springs, seven miles southwest of Milford. Pat said Robert "was a good, steady boy that you could depend on."[26] He said that Robert "gave no signs of the desperate career that he subsequently adopted, but that on the contrary he was quiet and inoffensive."[27]

Both Robert (Butch) and his mother worked on the Marshall ranch. James Marshall, shown here, was a rancher and outlaw. (*Jayne Crook*)

Ryan indicated that Robert's only offense he was aware of was stealing a saddle.[28] Lula wrote that she would defy anyone to prove that. She said that Robert would not have stolen a saddle because Mike Cassidy had given him both a saddle and a gun.

Another story is that young Robert went into town to get a new pair of overalls and found the store closed. Allegedly he helped himself inside and tried on a pair of overalls, which he kept, leaving an IOU note. The store-owner found the note and swore out a warrant for his arrest which Robert didn't appreciate or understand as he considered his word good.

When Robert was sixteen he worked on the nearby Jim Marshall ranch, nine miles south of the Parker ranch. Annie also moved to the Marshall Ranch at this time with all of the younger children, including four boys and three girls. Annie ran the dairy on the ranch, making and selling butter and cheese for extra money. They lived in a small house west of the big ranch house.[29]

James Marshall, sometimes called Jim, was born in Portland, Maine, in 1845. He married Clara Elizabeth Slade Mathis, a widow with four children, around 1873 near Washington, Utah. They moved to Panguitch where she bore three more children. Jim kept a ranch and also worked as a bootmaker.[30]

Jim Marshall was indicted for extortion in 1885 and fled his ranch.[31] Sometime later he showed up in the Brown's Park area and was recalled as a big-boned, red-faced freighter who hauled goods with his wagon team for Charlie Crouse.[32] A local rancher later wrote that Jim Marshall, Bill Brown, and Dan Parker were members of the Crouse gang in Brown's Park in 1890. He described Marshall as "a man about whom a stranger would say at first sight: I wouldn't trust him out of my sight, or in my sight, if his back was towards me. He had a hatchet face, with scissor-bill, foxy eyes set close together as the eyes of a pickerel, tall, lean and hungry, with sin and debauchery plainly written all over." He was known to drink to excess and apparently died in 1898 while bringing freight from Rock Springs to Brown's Park.[33] The landmark Marshall Draw in Brown's Park is named after him. One lawman who tracked Marshall described him as the worst outlaw in the area.[34]

Annie oversaw the dairy at Marshall's ranch for two summers. During the second summer, a small time outlaw named Mike Cassidy drifted into the area and started working on the Marshall ranch. Robert immediately took a liking to Mike Cassidy. Mike gave Robert a pistol, taught him how to use it, and educated him in the finer points of rustling cattle with a creative branding iron. Mike fell in with a couple of local shady fellows named Fred and Charlie.

In an early newspaper account, Pat Ryan claimed young Parker was reading dime novels about Mike Cassidy and idolized his way of life while working on Ryan's ranch. This was most likely Ryan exaggerating for the newspaper reporter. No dime novels have ever been known to exist about the relatively minor outlaw Mike Cassidy.

4. Leaving Home, 1884

LULA WROTE, "although Mother was quite naïve, she knew something questionable was going on out in the corral at the Marshall Ranch." She could see that Robert (Butch) admired Mike Cassidy and this was leading Robert down the wrong path. She decided to move the family back to the Parker ranch. Annie was pregnant with Lula then, and she was born April 5, 1884, just before they moved back to Circle Valley. But the die had already been cast for Robert LeRoy Parker.

Once a person is into the game, it's hard to get out. Robert got further into the game, which led to his leaving home at age eighteen in the spring of 1884. Lula said Robert accepted the blame for some stolen cattle taken by a couple of local men, "Fred and Charlie" who had families. There is no legal record of this occurrence.[1]

Another account indicates that Robert, along with some other men, possibly Fred and Charlie, were watching over the town herd of cattle. Some of the cattle were stolen, and the thieves convinced Robert to sign a bill of sale for the livestock.[2]

One June afternoon in 1884, Robert explained to his mother that he'd be leaving home early the next morning. There was no future, no excitement, at the ranch for him.

Annie attempted to persuade him to stay, but he yearned for work that would bring "hard, solid gold" to his hands. Telluride, Colorado, had been the land of promise for pioneer boys of Utah for several years,[3] and he and his friend Eli Elder planned to look for work there. Annie pleaded for Robert to stay at least until his father got home, but he told her he had already waited too long.

Early the following morning, Robert gathered his few belongings and Annie put together a few provisions for the road. After a quick breakfast, he told his mother that he'd return soon. Annie told him, "LeRoy, no matter

This photograph, taken in 1988, shows the remains of Parker Ranch buildings near Circleville, Utah. Butch left this ranch in 1884. (*Author's photograph*)

what happens, hurry back. Always remember that your father and I need you as you need us."

Then Robert left with his mare Babe and a young colt named Cornish.

When Maximilian returned home that evening, he was surprised and sorrowed that his son was gone. The next day he learned Robert had signed the bill of sale for Fred and Charlie for stolen cattle. Maxi was furious and tried to clear Robert's name with Constable James Wiley. Wiley told him not to worry that the rightful owners had their cattle back and that was all that mattered. But Maxi argued that Robert would never be able to return and "hold his head up."[4]

Matt Warner, a Utah cowboy and outlaw who comes into the story later, claimed that Parker left home after being accused of stealing a couple of horses from friend and neighbor Jim Kittleman. But Lula wrote that Robert would have never stolen from a close friend that he considered family.

It was reported that Mike Cassidy left the Circle Valley area in 1885 after running into some trouble,[5] possibly going to Mexico or to Fort Worth to run a saloon.

✧ ✧ ✧

WHEN ROBERT LEROY PARKER left home in 1884, he headed east. From 1884 to 1889, he likely drifted from ranch to ranch in the Utah, Wyoming, and Colorado area. His name shows up in several historic accounts.

Stories exist that he spent some time in Hanksville working for Charlie Gibbons. However, according to Charlie's record, it was several years later that Robert was around Hanksville.

There are stories that Robert worked on a ranch near Burntfork on the Wyoming-Utah border. Cowboy James Reagan claims he knew Robert "on Henry's Fork in Wyoming on the Utah line."[6] The Stoll family of Burntfork, who have been in the area for generations, indicate that Robert spent time at their ranch. Will and George Stoll were some of the original Carter cowboys of Fort Bridger and some believe Robert worked on that outfit too.[7]

People in Meeteetse, Wyoming, claim Robert signed a petition for a new bridge there in 1886. The petition shows a signature of Robert Parker.[8]

According to several old-timer reminiscences, Robert labored on different ranches from 1884 through 1886. Some of these ranches included: Coad Brothers Cattle Ranch on the North Platte in western Nebraska, ranches in the Miles City, Montana area,[9] and the Two Bar which was a part of the huge Swan Land and Cattle Company headquartered near Chugwater, Wyoming.[10]

Ann Bassett wrote that Parker appeared in Brown's Park in 1886.[11] Ann said Parker rode in horse races for Charlie Crouse. She reported, "When the thoroughbred gelding appeared on the track, he was ridden by a slender, brown-haired young fellow of about nineteen years. Small for his age he was a quiet, unobtrusive chap. Hearing rumors of this projected horse race, he had come to Crouse's ranch a few days previously. Crouse had sized him up with favor and hired him as jockey. And he rode the Brown's Park horse to a glorious victory. We were tremendously proud of that racer, he not only could run, but he was a handsome animal. His rider was hailed with enthusiastic acclaim. He modestly told us his name was Ed Cassidy. Later he became widely known as 'Butch' Cassidy, outlaw."

Ann Bassett wrote that Robert was quiet and kept to himself, working for Charlie Crouse for about a year before he moved away. She explained, "He was always well mannered. I never saw Butch Cassidy drunk nor wearing a gun—in sight. I have no personal knowledge of any of his deeds of outlawry, but I do know that he never lived in the Park after he was 'wanted' by the law. Occasionally he came that way, stopping for a meal, or overnight, at different ranches. But he took no part in the social life, nor ever attended a party after that which followed the race."[12]

At this time Robert first met a cowboy called Elzy Lay, short for William Ellsworth Lay, and they became close friends. Ann Bassett wrote that Elzy started working for the Bassetts in the summer of 1884 and was in and out of Brown's Park after that.[13]

After leaving home, Elzy drifted into the Brown's Park area. While in Brown's Park, he worked for and became friends with Matt Warner. Matt owned a ranch on Diamond Mountain near Brown's Park. The two were involved in robbing a merchant from Rock Springs and distributing the clothing to area residents.

Dan Parker left home soon after Robert. Annie later wrote of Dan's departure, "He went from home at the age of 17 years to try his luck in the world, because his parents were poor and family large and he hoped to be able to help them." Annie said that Dan worked "on a farm with his father" and "he was an obedient son and very affectionate to his mother."[14]

Dan soon fell in with a rough crowd. Dan allegedly helped the outlaw Joe Walker rustle some cattle near Woodside, Utah. Author Pearl Baker stated: "He punched cows, herded sheep, or did whatever range work he could get in the La Sal–Blue Mountain area." He worked for a time on the Carlisle Cattle Ranch near Monticello, Utah.[15] Dan was accused of stealing several sheep from a nearby ranch but was able to avoid trouble by switching out the hides skinned from the stolen sheep, which were to be used as evidence, with hides of sheep belonging to the Carlisle herd. Dan used several aliases, including Kid Parker, Dan Parks,[16] Joe Simms, Kid Jackson, and Billy the Kid,[17] but Tom Ricketts was the most popular.

The Parker family in 1895 when Butch was in prison in Wyoming. *From left:* Leona, Mark (on horse), Eb, Joe Rawlins (in buggy), Lula (with blurred face), Annie, Nina, and Sue Knell. *(Brigham Young University, G. E. Anderson Collection)*

Colorado Avenue, Telluride, Colorado, circa 1890. The bank robbed by Butch is the second building from the left with the bank sign. (*Courtesy Telluride Daily Planet*)

5. Telluride, 1889

W HEN ROBERT FIRST arrived in Telluride, he got a job "packing
ore from the mine; down the mountain to the mill on mules."
Although the work was physically demanding, he enjoyed it,
quickly learning how to skillfully place the packs on the mules.[1]

Lula wrote that he sold his horse Babe, but kept his colt Cornish down
on a ranch by the river. In the beginning he checked on the colt often and
started to break her. The rancher keeping the colt showed interest in buying her, but Robert moved the colt closer to town so he could spend more
time gentling her. When the rancher discovered the unbranded colt missing,
he swore out a warrant accusing Robert Parker of stealing the colt.

Parker was quickly arrested and jailed in Montrose. A friend of Parker's
wired Maxi Parker in Circle Valley for help. When Maxi arrived, he found
Robert sitting in an open cell. He told his father the colt belonged to him,
and he planned to stay in jail until his horse was returned to him. With Maxi
backing his son, the rancher gave in. Maxi attempted to persuade Robert to
return home with him, but his son wanted to stay and make more money.[2]

Parker soon met another Utah Mormon cowboy named Matt Warner.
Warner wrote that he met "Roy Parker" in Telluride. Matt was making the
rounds in western Colorado racing his horse Betty that he'd bought from
Charlie Crouse of Brown's Park. Matt made plans to race against a Mulcahy
colt in Telluride.

Matt wrote, "I noticed a neat dressed cowboy hanging around the bar
like he wanted to talk to me. I liked his looks and sidled over to him, and
we begun to buy drinks for each other."[3]

Parker warned Matt, "I know the Mulcahy colt. It has never been beat.
You are going to lose." Matt became upset and told Parker to put his money
where his mouth was. Parker said he would bet everything he had which
included, "three saddle horses, my saddle, bridle, chaps and spurs." Matt

Jen Parker Penaluna, sister of Robert LeRoy Parker, with her husband Tom and her daughter Margarette. Tom and Robert were good friends. (*courtesy Jacquie Tobin*)

proposed that they bet each other's riding outfits and Parker agreed.[4]

The two hit it off so well, Matt proposed Parker be one of the judges for the upcoming horse race, claiming, "I'd rather have you for a judge, even if you owned the Mulcahy colt, than trust one of these city pimps or gamblers."[5]

Matt won the race, and Parker presented his saddle, spurs, chaps, and gun to Matt. Matt tried to persuade Parker to keep the outfit as payment for judging the race. Parker refused. Matt said Parker was "stubborn as a mule" claiming Parker told him "a bet's a bet and I never squawk when I lose." Matt finally convinced Parker to become his partner in future races. Matt related that the two rode all over southwestern Colorado racing Betty and making lots of money while having a wild time.[6]

Matt was raised in Levan, Utah, approximately one hundred miles north of Circleville. Believing he was responsible for the death of a boy in a fight over a girl, Matt left home at an early age. Matt's real name was Willard Christiansen and his brother-in-law was the seasoned outlaw Tom

McCarty. Tom was well known in Utah because his family had nearly started a large Indian uprising when the McCarty's murdered some young Indian warriors.[7]

Matt reported that they ran into Tom McCarty in Cortez. Tom had a ranch near Mancos, Colorado.[8] Matt said Tom "had a cabin hide-out eight miles out of Cortez in the foothills." Another report places the cabin at Aztec Springs, twelve miles below Cortez.[9]

The trio later raced against a local Indian's race horse, nearly resulting in a fight when the Indian refused to pay up. Soon Parker and Matt exhausted the area with racing Betty. One day at Tom's cabin when they were restless and the day was dull, they planned a bank robbery.[10] Matt wrote, "Our plans were accordingly laid very carefully to go to a certain bank and relieve the cashier of his ready cash."[11] But they waited until the time was right.

✧ ✧ ✧

SOME EVIDENCE SHOWS that about this time Parker worked as a butcher in the little town of Ophir, Colorado, not far from Telluride. The meat market was owned by Jack Elliott.[12] Parker's sister, Jen had married Tom Penaluna and lived in Ophir for several years where they operated a saloon. Tom and Robert were friends, and Tom nearly had Robert convinced to return home early in his outlaw career.

Early in the summer of 1888, Parker went to work for Harry Adsit on the Spectacle ranch near Norwood, Colorado.[13] Adsit owned and controlled 19,200 acres at the base of the Lone Cone Mountain (Adsit described it as a circular dome twelve thousand feet high and twenty miles in circumference).[14] Adsit wrote that he "owned five thousand well-bred cattle and two thousand head of range horses."[15] Perhaps he ran cattle in multiple counties and held other leases, as he would have needed close to 100,000 acres to support these large herds.[16]

Adsit said two cowboys rode up to the ranch and asked for work one day, claiming their specialty was breaking broncos. He wrote that one of the cowboys was Parker and said "their work demonstrated that they were experts on riding and breaking horses and they continued their work for a year." The other cowboy was likely Matt Warner.

The foundation for Adsit's two-room cabin was found a few years ago by author Howard Greagor. Harry Adsit and his wife stayed on one side, and Butch and his cohorts occupied the other side.

In the fall, Parker slipped away and built a well-concealed corral at Stockdale Point. There he corralled thirty head of steers belonging to rancher Alfred Dunham. Dunham found the corral the next day and retrieved his steers. He considered filing charges when he learned who was responsible for constructing the corral, but never did.[17]

Adsit wrote that Parker had an uncanny ability for handling beef and an affable personality. He described Parker "as above average in height, good features, sandy hair, piercing blue eyes and rapid fire way of talking which later served him well, he cared not at all for liquor or cards, although he occasionally held the candle while the boys played poker on a saddle blanket in the open." Adsit stated Parker would tell him of his ambitions at the campfire and "would declare that he would make a mark in this world—and he did."[18]

After a year, Parker told Adsit that he wanted to visit his folks in Utah. Adsit told him to pick out two of the best four-year-old horses that he had broken and accept them with his compliments. It was said that if Adsit took a liking to someone "he almost always made them a gift of a nice, young horse."[19] Author Howard Greagor wrote that Parker was using the name Bud Parker at the time.[20]

Adsit surmises that it was on his ranch that Tom McCarty, Matt Warner, and Parker planned the Telluride Bank robbery in June 1889. For Parker, this was the big turning point from being a high-spirited cowboy to becoming a full-fledged outlaw. Two weeks after Parker left his employment at Harry Adsit's ranch, the bank in Telluride was robbed.

On Monday, June 24, 1889, McCarty, Warner, and Parker robbed the San Miguel Valley Bank of approximately $21,000.[21] The trio had come to Telluride three days earlier to case the bank and visit the local saloons.[22] Tom McCarty wrote, "About 11 o'clock in the forenoon we quietly rode our horses up to the bank."[23] Matt said that Tom stayed outside and held the horses while Matt and Parker went into the bank to rob it. Only the cashier, C. Hyde, was in the bank at the time. Matt immediately shoved his gun in the cashier's face, and Parker jumped behind the cage. Parker quickly filled sacks with money and gold from the counter and the vault.[24] Tom explained, "After the money was in our possession we bid the banker to stay inside and keep quiet or his life would pay the penalty."[25]

The three fired their "pistols in different directions to intimidate" the people on the street. Apparently they had made a deal with Jim Clark, the town

Matt Warner was likely a teenager when this photo was taken. (*Author's collection*)

marshal, to be out of town during the robbery. His cut of the loot was left for him in a hollow log outside of town. Sheriff J.A. Beattie led a posse in pursuit of the robbers.

All went as planned until the robbers sped out of town and were recognized by Harry Adsit who was riding into town.[26] Adsit said, "As they neared me, I recognized my two boys. I shouted, 'What's up?' They replied, 'Haven't got time to talk. Adios!' Butch's hat was missing. As I continued my way wondering at their delay in going home, I looked up and saw a mile away, a posse approaching."

Adsit continued with further details of the chase:

"Did you see them?" the sheriff asked. "Yes," I replied. He then summoned me as a member of the posse—he said "You have a fresh horse and here's a Winchester, now lead out." I asked them what they had done. He replied that they had held up the San Miguel Valley Bank. The posse was made up of clerks and others that could not ride well in a covered wagon.

As I turned to lead out, a gambler, a former cowboy, rode up alongside and told me the story. He said no one had been killed or injured, that one of the boys had shot at the feet of the cashier to make him stand still—that shot had started his mount bucking and the horse bucked his hat off. That was Butch and it would have been embarrassing had he been thrown.

The posse was far behind us and as we crossed the Miguel on their trail, I noted they had left the main trail into the timber. I pulled up my horse and told my friend that unless he wanted to die, we had better stop, for awhile, that I was a pretty fair shot as well as the boys and if we tangled [there would be] funerals.[27]

The bandits had arranged for relays of fresh horses along their escape route. One of the bandits in charge of relay horses told an alternate version of Adsit's stop. He wrote that Adsit actually came upon the bandits when they had stopped for lunch. "We extended an invite [to Adsit] to partake, but the offer was respectfully declined for reasons best known to himself."[28]

Then Adsit gave the bandits time to get on their way before he resumed his search. Adsit told the newspaper, "We remained still for probably half an hour, then ambled slowly up the trail—and soon discovered where they [the bandits] had returned to the trail. In a short time we met L.L. Nunn, the president of the bank, and when informed his bank had been robbed, he said, 'What shall I do?' I told him I had ridden my horse forty miles and as he had a fresh horse, I would suggest we change.

"Shortly after we changed, I saw [the bandits] riding down [t]he side of the mountain towards the Ames power plant. We followed down and at Trout lake we were informed that they had just passed sho[o]ting as they went [by] and if we speeded up we would overtake them.[29]

"I thought we were going too fast and slowed up. We finally reached the head of the West Dolores [River] where we found they had divided the money, $500.00 and $1000.00 wrappers lying on the ground.[30] Our horses were grazing as the sheriff came poking along. He was not the type of aggressive wild west officer." Sheriff J. A. Beattie was of advanced age.[31]

The sheriff then ordered Adsit to try and head off the outlaws near Rico. Adsit and two men left and attempted to stop the outlaws, but Adsit claimed they still missed them. After changing horses three times and riding over a hundred miles at top speed, Adsit demanded rest.

"The sheriff returned at daylight next morning, leading the dappled brown colt I had given Butch. He had found him on the mesa, almost dead

Telluride main street (Colorado Avenue). The bank sign shows in the upper right of the photograph. (*Telluride Daily Planet*)

from exhaustion. We all started our return, picking [up] our exchange horses enroute," Adsit wrote.

Ten days later Adsit received a letter from Parker:

> Dear Harry: I understand the sheriff of San Miguel county is riding the dapple brown colt you gave me. I want you to tell Mr. Sheriff that this horse packed me one hundred and ten miles in ten hours across that broken country and declared a dividend of $22,580.00 and this will be your order for the horse. Please send him over to me at Moab, Utah, at the first opportunity.

Adsit wrote, "I handed the letter to the sheriff and demanded the horse as it carried my brand, the Circle Dot, and suggested he go to Moab and get his men. He refused my demand and claimed as I had given the horse to Butch, he no longer belonged to me, and as the bank and the county refused to put up any money, he would keep the horse to help pay his expenses. I had the pleasure of paying my own expenses in the chase."

It appears that Adsit never revealed who Parker was. In a 1938 newspaper article he declined to give Parker's real name in order to protect the bandit's family who lived in Southern Utah.

Dan Parker may have had a minor role in the robbery by waiting with one of the sets of relay horses outside of town. Historian Jim Miller says that Dan cut the telegraph wires prior to the robbery.[32] U.S. Deputy Marshal Joe Bush was quoted during Matt Warner's trial in Ogden as saying he had chased the robbers of the Telluride Bank. He alluded to the fact that one of the four he chased was Dan Parker. Dan was in the area working on the Carlisle ranch, so he could have been involved. At the time of Matt's trial, Dan was serving time in prison.[33]

The outlaws made their escape down Dolores Canyon to a hideout on Mancos Mountain.

Bert Charter was also suspected of participating in the robbery. He had been another partner of Tom McCarty's according to an informant named "Rambler." Rambler said Charter was to provide horses at the predetermined relay stations on Keystone Hill, Johnson's horse camp, West Fork, Hot Springs, and Mud Springs. He further said that Tom McCarty and his "little band" remained in the vicinity of Mancos until "a thorough search of the lower country by the Navajos was over."[34]

Other accounts indicate the bandits were chased to Moab. North of Moab they crossed the "Grand River" (now known as the Colorado) on the ferry. They reached the ferry at four in the morning and had to wake up the ferryman, Lester Taylor. The boys feared they might be running into a trap with lawmen at the ferry, but they had outdistanced the law and were able to cross without incident. They paid the ferryman, along with three others whom they knew, with gold coins to keep their mouths shut.

They headed north to Thompson Springs, hiding out in the Book Cliff Mountains. The posse was right behind them so they traveled into Brown's Park to Charlie Crouse's ranch. Charlie let them hide out in a cabin on Diamond Mountain for a few days until the posse arrived at Charlie's ranch. Matt wrote that they then went south to Robbers Roost. Butch went into Green River for supplies where he was recognized by his uncle Dan Gillies.[35] According to Matt, the bandits ran into Sheriff Farrer of Green River and got the jump on him, sending him back to town without his pants. Matt reveals the group eventually went north up into Wyoming where they separated.[36]

Stories exist within the family that some of Robert's other brothers assisted him with his robberies. One story is that one brother wanted to join the gang. Robert told him that he was too slow and stupid to be an outlaw. This insult was Robert's way of protecting his sibling from a dangerous life.[37]

✧ ✧ ✧

AFTER ROBERT HAD LEFT the area, more of the Parker family spent time in Telluride. Lula mentions that Maxi and her brother Arthur[38] went to Telluride to open a stable. Maxi was forced to return home as the high elevation gave him health problems.

While living in Telluride, Arthur rode in a Fourth of July horse race that ended tragically. The horse he was riding "stumbled and fell, rolling over," inflicting injuries to Arthur that led to his death on July 7, 1890. He was only 21 years old.[39] One writer said that Arthur helped Butch rob the bank in Telluride. This is highly unlikely as he resided in Telluride a year after the bank robbery occurred.[40] The following is a newspaper account of his death:

ACCIDENTAL DEATH

We deeply sympathise with Mr. and Mrs. Max Parker, over the death of their eldest son Arthur, which sad event occurred at Telluride, Colorado, so long ago as the 7th of July of the present year, particulars of which however, have only just come to hand. It seems that on the 4th of July, Arthur Parker was engaged in riding a horse in the public races taking place during the festivities of that day, at Telluride, and that in the excitement of the contest his horse stumbled and fell, rolling over upon his rider and inflicting injuries upon the young man which three days after terminated in his death. Arthur Parker was born in Beaver City, 21 years ago, but several years since moved with his parents to Circle valley in Piute County.

The bereaved parents desire to express their heartfelt gratitude to the many kind friends who assisted in the soothing the last moments of their boy, and when he had passed away, aided in defraying the funeral expenses.[41]

Lula said, "I remember when we got the news of Arthur's death. Uncle Dan Gillies, who ran the post office at Circleville at the time, brought the message, which had been sent on from the Salina telegraph station. Mother was distraught. It was impossible to reach Telluride in time for Arthur's funeral. He was buried before we received the word. Even though I was a little girl, I can still see Mother pacing the fields, trying to wear out her grief. But around us she put on a good front and hid her sorrow."[42]

Dan Parker. (*Author's collection*)   William Brown. (*Museum of Northwest Colorado*)

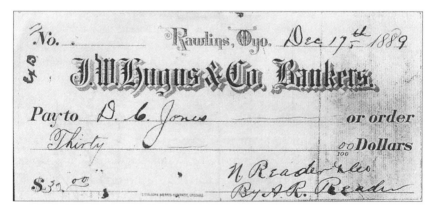

One of the checks stolen during the 1890 stage robbery near Baggs, Wyoming. This check was used as evidence during Dan's trial. (*Author's collection*)

6. Dixon to Rawlins Stage Robbery, 1889

ON A COLD AND WINDY Friday afternoon,[1] December 20, 1889, near Baggs, Wyoming, two men dressed in disguises[2] (which included a mustache and whiskers made from buffalo rope and held in place with a string) held up the Dixon–to–Rawlins stage. The driver, Abraham Coon, was carrying one passenger, J. C. Allen, who was riding up top with the driver. The stage was carrying the U.S. Mail. The two bandits brought the stage to a standstill as it was heading north, four miles from Muddy Station. Both bandits rode horseback and leveled their revolvers at the driver. "Stop boys and throw up!" demanded the older of the two bandits. He was later identified as William Brown.[3]

Once the stage stopped, Brown yelled, "Throw up your hands young fellow or I will kill you," and ordered the two men off the stage. Brown told the men to walk about thirty feet away with their backs to the stage.[4] Brown dismounted and rummaged through the mail bag. The younger bandit, later identified as Dan Parker, stayed on his horse with his six-shooter leveled at the two passengers.[5]

Dan Parker had decided to break out of his brother's shadow. His life would never be the same after this robbery.

Before Brown could completely search the mail, a freight wagon driven by Fred Elliot approached the idle stage along the lonely road. Brown instructed Dan, "You guard them and I will go and hold up this team." Fred Elliot told Brown that he had no money or gun. Brown responded that he and his partner were working men, like Elliot, and told him to pass on by the stage.[6] As Elliot passed the stage, he threw up his hands as a salute to Coon and Allen, who he said later "looked pretty lonesome."[7] While Parker was distracted watching Elliot, passenger Allen took a satchel containing $500 in gold and set it under his foot, pushing it into the mud.[8]

Once the freighter passed by, Brown returned to the stage, pulled out the mail bag, cut it open, and spread the contents out on the ground. He proceeded to open the letters in hope of finding some valuables. After finding little, he put the contents of the registered mail in his pockets, gathered up the letters, stuffed them into the mailbag and threw the bag back into the stage.[9]

Brown walked over to passenger Allen with his gun drawn and asked, "How much money have you got partner?" Allen handed Brown his pocketbook which contained $150.[10] Brown asked him, "Are you sure this is all?" Brown then pointed his gun at Coon and asked how much he had. Coon responded, "Four bits." Brown further questioned him. Coon responded that he was free to search him, but Brown joked, "No, you keep that, and when you get into Rawlins, drink to the health of Frank Jackson."[11] Brown ordered the two back on the stage and on their way. He mounted his horse and as they began to leave, Dan Parker fired three shots under the horses pulling the stage.[12]

The robbery provided little profit for the outlaws' troubles. A witness testified that Brown told him they had retrieved $100 and some checks. The witness also testified Dan told him that they had to dispose of the checks because they were useless.[13] One newspaper reported that "about $300" was stolen from the mail sacks and the passengers' pockets.[14] One of the checks used later as evidence was written to D.C. Jones of Dixon from A.R. Reader. Reader would later employ Harry Longabaugh (the Sundance Kid) at his Savery ranch.[15]

Allen allegedly returned to the scene after the robbery to recover the satchel that he had smashed into the mud. This led postal officials to suspect him as an accomplice.[16] He was held for a short time under a bond of $500 by the local authorities.[17]

A reward of $1,000 was offered by Deputy U.S. Marshal T. Jeff Carr on behalf of the U.S. Post Office Department for the arrest and conviction of the two stage robbers. Carr distributed circulars throughout Colorado and Wyoming with descriptions of the two robbers. The description of the younger robber matched Dan. It stated, "The robber, age about 22 or 24 years, about five feet eight or nine inches high, slim, complexion pale and swarthy looking, hair dark, face spare and apparently smooth, dark cloth suit, light colored cowboy hat, no overcoat, rode a bay horse or mare in good condition, weight about 900 or 1,000 pounds."[18]

Marshal Joe Bush. (*Brigham Young University, G.E. Anderson Collection*)

U.S. Marshal T. Jefferson Carr. (*Wyoming State Archives*)

On February 14, 1890, J.S. Hoy of Brown's Park reported that the two stage robbers had been hiding in Brown's Park. Hoy wanted to be deputized so he could detain the outlaws. He named the two outlaws as Dan Parks (or Parker) and the other as Brown. Hoy said Marshal Carr had trailed the two outlaws to Provo where he lost them, but believed they would soon double back to Brown's Park.[19]

Dan, it appears, went south to Parowan, Utah, to hide. It was during this time he received a letter from his brother, who was now going by the name George Cassidy. Cassidy told Dan of his ranch in Wyoming and how he longed for their family in Circleville.[20] The envelope was addressed to Lorenzo Watson of Parowan, at whose place Dan was hiding.[21] The transcript of the original letter reads as follows:

Dear Lorenzo
Kindly pass this letter to Daniel S. Parker
As always,
Bob Parker

Lander, Wyo. March 13, 1890
My Dear Brother,
It has been so long since I have written I suppose you have almost done looking for a letter from me but do not dispare for you shall have one after

so long a time you must forgive me for not writing before I have no excuse to offer only my negligence and I will try to be more punctual for the future.

I was very sorry to hear that you are in hiding again, but you Know I am not one to point a finger only be carefull, for I am inclined to think as Grand father Parker did about the wild cat in Duncan woods. I do wish I could come and see you all and I intend to if nothing happens to prevent this summer coming for I almost feel homesick when thinking how long it is since I saw my Mother it seems almost an age since I saw any of you.

When you get this letter you must write me and tell me all the news and what the prospects are for a safe reunion. I hope we may have a grand revelry but I should think it doubtful according to your letter.

I am now located at a good house about 18 miles from Lander[22] and have taken to raising horses which I thinks suits this country fine. H— and I have thrown our lots entirely together so we have 38 horses between us and we would have more but it has been a cold winter with plenty of snow and wind. (and you must excuse the pencile, but the ink froze.)[23]

Business here is very dull and Money hard but you know I am well. I should be in perfect health if I did not have such a good appitite and eat so much 3 times each day. I must draw my letter to a close give my love to Uncle Dan and family and tell them I should be happy to see them give my love to Father Mother Brothers and Sisters and receive the same yourself—

This From you brother
Bob

P.S. Direct your letters to George Cassidy as before and burn this up as you read it.[24]

Dan was arrested near Moab, Utah, by Deputy U.S. Marshal George [Joe] R. Bush.[25] In September, 1890, Marshal Bush testified he was initially after Dan for horse stealing, until Dan revealed the stage robbery.[26] Dan however mistakenly testified he was arrested in Vernal, Utah. He said he was arrested for the stage robbery, "On or about the first of September 1890, by a man by the name of Bush at the Vernal Post Office." Dan later testified that he had first met Bush in Moab where he had been arrested for another charge. Dan testified that he had been arrested by a Mr. Allred and that Bush later came to take him from the officers in Moab.[27] The postal file gives Dan's arrest as August 28, 1890, by Deputy U.S. Marshal J.R. Bush at Blue Mountain Gulch, Utah.[28] The *Salt Lake Tribune* quoted Bush as saying, "I went in with a posse after them, but only succeeded in getting Parker, after chasing the gang from Wyoming to Utah, thence to New Mexico, thence back to the Blue mountains and finally to the LaSal mountains, where Parker was captured after a desperate resistance."[29] The *Cheyenne Leader* reported, "Parker was captured by a constable there (Bennett, in Uintah county, Utah) and turned over to Bush at Moab."[30]

Annie Parker said Dan was held for "more than a month in Salt Lake City" after being arrested. "From there he was taken to Rawlins," Wyoming for his "preliminary hearing, and finally tried in Cheyenne, March 1891."[31] Dan was held in Salt Lake City for a short time due to complications created by Wyoming's statehood.

Dan was actually confined at the Utah Territorial Prison at Sugarhouse in Salt Lake City on September 4, 1890 and released from there on September 23, 1890, to answer his charges in Wyoming. He was described as having a light complexion, grey eyes, and sandy hair. His height was given at 5 feet, 10 ¼ inches, and he weighed 150 pounds. His age was noted as twenty-five (he was actually twenty-two at the time).

Dan was then taken to Rawlins for his preliminary examination. He was received at the Wyoming Penitentiary in Laramie on October 19, 1890, where he was held for safekeeping with a $3,000 bail. Dan would spend approximately seven months in one of the new metal cells on the south wing of the penitentiary.[32] Dan was later released for trial to the U.S. Court in Cheyenne on April 7, 1891.[33]

William Brown was arrested during a ranch dance by Deputy U.S. Marshal Frank M. Canton on January 8, 1891, in Johnson County, "at a little place called Piney" near Buffalo, Wyoming.[34]

Dan was mostly an amateur outlaw and "while covering his men with a revolver, he was considerably excited and quite nervous."[35] William Brown, on the other hand, proved to be a much more seasoned criminal. Brown, being older, likely had a big influence on Dan.[36] Deputy U.S. Marshal J. R. Bush was quoted as saying, "He [Brown] is a bad man to fool with. He has been into too many scrapes to weaken now. If he ever weakens there are lots of men in the country who will try to kill him."[37] William Brown had many aliases including Dolph Lusk, Frank Rogers, John Day, Dave Ray, George McGovney, Red Bill, and Jim Moore.[38] He was using the alias J. H. Day when he was arrested by Frank M. Canton.[39]

Dan proved he didn't have nerves of steel when he was questioned. After his arrest, he was turned over to Deputy U.S. Marshal T.J. Carr. Up until that time, which had been about a month, Dan had maintained that his name was Tom Ricketts. However, when Carr pushed him into telling the truth, he broke down and admitted his name was Dan Parker and he was "of the Parker family of southern Utah."[40] He also disclosed the names of all his family members, except Robert LeRoy.[41]

A continuance was denied by the judge on April 10, 1891. Both Parker and Brown's attorneys had requested additional time to bring in witnesses from Utah.[42]

Dan knew that his future looked bleak. On April 15, 1891, the *Cheyenne Daily Sun* reported a foiled escape plot by Dan Parker and three other prisoners: Kinch McKinney, Bates, and Dave Hazely. A prison official suspected something when he saw Parker and Hazely spending a great deal of time together and had assigned a spotter to them. The plot was to simply overpower the guards and get their guns and horses. Dan shared a cell with Kinch McKinney.[43]

The trial was held in the U.S. District Court in Cheyenne, Wyoming, on April 17 and 18, 1891. U.S. Attorney for Wyoming Benjamin F. Fowler prosecuted, assisted by Willis Van Devanter. Brown and Parker were defended by attorneys C.E. Dodge and A.C. Campbell.[44] Judge John A. Riner presided.

Ironically, William A. Richards, the future governor of Wyoming served on the jury. Richards would later pardon Butch Cassidy six months early for good behavior.[45]

Dan maintained his innocence and his parents strongly supported him. Annie wrote, "We firmly believe" Dan was "hastily tried and unjustly condemned, for a crime of which he is wholly innocent." She boldly stated, "Marshal Bush, who arrested our son, was heard to say that he would convict his prisoners if he had to hire witnesses in five counties."[46] She further stated, "We believe that the witnesses were bribed; and that the reward offered by the State was the means of convicting an innocent man."[47]

Even after Dan had been in prison for several years, he maintained his innocence. Annie said he was "advised to plead guilty as a better standpoint from which to ask for mercy," but, "he says he will die before he will take upon himself that unmerited disgrace."[48]

A Cheyenne newspaper reported, "Parker is about 18 years old and is quite intelligent, using good language while on the witness stand." Several witnesses at the trial stated that Dan had testified at his preliminary hearing that he was at Dry Valley, near Moab on the December 20, 1889, when the robbery took place. Dan, however, testified this time that he was at Ashley Fork nearly 250 miles away from Dry Valley, on December 20, 1889. Dan admitted that he had testified falsely at his preliminary hearing.[49]

Dan even signed a deposition stating that he could prove he was two hundred miles away from the location of the crime, but he was unable to provide the means to have his witnesses come to Cheyenne to prove his innocence.[50] Annie dramatically said that Dan "wrote to his father and begged him to come to him, but the letter arrived when his father was lying very ill, so ill that the news it contained was withheld by his friends for fear it would cost [him] his life."[51]

Abraham Coon testified that at the time of the robbery, he didn't recognize the younger robber as Dan Parker because of his disguise. Later, Coon said that he recognized Dan as the robber by general appearance.[52] It would be a fellow outlaw's testimony that proved extremely damaging. Joseph Murr testified that in April 1890, during a dance in Moab, William Brown told him that "he had to skip out of the northern country" because "he had robbed a stage up there." Brown allegedly told him "that he and a fellow by the name of Parker robbed a stage somewhere about Rawlins."

A few days after the dance, Dan Parker allegedly arrived to stay with Murr answering to the name "Tom Ricketts." Murr testified that Dan told him on several occasions that he and Brown had robbed a stage close to Rawlins. Murr further stated that Brown proudly shared with several people the incident because he liked to brag about it.[53] Brown allegedly smiled at Murr's statement during the trial and seemed to be amused with the testimony.[54]

Following the trial, a Cheyenne newspaper quoted Murr on the travels of William Brown and Dan Parker after the stage robbery. The newspaper stated:

> The two men started out to rob the store at Dixon, but learning that there was no money in the store they decided to rob the stage, giving as a reason that they wanted some money to spend on Christmas. After holding up the stage they went to Utah and drifted down into the northern part of New Mexico where a plan was hatched to rob the Durango, Colo[rado] bank. The scheme was for Brown, Parker, Murr and two other men to ride into the town, go up to the bank, and hold up the cashier. Brown was to gather up the money, while Parker kept the official quiet. Murr and the two other men were to stay outside and keep the citizens at bay in true

Jesse James style. After robbing the bank they intended to go up and rob the Denver & Rio Grande train near Grand Junction and then escape into Utah.

This plan was spoiled when Marshal Bush appeared on the scene.[55] There was also a report in the *Meeker Herald*, that the Vernal Co-op was robbed two weeks after the stage robbery and the same robbers were suspected.[56] J.S. Hoy named Bill Potter and William Brown as the two robbers of the Vernal Co-op. He also said that Dan Parker was hiding at the "Crouse Roost" in Brown's Park at the time.[57]

On April 18, 1891, Dan Parker and William Brown were found guilty of robbing the U.S. Mail. The jury had only deliberated two hours. The verdict was read, "We, the jury in the above entitled case find the defendants William Brown and Dan Parker, guilty as they stand charged in the indictment."

The newspapers said, "Review of the evidence in the case . . . was so complete that conviction was a foregone conclusion." During the closing remarks, the defense attorney, Mr. Campbell, knew a conviction was likely coming and tried to make a strong plea for the prisoners. He described a bleak picture of life imprisonment in an attempt to touch the jurors' hearts. At this point in the trial, William Brown broke down and cried.[58] Dan was described as "making light of the matter."[59]

Judge Riner had no choice but to sentence the two to life once they were found guilty. Prior to 1871, the same crime had been a capital offense punishable by hanging and had been the fate of over two hundred men.[60]

On April 22, 1891, a motion for a new trial was filed with the court on the grounds that the trial transpired before the defendants could provide their witnesses. This motion was overruled.[61] Brown and Parker were sentenced on April 24, 1891, "to be imprisoned for [the] term of natural life at hard labor in the Detroit House of Corrections."[62] The newspapers described Parker and Brown as being ill-prepared for their guilty verdict when it was given.[63] Judge Riner later said that the sentence was excessive in consideration, being that Dan "was a mere youth" at the time of the offense, however there was no exception in the law.[64] The life sentence was a result of robbing the U.S. Mail with the use of deadly weapons and putting the life of the carrier in jeopardy. The law states, "Any person who shall rob any carrier, agent or other person entrusted with the mail . . . [and] put his life in jeopardy by the use of dangerous weapons, such offender shall be punishable by imprisonment at hard labor for the term of his natural life."[65]

Parker and Brown were sentenced to the Detroit House of Corrections because robbing the U.S. Mail was a federal crime and the Detroit prison had contracted with Wyoming to hold federal prisoners. A short time later (Oct 1891), the Department of Justice approved the proposal to keep federal prisoners at Laramie. If it had been changed earlier, Dan would have remained in Wyoming and would have been present when his older brother Robert arrived for his two-year sentence for horse theft.[66]

U.S. Marshal Joseph P. Rankin delivered Dan Parker and William Brown to the Detroit House of Corrections on April 30, 1891.[67]

On October 1, 1891, both Frank Canton and Joe Bush each were paid a reward of $1,000 for the capture and conviction of Dan Parker and William Brown.[68]

On November 19, 1891, nearly seven months after Brown and Parker were delivered to Detroit, their lawyer, A.C. Campbell, filed a bill of exceptions for Brown and Parker. However, Judge Riner said, "The move was made too late, and the highwaymen have left all hope behind. They are in for life."[69]

Dan began his life behind bars for a few hundred dollars.

Some of Butch's friends in his Wyoming years included (right) Eugene Amoretti, Sr., a Lander banker; (below right) Eugene Amoretti, Jr., neighbor and friend; and (below left) Margaret and John Simpson, neighbors. (*Amoretti photographs are from the Wyoming State Archives. The Simpson photo is from the Author's collection.*)

7. The Wyoming Years, 1889~1894

AFTER ROBERT PARKER, then known as Roy Parker, split from Matt Warner and Tom McCarty, Matt and Tom spent the winter of 1889–90 in the Star Valley area, on the border of Wyoming and Idaho. Tom wrote that he felt secure since the deep snow closed the roads in and out of the valley for the winter.[1]

Parker drifted back into Brown's Park where his friends Charlie Crouse and the Bassett family resided. He especially enjoyed the Bassett family as they reminded him of his own family. Parker liked to borrow and read books from Mr. Bassett's library.[2] Ann Bassett often said that Butch never *lived* in Brown's Park after he was "wanted" but only made visits.[3] Josie Bassett claimed Butch worked for them and spent the winter in their bunkhouse. Josie called him "Bob Parker" instead of Butch and described him as "a big dumb kid who liked to joke."[4]

With the Telluride robbery, Parker crossed the line from small-time rustler to a full-fledged outlaw. At this point, he dropped the name Parker and started using Cassidy after his boyhood hero, Mike Cassidy.[5]

CASSIDY WOULD LATER drift up into Rock Springs. At the time, the only jobs available were in the coal mines, and those did not interest him.[6] Cassidy landed a job at a butcher shop where he received his nickname "Butch." He worked for W. H. Gottsche who owned the butcher shop located at 432 South Front Street during 1889.[7] The shop was known as "The Family Market." Cassidy worked with Otto Schnauber who described him as "a good worker and fine young man from a good family." Schnauber worked for Gottsche and would later operate the "Pacific Market" at the same location.[8] Cassidy likely got to know the local butchers while previously supplying rustled cattle to the various shops in town.

W. H. Gottsche owned Currant Creek Ranch southwest of Rock Springs and northwest of Brown's Park. Cassidy spent time at the ranch which supplied beef to the butcher shop in Rock Springs.[9] The inscription, "George Cassidy 1889" has been discovered at the ranch.[10] Butch was reported to have gathered wild horses and retained them there.[11]

In his biography, Matt Warner maintained that Cassidy got his nickname "Butch" from a gun that Matt owned that had such a kick that it was called Butch. The gun dropped Cassidy on his rear, and he was known as Butch thereafter.[12] Matt was also known as a good storyteller, so the butcher shop version is more likely, albeit difficult to document. Many of the owners and employees of the old butcher shops claimed Butch worked at their establishments. If he did work at a butcher shop, it was only briefly.

Lula wrote regarding Butch's time in the butcher shop: "My brother had a disarming way with people. It wasn't long before he had befriended nearly everyone in town. He always gave good measure with the meat, and housewives had the highest confidence in him."[13]

Whatever the origin was for the nickname "Butch," during this time he really went by the name "George Cassidy." The nickname Butch didn't come into frequent usage until years later in the press (after 1896).[14]

Stories exist of Cassidy being arrested in Rock Springs for "rolling a drunk," although no records have been located to confirm this. Cassidy was supposedly seen talking with the drunk earlier in the evening although the saloonkeeper allegedly stole the money. Cassidy was "so furious at being falsely arrested for such a petty, sneaking crime that he swore vengeance."[15]

Some historians believe Cassidy traveled into the Hole-in-the-Wall country, near present-day Kaycee, Wyoming, and homesteaded a ranch that was later known as the Blue Creek Ranch. A double cabin exists on the ranch that is rumored to have been built by Cassidy. It was reported that "Jim Stubbs paid Cassidy $1500 in gold pieces for the Blue Creek ranch" in the summer of 1894.[16] Other reports have the date as 1889 or earlier.[17]

John Brown Parker filed the original homestead application on the ranch on March 16, 1892, in Buffalo, Wyoming, but he was not related to Robert LeRoy Parker. He later relinquished it to Jim Stubbs.[18] John Brown Parker was reported to be a surveyor and his services were in high demand. John Brown Parker was described as being "tall, rather stoop-shouldered fellow of medium complexion with a fancy mustache—folks didn't like him very well, for he was inclined to be somewhat over-bearing."[19]

Cassidy spent little to no time in the actual Hole-in-the-Wall area. He may have passed through the area or stopped to visit a friend, but he did not live there. It was later that the media associated Butch Cassidy with the Hole-in-the-Wall even creating an outlaw gang named after the Hole. Hole-in-the-Wall is a misnomer as there is no actual hole nor is it a box canyon. A small ranch behind the Red Wall was known as the outlaw ranch. A notch in the Red Wall to the east of the ranch was used as access. The Hole was used by the two outlaws—George Sutherland Currie known as "Flat Nose" Currie and later by Harvey "Kid Curry" Logan.

Cassidy did settle in Fremont County and went into a partnership with a cowboy named Al Hainer. Little is known about Al Hainer outside of the time he was partners with Cassidy. Some surmise that he was another Mormon cowboy from Utah. Together the two started a horse ranch or operation on Horse Creek north of Dubois, Wyoming, some time around 1889.[20] The two had considerable money,[21] likely Cassidy's share of the Telluride bank robbery loot. One report states they purchased the Charley Peterson place on Horse Creek.[22]

Eugene Amoretti, Jr., a friend and neighbor, said Cassidy deposited $17,500 in Amoretti's father's bank in Lander. He recalled, "The cashier and I were sitting behind the netting in the bank when a man came in. He threw a leather belt on the counter and said, 'Count her out.' The cashier took the belt and found the bills amounted to $17,500."[23]

Will Simpson said "a considerable amount of [Cassidy's] money went over the fero table in Lander."[24]

Lander banker Eugene Amoretti was a friend to Cassidy during this time. According to Larry Pointer, "Amoretti was probably the only banker in the West who could say Butch Cassidy was his friend. His bank in Lander was never robbed during the entire outlaw era."[25] Eugene Amoretti, Jr. later owned the EA ranch on Horse Creek, north of Dubois. The EA ranch was located next to Cassidy's cabin on Horse Creek, and some believe Amoretti later purchased Cassidy's Horse Creek ranch and incorporated it into the EA.[26]

Cassidy met and made friends with attorney Douglas A. Preston. Preston opened a law practice in Lander in 1889,[27] moving his practice to Rock Springs in 1895. Lula said that they met in Rock Springs when one evening Cassidy saved the life of Preston in a saloon brawl. From that time forward Preston

EMBAR CATTLE CO.

Branding Iron of the

EMBAR CATTLE CO. EMBAR, WYO.

Cattle are branded on the left side or hip and horses on the left shoulder.

The breeching brand has been put on calves since 1892.

Cattle are marked with an underslope from each ear.

Rewards will be paid for information concerning depredations which have been or are proposed to be committed upon stock or other property, and for the return of such as has been stolen.

Embar Cattle Company brand and rewards notice from an 1890s newspaper. (*Author's collection*)

defended Cassidy, both in court and more informally. Preston confided to a close friend that Cassidy had indeed saved his life, and he felt indebted to him.[28] Preston continued to be a close and trusted friend to Cassidy throughout his time in the United States. Later Preston served as the Wyoming Attorney General.

At Horse Creek, Cassidy became good friends with his neighbors the Simpson family. He endeared himself to the Simpsons when he rode 120 miles round trip in a blizzard to Fort Washakie for medicine for the Simpson's child who was ill from influenza.[29] Cassidy and Hainer spent Christmas 1889 with the Simpson family at their cabin on the mouth of Jakey's Fork on the Wind River. Cassidy was said to bring "the spirit of frolic with him."[30] Children gathered around him. "Butch Cassidy set the pace, with his tow-colored hair in wild disorder and his puckered blue eyes blazing."[31] Simpson's son, Will, eventually became an attorney and prosecuted Cassidy in 1892. Will's son, Milward, later became Governor of Wyoming and his grandson Alan was a U.S. senator from Wyoming.

Another neighbor, Andrew Manseau, said "Butch Cassidy and Al Heiner spent one winter on a place above me. They had some race horses and bought blue joint hay from me. I charged them big prices." Manseau said he "slept with Cassidy" several times when he was "wintering in

This cropped page from the November 15, 1890, Occidental Hotel register shows Cassidy and Hainer's names. It is dated near the top of the page. *(American Heritage Center, University of Wyoming)*

Dubois."[32] It was common in that time for men to sleep in the same bed.

Cassidy and Hainer were in Buffalo, Wyoming, on November 15, 1890, as they both registered at the Occidental Hotel, staying in Room 25 as "Geo. L. Cassidy" and "Al Hainer" of "Lander City." Matt Warner indicated in his book, *Last of the Bandit Riders,* that Butch, Matt, and Tom McCarty made a raid near Buffalo in Johnson County for looking for cattle around this time.

A neighboring ranch in the area was the Embar on Jakey's Fork owned at the time by Robert Augustus Torrey, a retired Army post commander.[33] It is possible that Cassidy and Hainer worked on the Embar Ranch at this time. Torrey later shifted the ranch operations over the Owl Creek Mountains. By 1892 he had turned the ranch over to his younger brother, Judge Jay Linn Torrey, who ran it with help from his nephew Virgil Rice and foreman Jacob "Jake" Price.[34] Judge Torrey would later become a nemesis of Cassidy.

Will Simpson explained, "Cassidy abandoned the ranch in probably 1891 or 92 [originally he had written 1893, then crossed it out] and for a time lived on the Owl Creek [in the Big Horn Basin]."

Researcher Pat Schroeder and I found tax records in the dusty basement of the Lander courthouse which indicate that Butch and Hainer owed $21.77 in back taxes in 1890 on their ranch near Dubois. Records confirm that they likely abandoned the ranch because while Butch was in prison, delinquent taxes of $19.78 were due in 1894 and $4.32 in 1895.

After moving to the Owl Creek area, Cassidy became friends with William H. "Billy" Nutcher and Jacob C. "Jakie" Snyder. Billy owned a ranch on Owl Creek with John D. McCullough. Billy later sold Butch the "stolen horses" that sent Butch to prison in 1894. Billy's younger brother Joseph (or

Joe Nutcher's mug shot from the penitentiary. (*Wyoming State Archives*)

Jakie Snyder's mug shot. (*Wyoming State Archives*)

Joe) served time at the Wyoming Territorial Pen in Laramie after being convicted of stealing horses from the Embar ranch.[35]

The Big Horn Basin had ongoing battles between large cattle ranchers and small-time ranchers, much like those of the Johnson County War. Rustling and killings occurred on both sides. Some believe that Butch was involved, causing him to be framed and sent to the pen to get him out of the way.

Lander town marshal Hank Boedeker recalled meeting Butch and his two friends Al Hainer and Jakie Snyder as they were riding into town. Hank wanted their guns. He told them, "Fellas, I want your guns. I won't have you getting someone into trouble and getting yourselves into a mess here in town. I know that won't happen if I have possession of your guns." Jakie did not want to give them up, but Butch responded, "It's all right boys. We're giving him our guns." Hainer unbuckled his guns, but Snyder did not until "Cassidy gave him one of those hard looks he could pass out when he felt that way and Snyder unbuckled his guns."[36]

Cassidy "liked to go onto the famous Embar ranch up Owl Creek out of Thermopolis to brand colts."[37] This statement indicates that Cassidy continued to work for the Embar after its relocation to the Owl Creek area. At some point, trouble developed between Butch and Jay L. Torrey who owned the Embar ranch. Torrey played a role in Cassidy's incarceration and appears to have tried to influence the judge to lengthen Butch's sentence. Torrey later became famous for organizing "Torrey's Rough Riders," a Spanish American War calvary unit made up of cowboys, although they saw no action.[38] Not far from the Embar ranch was the wild town of Embar. Cassidy liked to stop at Smith's Embar Saloon.

Elzy Lay was also in the Lander area at the time. In January 1893 he and Frank Wilson ran into trouble. They convinced the local jeweler, F. G. Burnett, to trade their old rifle for a new Winchester. The owner of the new rifle, Jim Carter, was so upset when he found out about the trade he asked Sheriff Charlie Stough to arrest them. Stough caught Lay and Wilson on the North Fork of Owl Creek and brought them to Lander. They convinced Stough they meant no harm and were released. A few months later, in April, Wilson was convicted of burglary and sent to the Wyoming penitentiary.[39]

Another friend of Butch's at this time was Emory Burnaugh. Emory would later testify in Butch's behalf at his second trial.[40] Emory married a one-time girlfriend of Butch's, Alice Stagner.[41] Alice's father, Speed Stagner, lived near the ranching community known as Mail Camp at the base of Blondie Pass in the Owl Creek Mountains. Alice's mother was a Cheyenne Indian. According to the Burnaugh family, Butch spent two winters at the Burnaugh ranch.[42] Alice was quoted as saying of Butch, "He was the most well-mannered man I ever knew. He was never violent, never threatened and he never killed anyone."[43]

Butch had a couple of other girlfriends in the area. He split his time between Dora Lamoreaux and Mary Boyd who were both acquaintances of Alice Stagner.[44] Dora was part Sioux and Mary was part Shoshone.[45] Dora recalled that, "We rode horseback and we danced. He was a gentleman and I was a lady."[46] Old-timers indicate that Cassidy "had intentions of settling down and establishing a home for Mary." Mary later claimed she was the common law wife of Cassidy.[47]

On August 9, 1893, in the *Cheyenne Daily Leader*, it was reported that Elzy Lay made "A Ride For Life." Alice Stagner Burnaugh had become ill with her first pregnancy. Lay rode fifty miles in eight hours to Fort Washakie, returning the next day with a doctor to deliver her first born, Winnie.[48]

There is an 1895 newspaper account of a wagon ride that Emory Burnaugh took with Cassidy and Hainer over Blondie Pass:

A year or two ago Charles E. Burnaugh had the contract for carrying the mail between the Post and Embar and consequently had to cross the hill six times a week. On one occasion Burnaugh met Al Hainer and his former side partner, Cassidy at Smith's Embar Saloon and the three drank to future and past friendships until the trio became mellow, reaching a point where they overcame the ills of life, the three mounted Burnaugh's buckboard and started over the mountain. They climbed the hill on the Owl creek side and at last reached the apex of Owl creek mountain where a glorious view of the great valley of the Wind river range was presented to their view. As they started down the steep mountain side above mail camp something interfered with the working of the brake, but the reins were in the hands of Burnaugh and he managed the team so that they held the wagon, but his jolly companions were out for a lark and one of them commenced a fusillade with his revolver which frightened the team to madness while the other opened a keen jack knife and deliberately cut the reins just beyond the handhold of Burnaugh. Away went the buckboard with its load of freight and away went horses and men down the mountain side. They went safely to the first angle in the road and made the sharp curve to the left which goes straight to the deep chasm where the road angles to the right and this they made safely and then down, down, down, the deep and dangerous dugway until finally they came out at the mail camp safe and sound and well sobered by the adventure.[49]

Christian Heiden whose parents homesteaded on Owl Creek near the Embar ranch said that his uncle ran the Saloon near the Embar. He said, "I can well remember my first glimpse of Butch when [he], with his pals Jakie Snyder and Al Hainer, came galloping up to the place. He was dragging a mountain lion he had roped that day and tied him to the hitching rail, where the lion snapped and spat at the assembled cow-punchers who had piled out of the saloon to tease him."

Heiden said he drove the stage from Embar to Meeteetse and got to know Butch well as he often rode along with him. Heiden remembered, "Butch and his pal Snyder rode with me one time up to Meeteetse. We stopped at Rose Williams's log cabin for a meal. Rose was a widow and served meals and sometimes whiskey.[50] That day she served us a somewhat meager meal of jackrabbit, and Butch asked me if that was the usual bill of fare. I told him it often was. Butch suggested that we go hunting and we started out on horseback. We ran on to a few buffalo, the last I ever saw, and then some deer. Butch wouldn't bother with them and later shot a two-year-old calf. 'What's the brand?' I asked, as he examined the kill. 'Never mind the brand,' he said, 'It's meat we're after.' We took it back to the widow Williams. I never saw Butch shoot anyone, but he always packed a wicked-looking Colt .45 with a big wooden handle on it. He was very quick in his actions and quick-witted."[51]

Butch was always up for a practical joke. Another prank resulted when "Cassidy and several exuberant fellow spirits hitched four unbroken horses to the old overland stage coach, filled the inside with rouged women and, having disposed themselves on top of the conveyance wherever there was room to hang on, let her go reeling down the main street to the banging of their six-shooters and the shrieking of the female passengers, Lander was startled, but Lander was not shocked."[52]

Yet another time Butch, Hainer, and their friend Whitney (most likely Fred Whitney) borrowed John Lee's buckboard. Butch and Whitney climbed into the buckboard and started down Main Street in Lander when Butch lost control probably due to excessive speed and alcoholic beverage. They crashed into a hitching rail that broke the team free and destroyed the buckboard in front of Coalter's Saloon. Whitney landed in the street and Butch on the sidewalk. Butch apparently got up and dusted himself off and called out to Lee, "John, come and get your buckboard."[53]

Butch may have helped run the Quien Sabe ranch for his friend Tom Osborne and perhaps he even owned this ranch on Copper Mountain northeast of present-day Shoshoni. Tom was sent to prison for murdering a man who had cheated him out of his Quien Sabe ranch. It was rumored, but undocumented, that Osborne deeded the ranch over to Cassidy while Osborne served his prison term. However, Cassidy also was sentenced to prison later in 1894. The Quien Sabe ranch was certainly a gathering place for outlaws at this time.[54]

In 1894, Butch and Hainer owed delinquent taxes for land near Lost Cabin in the amount of $19.98. The Quien Sabe ranch is in the same area as Lost Cabin so it's possible that the taxes were for the Quien Sabe ranch.

Butch's horse deal with Billy Nutcher (shown here) led to Butch's incarceration.
(*Jay L. Torrey Collection, American Heritage Center, University of Wyoming*)

Uinta County Jail Record showing "George Cassady" as prisoner 435 and Al
"Hayner" as number 436. (*Uinta County, Wyoming, Sheriff's Office*)

8. Arrests and Trials, 1892~1894

I N THE FALL OF 1891, Butch was at "Mail Camp" at the base of the Owl
Creek Mountains.[1] He purchased three saddle horses, a sorrel, a grey, and
a brown from Billy Nutcher.[2] Billy claimed he traded cattle for them in
Johnson County the previous fall and the "title was okay and he would warrant it."[3] Butch claimed that J.S. Green and C.F. Willis had witnessed the sale
between Cassidy and Nutcher. Cassidy declared Green and Willis had both
known him as well as Hainer in Utah prior to this time.[4] Unfortunately,
Butch failed to obtain a bill of sale.

A complaint was filed by Otto Franc[5] against George Cassidy and Al
Hainer on behalf of the Grey Bull Cattle Company for the theft of one horse
valued at $40. Otto was the Justice of the Peace in Fremont County at this
time.[6] Otto Franc owned the Pitchfork Ranch on the Greybull River. The
Grey Bull Cattle Company was owned by Richard Ashworth, an Englishman,
who was out of the country most of the time. The alleged theft was reported
to have occurred on October 1, 1891.[7]

Horse theft had become a foremost concern for area ranchers. Local
newspapers referred to it as "a gigantic horse stealing industry."[8]

It was not an advantageous time to be possessing horses without a bill of
sale.[9] The ranchers began to organize to combat the problem in late 1891.

Rancher John Chapman volunteered to track the accused bandits.[10]
Chapman had a vested interest in capturing horse thieves, having had somewhere between 80 and 200 horses stolen from his ranch.[11] Chapman talked
with James Thomas in the Owl Creek Mountains who remembered seeing
Cassidy and Hainer with some horses they planned to take to Evanston, Wyoming.[12] Chapman received further confirmation that the two had traveled to
Evanston in Uinta County when he spoke to the agent at Fort Washakie.[13]

Early Big Horn Basin pioneer Stub Ansell said he witnessed Butch es-
caping the law at the J. K. Moore Hotel in Fort Washakie. Stub explained:

He [Butch] asked Stub to get him two boxes of cartridges for his forty-five colts, which he did. He took them to his room on the second floor, as he thought nothing more of the matter. Shortly after the sheriff and his deputy from Lander rode up and dismounted, came in and were telling the proprietor of the office that they were on the trail of Cassidy and were going to take him in. Just about that time, Stub says, Cassidy came down the stairs with a forty-five in each hand. The officers did not see him until he was right back of them with his six shooters. He backed out of the door towards the barn, then running towards the barn where he had a saddle horse tied. He jumped on his horse and dashed away. The officers were so surprised that they never fired a shot.[14]

Sometime later, Butch and Al showed up in Auburn in the northwest part of Star Valley, near the Idaho-Wyoming border. Both Matt Warner and Tom McCarty had married local Auburn girls a few years earlier and the families of the girls remained in the area.[15] Butch and Al spent the winter in a small log cabin on the Hugh Morgan place.[16] It was reported that Al played cards with locals during the winter while Butch spent his time on the George Davis ranch. Neither drank or danced while they were in Auburn. Locals liked the men and said Butch was an excellent shot and "could drive nails with his bullets." George Davis had hay for sale, which the two needed for their horses.[17]

Some reports have Cassidy and Hainer working at a sawmill most likely located on Stump Creek outside of Auburn.[18] Auburn today is located in Lincoln County, but in 1892 it was a part of Uinta County.[19] The sawmill may actually have been located west of Auburn in Idaho.

John Chapman had traveled to Evanston during the fall searching for the two suspected horse thieves, but with the approaching winter in Star Valley, he decided to wait until spring before continuing his search. Otto Franc reported in his personal journal, "Chapman returned from his horse thief hunting trip" on December 26, 1891.[20]

In January 1892, it was reported that ten horse thieves were killed in a skirmish while rounding up stolen stock near Red Lodge, Montana.[21] The ranchers were fed up and took extreme measures. The Chapman brothers had recently lost 150 head of horses and nearly 400 had been stolen in the area.[22] Vigilantes organized to fight the thieves, killing an additional four men in February 1892.[23]

J.K. Moore Hotel in Fort Washakie. Butch eluded officers here in the fall of 1891. (*Wyoming State Archives*)

In April a seven-man posse arrived in Star Valley for Cassidy and Hainer.[24] Some say the passes into the valley were still covered in snow, and the posse had come in on foot using snowshoes.[25] John Chapman had sought assistance from Uinta County authorities. Sheriff John Ward allowed his tough and able deputy sheriff, Bob Calverly, to assist Chapman.[26]

George Davis was the first postmaster of Auburn and apparently delivered mail to the outlaws. Deputy Calverly and John Chapman were able to locate Cassidy and Hainer by following Davis to their location.[27]

On April 11,[28] the posse arrested Al Hainer without incident near the sawmill as he watched the loggers working. They took him to the Harrison store in Auburn.[29] Two posse members stayed with Hainer while the other five went for Butch. Butch lay asleep inside the cabin on the George Davis ranch. The lawmen called out that they had him surrounded and to come out and give himself up. Butch responded with, "Let's get to fighting!"[30] When he didn't come out, Deputy Calverly entered the cabin.

Calverly described what happened, "I arrested Cassidy on April 11, 1892. . . . I told him I had a warrant for him and he said: 'Well get to shooting,' and with that we both pulled our guns. I put the barrel of my revolver almost to his stomach, but it missed fired [misfired] three times but owing to the fact that there was another man between us, he failed to hit me. The fourth time I snapped the gun it went off and the bullet hit him in the upper part of his forehead and felled him. I then had him and he made no further resistance."

Calverly used a Colt 1873 Double Action 44.–40 which has a cylinder that can easily rotate unless the hammer is fully pulled back which could explain the possible misfires during the scuffle.[31]

The *Fremont Clipper* in Lander told a different version. Cassidy and Hainer were arrested on April 8, 1892. Cassidy gave "considerable resistance" and when ordered to throw up his hands, he responded, "Never to you damned sons of bitches!" In a "desperate struggle" with Bob Calverly, Cassidy was "beaten senseless" and "cuffs and shackles were applied to his limbs."[32]

Another report claims Cassidy responded, "No, I'll be damned if I do," at the same instance drawing a gun from a pair of overalls he was wearing over his trousers.[33]

John W. Chapman was said to have had a high regard for Cassidy and assisted in caring for his wounds at the time of capture.[34] According to a local Auburn history, Butch was beaten repeatedly on the head. He had thirty-five gashes aside from the bullet wound.[35] When he was taken to the Harrison store, some of the townspeople bandaged his head.[36]

Another report claims one member of the posse was a "coward" and waited until Butch was handcuffed then started pushing him around saying, "Well, Cassidy, we've got you down again," to which Butch responded, "Like hell you've got me down. I want you to know that I slipped and fell down." Butch reportedly said he preferred death to capture.[37]

✦ ✦ ✦

TENSION WAS BUILDING in Wyoming at this time as members of the Wyoming Stock Growers Association had essentially declared war on homesteaders and owners of small ranches. Butch was caught in the middle. The fight was over land and open-range grazing. Owners of large ranching operations thought the settlers were rustling their cattle and claiming the best waterholes and hay meadows for their homesteads.

About the same time as Butch's arrest, an "invading" vigilante group of about fifty out-of-work Texas lawmen and Wyoming stockmen stopped at a cabin near present-day Kaycee, Wyoming, and killed Nate Champion and "Nick" Ray after an all day siege on April 9, 1892. This event was the beginning of what later became known as the "Johnson County War."[38]

On April 22, 1892, the *Fremont Clipper* called it "War in Wyoming" and the "Rustlers War" and explained that "the rustlers comprise all of the small ranchmen and settlers in the country."[39]

Colonel Jay L. Torrey (with flag) and his Rough Riders staff which included Bob Calverly (far right), who arrested Butch in 1892. (*Wyoming State Archives*)

As a result, several smaller ranchers and settlers in the Big Horn Basin banded together to "devise a means of protection and defense." They adopted several resolutions which stated their objections to being labeled "rustlers" and "deserving of death" for their "ownership of cattle or an acre of ground." They further stated that "should armed invaders attempt to take by violence the lives or property of our fellow citizens we will meet them with such force as will be adequate protection."[40]

BUTCH WAS FORTUNATE to be alive. If Calverly's revolver had not misfired, he could have been killed. A few days later, a vigilante posse led by the same John Chapman cornered and killed two suspected horse rustlers in Jackson Hole, Spencer and Burnett. This posse was operating from a list of "rustlers" to be "eliminated," generated by the big ranchers during the Johnson County War according to testimony given by William M. Colloum at the Coroner's Inquest for Nate Champion and Nick Ray. One wonders if Butch was on the this list of men to be exterminated along with Spencer, Burnett, Champion, and Ray.

One newspaper indicated that Cassidy and Hainer had eight head of horses in their possession when captured (seven from the Grey Bull Cattle Company along with a stallion from Thomas Kent), considerably more than

Judge Jesse Knight presided over both of Butch's trials. (*Wyoming State Archives*)

Butch's attorney and friend Douglas Preston. (*Fremont County Pioneer Museum*)

the three horses from Nutcher. However they were never charged in connection with these other horses, making the report somewhat questionable.[41]

As Hainer and Cassidy were escorted from the store they shook hands with the locals. Cassidy later told F.N. Putnam that while coming out of rough Crow Creek Canyon, he was able to slip his hands out of his handcuffs to adjust the bandages on his head. He had small hands and large wrists, a trait common in the Parker family. Butch said he was waiting for a chance to grab a gun from one of the possemen and then "I was going to build up the cutest little smoke you ever saw." But the opportunity never came.[42]

Butch and Al were taken to the Uinta County Jail in Evanston and held there for two months. The jail records indicate that they were received on April 14. Butch was listed as prisoner 435, "George Cassady," and Al as prisoner 436, "Al Hayner." Butch was discharged (for transfer) on June 14, while Al was discharged a week later on June 22.[43] Two other Fremont County prisoners were held in jail at the same time, Jack Bliss and Kid Collier, who had been received on March 25, 1892.[44]

Butch was moved to the Fremont County jail in Lander where he spent a month or more. According to the Fremont County Jail Register, both "George Cassidy" and "Albert Hayner," twenty-five years of age, were received on June 10, 1892, as prisoners 148 and 149, respectively.[45] Obviously a discrepancy exists in jail records between Uinta and Fremont County, as the men could not have been both places on June 10. Fremont County Jail records indicate that Cassidy was released on July 29, 1892, and Hainer was released on July 30, 1892, as their cases continued.

On July 16, 1892, Butch and Hainer were formally charged with Grand Larceny involving the theft of a horse valued at $40 from the Grey Bull Cattle Company. Butch and Hainer each posted $400 bail and were released.

Butch's trial was delayed over a year as prosecutor James S. Vidal requested additional time for their witnesses to appear. Butch hired his friend Douglas Preston as his attorney. C.F. Rathbone assisted. Butch was given notice on March 14, 1893, to appear in court on June 12, 1893.

Beginning in early 1893, Billy Nutcher started taking out bank loans that he apparently did not intend to repay. Nutcher and his partner, John D. McCullough, borrowed $347.11 from one bank and $125 from another bank the following day. Interestingly enough, Sheriff Charles Stough of Lander acted as guarantor on behalf of Nutcher. Billy Nutcher was preparing to leave the area.[46]

✧ ✧ ✧

ON MAY 13, 1893, the Justice of the Peace Record Book for Fremont County shows Butch and Billy Nutcher were charged with riding two Embar horses on the open range. They were delivered to Justice of the Peace Ed Cusack by special deputy A. J. "Jack" Price (his brother Jacob Price was foreman of the Embar) on May 27, 1893. Butch pled guilty and was fined $25, however, Nutcher failed to appear. Nutcher appeared a month later for the trial of his brother Joseph but then vanished. Nutcher showed up years later in Mexico and California. Census information indicates he lived a lengthy life into the 1930s with a wife and children in California.[47]

In later years, Ed Cusack recalled that Jack Price and Virgil Rice, both deputy sheriffs, brought in Butch. He said Butch decided to plead guilty and was fined $50 and costs. He said Butch could not pay, and so he was sent to the county jail in Lander. Cusack said Price had a lot of faith in Butch, so Price paid the fine and Butch was released. Ed indicated it was his understanding that Butch never re-paid Price.[48]

Will Simpson, Butch's old friend who was also Butch's prosecutor for his two trials. (*Courtesy of Nancy Adams*)

Historian Pat Schroeder of Wyoming says her research shows that Cassidy and Nutcher sold the horses to Jacob Price who was manager of the Embar. They had not been paid, so they returned to retrieve the horses and were arrested.[49]

If Cassidy and Nutcher had truly stolen the horses, Cassidy was obviously fortunate to only be fined $25 and set free. The larger ranchers in the Basin, such as Torrey, were likely not amused at the small fine and release of Cassidy; they would be better prepared in the future to get him.

✧ ✧ ✧

COURT CONVENED ON Butch's earlier charges (the Grey Bull Cattle Company charges) on July 20, 1893, before Fremont County District Court Judge Jesse Knight. During the year's time, prosecutor Vidal had been defeated for re-election. The new prosecutor was Butch's old friend Will Simpson. Some said Will's parents were not happy with him for prosecuting George Cassidy whom they considered a fine man. Will Simpson was assisted by M.C. Brown, a former judge.

A delay requested by the defendants was denied on June 12, 1893. Two of their key witnesses, C. F. Willis and J. S. Green, were supposed to reside in Uinta County, but Sheriff Ward and Deputy Calverly could not locate them and wrote, "No such man found in Uinta County." Apparently the judge felt a year's continuance had already been sufficient time.

Sheriff John Ward issued a subpoena for Billy Nutcher, but he could not be found.

The defendants, Cassidy and Hainer, did not deny they were in possession of the horses, but insisted they purchased the horses from Billy Nutcher at Mail Camp and had two witnesses, Willis and Green, who could attest to the transaction. Unfortunately they were forced to proceed without the witnesses.

A member of the jury was Butch's friend and banker Eugene Amoretti, Jr.[50]

The trial was speedy. The next day, Judge Knight charged the jury and quoted the law, "Whoever steals any horse, mule or neat cattle at the value of $5.00 or upwards, or receives, buys or conceals any such horse which shall have been stolen shall be imprisoned in the Penitentiary not more that ten years or may be imprisoned in the county jail not more than 6 months."

The jury deliberated only two hours.[51] Jury foreman Seddon Jones delivered the verdict the following day on June 22, 1893. He read, "We, the jury find the above named defendants, George Cassidy and Al Hainer, not guilty."

Just three days before the verdict was given the enemies of Cassidy became aware the defendants would be found "not guilty," so prosecutors filed a second complaint on June 19, 1893. To avoid duplicate charges, Cassidy and Hainer were accused of stealing a different horse this time. This horse, belonging to Richard Ashworth, was valued at $50 on August 28, 1891.[52] Cassidy and Hainer were re-arrested and the new trial was scheduled for June 1894. Surety bonds were again obtained and the two were released.

IN NOVEMBER OF 1893, the banks that had loaned Nutcher money began proceedings against Nutcher and McCullough. Their attorney swore an affidavit for their property and swore that Nutcher "had absconded with the intention of defrauding his creditors." Nutcher's cattle were quickly rounded up and impounded by Jack Price. Conveniently his brother, Jacob assessed the value of the cattle along with George H. Smith.

Cassidy and Jakie Snyder won a "writ of replevin" against the banks disputing the ownership of property seized. It appears they later dropped their cases as the banks had yet to recover any stock.[53]

Butch then filed a complaint against Jack Price, for stealing eight neat cattle on January 29, 1894. Jakie Snyder filed a similar charge the same day against Price.[54] The trial was scheduled for February 9, 1894.

Jack Price appeared before Justice of the Peace Cusack objecting to the sufficiency of the bonds for each case. On February 19, the day Cusack was to rule on the ownership of the disputed cattle, Jack Price on behalf of the Embar forced the sale of the cattle by claiming they were being held in Embar pastures and refusing to hold them any longer.

Sheriff Stough published the "Order of Sale" in the newspaper. On March 12, 1894, it was reported that Jack Price sold the cattle to his brother Jacob Price for $100 and the horses were sold for $68 to John H. McCoy and Fred McClain.[55]

JURY SELECTION FOR CASSIDY and Hainer's second criminal trial started on June 30, 1894, and the jury was filled on July 2 after three separate attempts. This time, Will Simpson prosecuted the trial by himself, not skimping on witnesses as he subpoenaed twelve individuals compared to Douglas Preston's four witnesses.[56] The trial preceeded, and the jury retired on July 3, 1894. The foreman, George S. Russell delivered the verdict on Independence Day, July 4, 1894:[57]

"We the jury find the above named defendant George Cassidy guilty of horse stealing as charged in the information and we find the value of the property stolen to be $5 (the minimum for Grand Larceny). And we find the above named defendant Al Hainer not guilty and the jury recommends the said Cassidy to the mercy of the court."

Once the verdict was read, Butch was bound over for sentencing. Al Hainer reacted with harsh words when the verdict was read. He was judged guilty of contempt of court and bound over for sentencing on July 9, 1894.[58] It was rumored that Hainer sold out his partner Cassidy and that his outburst was a way of covering his tracks.

According to Will Simpson, Hainer's contempt charge may have been due to an attempt to attack Simpson before the verdict was read, as it was evident Cassidy would be found guilty.

Simpson stated: "Sunday morning an attempt was made upon my life by Hainer, a Mexican by the name of Armenti, and a half breed by the name of Lamoreaux, who jerked me off my horse in front of the livery stable about sunup and attempted to get me inside the stable. They were all drunk and all defendants being tried at the term of court except Lamoreaux. I was riding a rather wild horse and as I was jerked off the horse by Lamoreaux I held to the bridle and turned the horse around, and he kicked Lamoreaux up against the stable. This gave me an opportunity to get my six-shooter, which was between my overalls and my under clothes, and they all disappeared into the barn."[59] Ed Lamoreaux was a brother to Mary Lamoreaux who had been one of Butch's girlfriends.

Simpson also claimed that the same day Butch had horsewhipped one of the witnesses for the prosecution for giving false testimony. Simpson wrote, "On Sunday morning, Cassidy, who was in custody of Virgil Rice, a deputy sheriff, at the courthouse horse-whipped one of the witnesses, Arapahoe Dave, for giving his testimony to the effect that he had seen one of the horses in his [Butch's] possession on the Owl Creek mountains."[60]

TWO YEARS LATER, Al Hainer was arrested with another of Cassidy's friends, Jakie Snyder. Judge Jay L. Torrey swore out a criminal complaint against the two for stealing twelve head of cattle on October 22, 1895.[61] According to the Jail Register for Fremont County, Jakie Snyder and Al Hainer were received on October 30, 1895, for Grand Larceny. Jakie was found guilty and sentenced to five years hard labor in the pen in Laramie. Hainer was released on bail February 12, 1896. One begins to wonder if Hainer was working as an informant.

When Butch was released from prison in January 1896, Hainer was in jail in Lander.[62] Hainer would fade from history in the coming years. The 1896 Lander directory lists Hainer residing at the "Cottage Home Hotel" and working at a livery stable.[63] Hainer is listed as a woolgrower in Laramie in 1900.[64] He "ran a poker [game] for Jerry Sheehan in Fremont for a year or so" and then relocated to Oregon where he died around 1935 in an asylum.[65]

Jakie Snyder experienced numerous legal troubles in 1894 and 1895. He was charged with stealing a horse, robbing E.C. Enderly's store, and was a victim in a shooting "with the intent to kill" near Owl Creek. Snyder was later murdered by a jealous husband in 1909.[66]

✧ ✧ ✧

THE FREMONT COUNTY jail register indicates George Cassidy was received on July 4, 1894, as prisoner 192. He was discharged on July 10, 1894, for

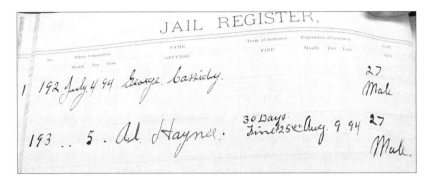

This Fremont County (Wyoming) jail register shows the names of George Cassidy and Al Hayner. (*Fremont County Sheriff's office*)

"two years in Penitentiary at Laramie City." The jail register shows Al "Hayner" being received on July 5 as prisoner 193 for "30 days and fined $25 for contempt of court." He was discharged on Aug 9 by H. H. Brower.[67]

On July 7, Douglas Preston filed a motion for a new trial. His reasons were lack of evidence and an error in the judge's instructions to the jury. Two days later Judge Knight denied the motion. Judge Knight did admit error on the part of the prosecution. The law states, "he who steals any horse . . . or receives any horse . . . shall be guilty of horse stealing." The prosecution excluded, "knowing the same to have been stolen." Judge Knight in denying the motion said that he "had given several other instructions which cured the mistake" and "that I had instructed the jury that the charge of the Court should be taken as a whole and that they were not at liberty to base their verdict upon any one single, instruction."

On July 10, 1894, Butch's sentence was pronounced by Judge Knight: "It is therefore considered, ordered, and adjudged by the court that you, George Cassidy, be taken by the sheriff of Fremont County to the Wyoming State Penitentiary at, or near, Laramie City in the County of Albany in the State of Wyoming and by him delivered to the rules and regulations of said prison, for the term of two years at hard labor."

Judge Knight also sentenced Hainer as follows, "It is therefore considered, ordered and adjudged by the court that you, Albert Hainer, be confined and imprisoned in the County jail of the County of Fremont, Wyoming, for the term of thirty days and that you pay a fine of twenty five dollars and that you stand committed until the fine shall be freely paid."

Judge Jesse Knight did admit to Butch that possibly he had not received a fair trial. But Butch wrote a note to the Judge and told him "he had no cause to complain, that he had received justice," consequently thanking him for a fair trial. However, at the time of his sentencing Butch felt differently and told the judge that he was "innocent and had been convicted on perjured evidence and bought testimony."[68]

Interestingly, the value of the horse changed from $50 to $5 in the second trial. Possibly Judge Knight had instructed the jury to determine the value of the horse. It is also possible that attorney Preston appealed. However, Butch, who had already been tied up in trials for two years, likely wanted to serve his time and move on. Butch was only sentenced to two years, when he could have been sentenced to up to ten years for grand larceny. Lula wrote he was bitter over being convicted of stealing a horse valued at only $5. But the lower value assured that his sentence was relatively light.

Years later, Judge Knight told the governor that Butch had learned he had been found guilty before the verdict was read and friends had offered a horse and assistance in an escape. Butch believed Judge Knight to be an honest man who would not be "governed by those persecuting him instead of prosecuting him." Butch said he would remain to accept his sentence. Judge Knight admitted that Torrey "was quite anxious . . . Cassidy receive a long term of imprisonment." Judge Knight said, "My own judgment was that while it was true a great deal of money had been expended in procuring witnesses and private counsel to aid the prosecution, still under the circumstances, if Cassiday was sentenced to a reasonable term of imprisonment, he was more liable to be benefited by the imprisonment and come out of the penitentiary a good man than he would be if he were sentenced even to the full extent of the law."[69] Fortunately, at that time, the authorities never connected "Bud Parker" of the Telluride Bank Robbery to George Cassidy.

Butch likely felt fortunate in comparison to his brother Dan who had received a life sentence just a few years earlier. It certainly took a huge toll on his mother, Annie, who was extremely distraught over having two sons in prison.

Top: George "Butch" Cassidy in his mug shot from the Wyoming Territorial Prison. *(Wyoming State Archives)*
Above: Butch's signature as "George Cassidy" on the trial affidavit. *(Fremont County Courthouse)*

9. The Big House Across the River, 1894-1896

CCORDING TO THE Simpson family, Butch spent the night before he entered prison at their home. Butch had convinced the jail deputy to ask clerk of court Ben Sheldon to allow him to take care of some unfinished personal business. He promised to be back by daylight and Sheldon responded, "If Cassidy said so, he'll keep his word."[1]

The next day, Sunday, Butch and five other prisoners (William Wheaton, Harry Gilchrist, William Nicols, Charley Brown, and Isaac Winkle[2]) were escorted to Laramie by Fremont County Sheriff Charlie Stough and Lander Town Constable Hank Boedeker.[3]

Butch entered the old territorial penitentiary in Laramie on July 15, 1894. Upon arrival, Warden A. W. Adams found Butch not wearing the customary leg shackles and demanded to know why. Before Stough could reply, Butch answered, "Honor among thieves, I guess."[4]

Adams interviewed Butch and gave him the rules and regulations of prison life. He became prisoner number 187. He stated his name as George Cassidy. Records were given as follows: "where convicted and Sentenced–Lander, Wyoming, County of Fremont. Term of Court–June 1894. Date of sentence–July 12, 1894. Place of Confinement–Wyoming State Penitentiary. Crime–Grand Larceny. Length of Sentence–Two(2) years. Sex–Male. Age–27. Nativity–New York City. Occupation–Cow Boy. Height–5 feet 9 inches. Color–White. Complexion–Light. Hair–Dark Flaxen. Eyes–Blue. Has Wife–No. Parents–Don't know. Children–No. Religion–None. Habits of Life–Intemperate. Education–Common School. Relations Address–Not Known. Marks, Scars and General Remarks–Weight 165 lbs. Features–regular, Small deep set eyes. Two (2) cut scars on back of head; small red scar under left eye (this scar was reported to have been received from Bob Calverly when he was arrested in Star Valley[5]). Red mark on left side of back. Small brown mole on calf of left leg. Comment: 'Good Build.' A. W. Adams, Warden."

Butch "did time" at the Wyoming Territorial Prison in Laramie. (*Wyoming–Territorial Prison–Laramie, Photo File, American Heritage Center, University of Wyoming*)

One-hundred-thirteen prisoners were incarcerated there when Butch arrived. Local news reported that the broom factory, once shut down, had begun operating again.[6] The prison was made up of two cellblocks each totaling forty-two cells (fourteen cells on a level, stacked three high). The north cellblock was made of adobe, and the cells measured six feet by eight feet. The south cellblock was added in 1889 and had steel cells measuring five feet by seven feet. Each cell was designed to sleep two prisoners in canvas hammocks.[7]

Butch then took a bath and was given clean prison clothes which included a shirt and striped pants. His head was likely shaved, and he was then escorted to his cell and given a candle, blanket, and a pillow.

According to the Stoner family, Butch shared a cell with Abraham "Rocky" Stoner, a rancher from Cokeville, Wyoming. The men were likely assigned a cell in the north end of the prison, which was the older section.[8] The cell was cramped for two prisoners. Butch later stayed on Stoner's ranch on Sublette Creek south of Cokeville and left money with Stoner for safekeeping. Stoner served two prison terms and was on trial when he died in 1909.[9]

Because Butch's prison term was only two years, he was not required to work in the broom factory. He was allowed to remain in his cell and could read books from the prison library. Butch likely wanted to be outside and may

Sheriff Charlie Stough (at right) took Butch Cassidy and five other men from Fremont County to the prison in Laramie. Below are the prison mug shots of Cassidy and the five other men. (*Fremont County Pioneer Museum and Wyoming State Archives*)

The petition requesting a pardon for George Cassidy was signed by prominent men. (*Wyoming State Archives*)

have worked in the prison garden. He may have also worked with horses on the prison ranch.

Butch was familiar with several of his fellow prisoners. He was friends with Joe Nutcher, whose brother Billy had sold Butch the horses that led to his incarceration.

He knew of Albert "Slick" Nard and likely wanted to stay clear of him. Nard had been hired by John Chapman to help bring in rustlers but later was involved in killings that sent him to the pen.[10] He turned on his partner, Jack Bliss, and helped kill him during his capture while acting as a lawman. Nard also assisted in the capture Joe Nutcher.

Butch's old friend Tom Osborne was also incarcerated as well as Kinch McKinney. Kinch had been Dan Parker's cellmate during his trial in

Left: John D. Woodruff, accompanied by Judge Torrey, made a visit to Cassidy in prison, but Cassidy refused to see Torrey. Woodruff, a state senator, later signed the petition asking for a pardon. (*Wyoming State Archives*)
Right: Governor W.A. Richards pardoned George Cassidy six months early for good behavior in January 1896. (*Wyoming State Archives*)

Cheyenne. Kinch was able to escape during Butch's stay and was gone for two months until being recaptured. As a result he had to carry a ball and chain on his ankle for a month.[11]

Old pal Jakie Snyder arrived later at the prison for stealing horses from the Embar.[12]

Another prisoner was an individual named William T. Wilcox. It is unclear what relationship Wilcox developed with Butch. However years later in the 1930s, Wilcox visited old friends of Cassidy using the name William T. Phillips and even confided to people that *he was* Butch Cassidy. Phillips also penned a manuscript about Cassidy and his exploits. Some of the information in the manuscript indicated he may have had a close connection to Cassidy.

William T. Wilcox was in prison at the same time as Butch and, years later, confided to some that *he was* Butch Cassidy. (*Wyoming State Archives*)

On Labor Day of 1894, a rodeo was held at the prison for the entertainment of the prisoners. If Butch was allowed to attend, he would probably have enjoyed the event as he loved a good show of horse skills.[13]

Nearly a year after Butch's arrival, a local photographer was hired to take pictures of 105 of the inmates. On May 22, 1895, Butch's mug shot was taken. By then his hair had grown back. Butch wore his jacket as it was still cool in Laramie in the third week of May.[14]

On May 25, 1895, N. D. McDonald was appointed as the new warden at the prison.[15]

Butch was a model prisoner; however his sister Lula shared that he became bitter in prison and said if people wanted to label him an outlaw, he would show them what an outlaw was. He planned to make his mark in the world when he was released.

During 1895, Judge Torrey went to the prison with Senator Woodruff and attempted to visit Butch.[16] Butch refused to see him and "expressed [he was] very much opposed to Torrey and his methods."[17] Butch felt he had been framed and that Torrey had played a part in that.

Abraham "Rocky"
Stoner may have been
Butch's cellmate in the
Laramie prison.
(*Wyoming State Archives*)

Fremont County District Court Judge Jesse Knight wrote to Governor Richards on September 28, 1895, recommending that Butch be pardoned early. Knight mentioned that Sheriff John Ward had visited the prison recently and had also suggested an early pardon. He hoped that Butch would leave prison rehabilitated and having an influence on others for good. Judge Knight said, "Cassidy's pardon would have much to do in causing him to become a law abiding citizen." Judge Knight saw potential in Butch long before he ever became the infamous Butch Cassidy. He said, "Cassiday is a man that would be hard to describe – a brave, daring fellow and a man well calculated to be a leader, and should his inclinations run that way, I do not doubt but that he would be capable of organizing and leading a lot of desperate men to desperate deeds."[18]

Governor Richards responded with his sole question: would George Cassidy do what was expected when released? But he concluded it was worth a try. He requested a petition signed by a few responsible men be forwarded to him. He hoped that this would place Cassidy under obligation to the individuals. As a result, several highly-respected men signed the petition. The

list included the sheriff, clerk of court, county commissioners, senator, judge
and leading citizens of Fremont County. Included were Judge Knight, Orson Grimmitt (Sheriff), W.S. Firestone, E.A. Earl, E.F. Cheney, Ben W. Sheldon, J.L. Baldwin, W.H. Rheim, H.A. Brower, John D. Woodruff, M.J.
Crowley, A.M. Sparhawk, and H.M. Farlow. The names are impressive and
show Butch was well-liked by people on both sides of the law.

Deputy Sheriff Harry Logue who served in Lander under Charlie
Stough stated, "Butch Cassidy was as fine a fellow as anyone would ever care
to meet, he never was half as bad as he was painted."[19]

Evidence exists that Butch did make some type of deal with the governor promising to commit no more crimes in Wyoming after his pardon. Such
promises were often typical when a prisoner was offered a pardon. Will Simpson confirmed this in a letter he wrote to author Charles Kelly in 1939. Will
states Butch "was not to turn a trick in Wyoming, and he assured me that
while he was on his get-away that had done nothing whatever to do with the
[recent] Wilcox robbery or the killing of Hazen."

Governor William A. Richards arrived in Laramie on January 18, 1896,
making a visit to the penitentiary. He sought the warden regarding some recently escaped prisoners as well as to see Butch in follow-up to the letters received from Judge Knight.[20]

Butch was pardoned six months early on January 19, 1896.[21] Butch told
Judge Knight that his bad feelings for Judge Torrey had ceased. In a letter
from Governor Richards to Judge Torrey, the governor wrote:

"He [Butch] assured me at the time of his pardon that he had no quar-
rel with you [Judge Torrey] or anyone else in Fremont County, that he had
enough of Penitentiary life and intended to conduct himself in such a way
as to not again lay himself liable to arrest . . . Cassidy has left Fremont
County and does not intend to again make his residence there."[22]

History proves Butch had other plans.

Butch boarded the train in Laramie along with warden N.D. McDonald. The warden was traveling to Boise to return a recently captured escaped
prisoner.[23] Butch rode with the warden as far as Evanston where Butch left the
train to travel to Cokeville. He'd promised to visit Rocky Stoner's wife, Ella,
to deliver the message that Rocky was doing well under the circumstances.[24]

10. Detroit House of Corrections, 1891~1897

I N DETROIT, MICHIGAN, Butch's brother Dan had already served three years in prison when Butch began his incarceration in Wyoming.

The Detroit House of Corrections warden stated on March 16, 1895, that since Dan's incarceration in 1891, "his conduct has been very good, in fact excellent and that "his health is good; no organic disturbance noticeable." The prison physician examined Dan and reported the same day that he found him to be "enjoying very good health."[1]

Prison life in the Detroit House of Corrections was intense. The general health of the prisoners was adequate; however, several deaths occurred primarily due to pneumonia, consumption, and tuberculosis.[2] William Brown, Dan's partner, would later develop tuberculosis and mental disorders. Brown was released from prison and committed to St. Elizabeth's Insane Asylum in Washington D.C. on July 10, 1900. A physical examination described that he believed he was still at the prison and suffered from delusions in which he thought he owned all the metal in the ground as well as several railroads. Brown's health continued to worsen. He died "rather suddenly" eleven days later at age forty on July 21, 1900.[3]

Butch's parents felt that Butch had received a fair sentence of two years in contrast to Dan's life sentence which they believed was "extreme and out of proportion to the offense." And as a result they began a letter writing campaign to the U.S. President for a possible pardon. They wrote to President Grover Cleveland through Senators Joseph Rawlins and Frank Cannon of the Utah Territory. Maxi and Annie maintained Dan's innocence and insisted that he had been at home in Circleville when the robbery occurred.[4]

Maxi's attorney drafted a letter to President Grover Cleveland on behalf of the Parkers and pleaded Dan's case by laying out several "statements of fact." He stated that Dan's attorneys were appointed by the court and were "called into the case without sufficient investigation and preparation," which resulted

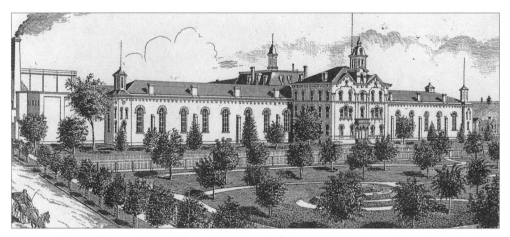

Detroit House of Corrections where Dan Parker served time from 1891–1897. (*Author's collection*)

in Dan "having no means to procure witnesses that would have proven his absence at the time and place, when said robbery was alleged to have been committed." Next the attorney embellished Dan's young age by stating Dan "was then only a boy—a few months past 17 years of age." In reality Dan was twenty-two years old at the time of the robbery in 1889. He claimed Dan's conviction "almost wholly and solely rested on the testimony of—one Abe Coons" whose reputation "for truth and veracity, and reliability as to his statements is very doubtful and questionable." The letter stated that Abe Coons was heard to say that "he could only identify and swear to one of the men or boys who held him up" and that Dan's innocence could be proven. He wrote that due to Maxi's own ill health "caused by exposure in the mountains and hard work" he was unable "to obtain such affidavits and other evidence" to prove Dan's innocence. He stressed how critically Dan was needed at home, saying that "his [Maxi's] health is permanently destroyed, and he is virtually unable to earn such support as his family need[s], and that the help and assistance of his son is daily and absolutely necessary." He continued by saying Maxi "is now confined to his bed, and no hopes are entertained for his recovery, and that his wife will thereby be left a widow with seven children, her oldest boy being only 14 yrs old."[5] Maxi was fifty-one years old at this time and would live to the age of ninety-four.

Maxi stated through his attorney that if Coons's testimony was to be believed then, because of Dan's youth, he was "certainly led into said crime by

Left: Senator Joseph Rawlins was instrumental in obtaining Dan's presidential pardon. (*Used by permission, Utah State Historical Society, all rights reserved*)
Right: Dan Parker in about 1900. (*Author's collection*)

said Brown, who was 30 years his senior . . . and adept in crime." In reality, William Brown was only seven years older than Dan, but he was an experienced outlaw. Maxi further argued that Dan had already served four years and eight months of his sentence, and this was his first offense. Maxi said that the "punishment is extreme and unwarranted by the evidence and that no repentance can ever be made manifest by [the] defendant and as he avers he might as well have received the punishment of death for having committed said offense as to be sentenced to imprisonment for life." Maxi ended with the statement "that the ends of justice have already been satisfied by the years of his incarceration: that his good conduct is guaranteed in the future."[6]

On Dan's behalf, Senator Joseph L. Rawlins confirmed Maxi's statements in a letter in 1895. He further claimed that Dan was at home in Circleville at the time of the robbery. He said, "I am personally acquainted with Parker's parents and they are respectable people, although quite poor." He said Dan had a respectable reputation up to the time of the alleged offense.

The first page of Dan Parker's Presidential Pardon shows President William McKinley's signature. (*Author's collection*)

Senator Rawlins said that he, as an attorney, had "carefully read the testimony of the principal witness against Parker and it leaves considerable doubt as to his [Dan's] identity." Senator Rawlins said he believed if Dan had participated in the crime, he had undoubtedly been led into the crime by Brown. He believed the "ends of justice would be subserved by the pardon of young Parker" and recommended the pardon be granted.[7]

Desperate, the Parkers even contacted Dan's prosecuting attorney, Benjamin F. Fowler, who consequently wrote on March 1, 1895, on Dan's behalf, "I am of the opinion that the Defendant has been sufficiently punished. In fact . . . I think that the statute is far too severe. Four years imprisonment in penitentiary

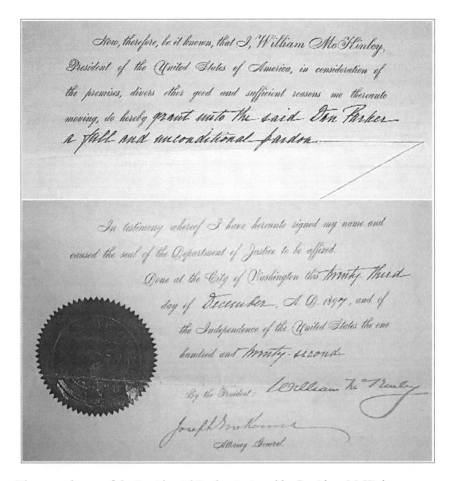

The second page of the Presidential Pardon is signed by President McKinley on December 23, 1897. (*Author's collection*)

should certainly be sufficient punishment for the acts which this young man has committed. As I remember young Parker, he was rather a bright, intelligent young man, and did not impress me as being of a vicious type."[8]

The first attempt to get Dan pardoned was unsuccessful. On March 24, 1895, President Grover Cleveland denied Dan's pardon application by writing, "I cannot find sufficient justification for interfering with the sentence in this case at this time—G. C."[9]

Although frustrated, Dan's parents were not dissuaded in their efforts to seek a pardon with the assistance of several officials. Senator Frank Cannon of Utah wrote to President Cleveland in 1896. He urged him to again review the case and stressed how the aged Mrs. Parker needed Dan at home. He stated, "Perhaps you may find the situation as it exists to-day justification for pardon."[10] This letter fell on deaf ears because President Grover Cleveland was completing his last of two terms of office and was replaced the next year by William McKinley.

President William McKinley acted on the pleas of Dan's mother and urging from Senator Rawlins. Senator Rawlins requested President McKinley grant the pardon as a "Christmas present for the unhappy mother."[11] President McKinley granted Dan's pardon on December 23, 1897.[12] Dan was released on December 28, 1897, after serving six years and eight months. Dan was thirty years old.

Once Dan arrived home safely, Annie wrote to President McKinley on January 8, 1898, thanking him. She wrote, "Please except [accept] the gratitude of a fond mother's heart for the joy you have brought into the house hold by granting a pardon."[13]

President McKinley was shot and killed less than four years later by an assassin on September 6, 1901.[14]

Annie was also grateful to Senator Joseph Rawlins for his efforts to get Dan released. In honor of Senator Rawlins, she had named her youngest son, born in 1894, after the senator. His full name was Joseph Rawlins Parker.

Dan immediately returned home to Circle Valley, Utah, after being released from prison. He lived peacefully with his family. Prison life had cured Dan of his outlaw ways.

11. Montpelier Bank Robbery, 1896

O N JULY 24, 1896, just six months after Butch's release from the Wyoming Territorial Prison, the Lander newspaper reported that Butch was wanted for stealing a herd of cattle. The newspaper stated, "Governor Richards is not well pleased with the pardon he granted to Cassidy. Cassidy it will be remembered, received his pardon at the hands of the Governor, and the first use he made of his liberty was to steal a herd of cattle, for which offense the authorities of Sweetwater County want him bad."[1] It is unclear if this was an erroneous report or if Butch was exacting revenge on Torrey.[2]

Butch had returned to the Brown's Park area and become reacquainted with his old friends Elzy Lay and Matt Warner. Elzy had married local girl Maude Davis from the Vernal, Utah, area. Warner wrote that Butch and Elzy were at his ranch on and off again.[3] Elzy's forte was training horses. Elzy's grandson said that he didn't break horses, but instead he trained them by gaining their trust.[4] This talent would serve Butch and Elzy well in the coming years.

Matt Warner had married and his wife pleaded for him to put his outlaw days behind him. In an attempt to find honest work, he took a job protecting some mining claims in the Dry Fork Creek area near Vernal, Utah, for E.B. Coleman. He was involved in a gunfight and killed two men who he claimed had ambushed him.[5] Warner claimed he, Coleman, and William Wall turned themselves into Sheriff John T. Pope promptly. Pope arrested the three, charged them with first degree murder, and brought them before the court.[6] The public was angry and attempted to lynch the gunfighters. According to Warner, Butch and Elzy were involved in fighting off the mob.[7]

Butch reportedly made a visit to the Vernal jail to talk to Warner in the presence of Pope and to offer his help in any way.[8]

Sheriff Pope decided to move the prisoners to a more secure location at Ogden, Utah. He transferred the prisoners during the night to avoid both the angry crowds and the possibility that friends of the outlaws might assist in their escape. Pope tied the outlaws' feet together under their mules and refused to let them down, not even to relieve themselves. Warner swore he would kill Pope for this treatment. Warner described the incident, "Sheriff John Pope and four deputies took Bill and me to Ogden. They are so scared of me and at me so much they handcuff me and tie my handcuffed hands to the horn of the saddle, pass a rope under the belly of the mule they put me on, and tie my ankles so tight they get raw and bled. They are so scared stiff that Butch Cassidy and his gang will follow us and try to rescue me. They slip away in the night with me and ride as fast as the route will permit. It nearly finished me. But I would rather have died than beg that yellow coyote, John Pope, to loosen the ropes. Instead I told him I would kill him when I got free."[9]

While Warner was being held in Ogden, Butch sent word telling him he would break him out if he wanted. Warner wrote back telling Butch to hold off and to hire some good lawyers. Warner's note said: "Butch, we're goners if we don't get some money quick to hire lawyers."[10] Butch, being out of prison only eight months, was flat broke. He knew of an ideal lawyer, his old pal Douglas Preston. However, he would need money to hire him. Butch along with his friends Elzy Lay and Bub Meeks decided to rob a bank. Bub Meeks had a vested interest because his brother David was married to the daughter of the other prisoner held with Warner (William Wall).[11] The *Salt Lake Herald* reported the trio considered banks in Logan, Utah, and Evanston, Wyoming, before deciding on the Montpelier, Idaho, bank.

Butch was familiar with the Montpelier area as well as the neighboring town of Cokeville. Wyoming, where Rocky Stoner's family lived. Warner said he held a grudge against Montpelier and town marshal Joe Jones for his attempt to arrest him years before.[12]

Prior to the robbery, the trio worked on a ranch eight miles north of Cokeville operated by Mrs. P. Emelle, whose husband was a jeweler in Montpelier. She explained, "They were the best workers [I] ever had, but always went heavily armed and made two mysterious trips."[13]

One of these trips may have been to Piedmont, Wyoming. On July 18, 1896, two well-dressed men rode into Piedmont. They were likely Elzy Lay and Cassidy, who rode a gray horse similar to a horse later used in the Montpelier robbery. The men checked into the Guild Hotel to await the train from Rock Springs. At 10:30 A.M., Douglas Preston arrived on the train and the three went to the hotel where they were overheard discussing Matt Warner's trial. The following day before departing, Preston, sent a telegram to Sheriff Wright of Ogden, Utah, "making inquiry as to the time Matt Warner was to be tried."[14]

Years later, Douglas Preston confided that he often met Butch in secret meetings in the desert between Brown's Park and Rock Springs.[15]

The trio may have obtained some relay horses from Nate Putnam of Auburn, Wyoming, who Butch had become acquainted with in 1892. Nate may have manned one of the relays as he was reported to have a great deal of money after the Montpelier robbery.

The three bandits used the aliases George Ingerfield (Butch Cassidy), Willie McGinnis (Elzy Lay) and Marty Makensie (Bub Meeks) while working for Mrs. P. Emelle. They quit their jobs just two days before the robbery and headed for Montpelier. Meeks stayed in a hotel to keep an eye on the bank while Cassidy and Lay camped outside of town. The next day Cassidy and Lay met Bub for dinner at the hotel and then observed the town.[16] The trio stopped at O'Conner's Saloon at 2:30 on the afternoon of August 13, 1896, for some liquid courage and waited for the bank to close. It had been seven years since Butch had robbed a bank.

Just before closing at 3:15 P.M., Butch and Bub Meeks entered the bank. Elzy Lay stayed outside as a lookout. Butch pulled his revolver and demanded access to the area behind the teller's cage which was granted through a door in the hallway. Bub stayed outside the teller's cage with his revolver drawn. Cassidy quickly entered the vault and gathered the gold and silver, but couldn't find any currency. He demanded that the teller, A. N. "Bud" Macintosh, tell him the location of the currency. When Macintosh responded that there was no currency, Butch hit him over the eye with his revolver calling him a "god damn liar" and Macintosh revealed the location of the currency. Ironically Bub Meeks scolded Cassidy for using unnecessary violence. Butch put all of the loot, later determined to be $7,165, into a special bag he had concealed under his vest.

Outside the bank, Elzy tried to force Cashier G.C. "Grover" Gray and his friend Ed Hoover into the bank and was having some trouble. Meeks who was watching from inside the bank told Lay to hit the "son of a bitch" over the head if he didn't cooperate. Gray and Hoover entered the bank and were forced to face the wall.

Cassidy and Meeks left the bank, mounted horses Lay had brought up, and the trio fled east out of town. Deputy Sheriff Fred Cruikshank grabbed the closest transportation—a bicycle —and followed, hoping to see what direction the bandits took. He kept them in view and saw that they headed towards Montpelier Canyon.[17]

A posse immediately organized and pursued, but couldn't keep up with Butch's relays of fresh horses. The posse traced the outlaws' trail for nearly a week before giving up. According to Meeks family sources, the bandits went to Commissary Ridge near the headwaters of the Green River then down to Piedmont, then into Brown's Hole.

A portion of the Montpelier loot was used to hire defense attorneys for Matt Warner during his murder trial in September. Douglas Preston made arrangements for Warner's defense team by hiring two of Utah's top defense attorneys, Orlando W. Powers and D.N. Straupp.[18]

A short time after the robbery, Warner's wife asked to meet with Butch and said she didn't want him to interfere with Warner's trial. In response, Butch wrote a letter to Rose Warner. Butch suspected her request to meet him was a trap:

> Vernal, Utah
> August 25, 1896
>
> Mrs. Rose Warner, Salt Lake:
> My Dear friend through the kindness of Mrs. Rummel, I received your letter last night. I am sorry that I can't comply with your request, but at present it is impossible for me to go to see you, and I can't tell you just when I can get there. If you have got anything to tell me that will help your Matt, write and tell me what it is and I will be there on time. I can't understand what it can be, for I have heard from reliable partys that you did not want Matt to get out, and I can't see what benefit it could be to you unless it was in his behalf. I may be misinformed, but I got it so straight that I would have to be shown why you made this talk before I could think otherwise. But that is neither here nor there, you are a lady, and I would do all I could for you or any of your sex that was in trouble. Of course, I am foolish (which you have found out), but it is my nature and I can't change it. I may be wrong in this, but if so, I hope you will look over it an[d] prove to me that you are all right, and I will ask forgiveness for writing you as I have. I understand you and Matt named your boy Rex Leroy after me, thank you. I hope I will be able to meet you all before long if everything is satisfactory. I'm sorry to hear about your leg.[19] If I can do anything to help you out let me know and I will do it. Lay and I have got a good man to defend Matt and Wall, and put up plenty of money, too, for Matt and Wall to defend themselves. Write me here in care of John Bluford, and believe me to be a true friend to my kind of people.
>
> George Cassidy[20]

On the second day of Warner's trial on September 9, 1896, the front page of the *Salt Lake Herald* ran an article on recently uncovered evidence that the Montpelier bank robbery had been committed to fund Warner's legal defense. The article correctly identified the three robbers as Cassidy, Lay, and Meeks and said all three were camping in the mountains outside of Ogden ready to spring Warner. It also claimed the money was used to secure D.V. Preston of Rock Springs, who had previously defended Cassidy, and other legal team members Judge Powers, D.N. Straupp and F.L. Luther.[21]

The next day both Douglas Preston and Orlando Powers emphatically denied the accusations calling the article a "gigantic lie" and threatened to sue the *Herald*, but no lawsuits were ever filed. Preston claimed that his fees had come from friends of William Wall and not Butch Cassidy and that he had received the money before the Montpelier bank robbery. The *Herald* story was called "The Fake of the Century."[22] The trial proceeded.

The plan worked. Warner was convicted not of murder, but of voluntary manslaughter, and was sentenced to six years.[23] He was released for good behavior after three years and was able to start a new life. When he was released from prison he was threatened with a second murder charge. Utah Governor Heber M. Wells made a deal with Warner that he would help him if he would arrange for Butch to turn himself in.

Charles Siringo reported that Charlie Gibbons of Hanksville held the gold from Montpelier for safekeeping for a time. Gibbons was unaware of the bank robbery while the money was in his possession.[24]

In September 1896, Butch and Meeks were spotted in Loa, Utah, about two hundred miles south of Salt Lake City. The *Salt Lake Tribune* reported the bandits spoke at length with two traveling salesmen, Joe Decker and W.C.A. Smoot, about Matt Warner's trial. Butch and Meeks claimed the first time they heard of being wanted in connection with the Montpelier robbery was when they read it in the *Salt Lake Herald*. Butch confirmed that he had offered to break Warner out of jail, but that Warner had refused his offer. Butch said the *Herald* report was based on wild claims from Mrs. Warner who did not want to see Warner released from jail. The outlaws claimed they could prove they were in Vernal at the time of the bank robbery. Ironically, they were carrying a large wad of money and said they were headed south to purchase cattle and drive them to Vernal. The salesmen reported that Butch was riding a fiery gray horse and Meeks a good gray horse. They were both well armed and each carried a .38-55 Winchester and horse pistols as well as saddlebags full of cartridges.[25]

Left: Elzy Lay was Cassidy's partner in the Montpelier, Idaho, robbery. (*Bob McCubbin photo*)
Right: Bub Meeks was identified by the teller as participating in the robbery. (*Author's collection*)

Butch and Bub may have parted company soon after this as reports soon place Butch in Wyoming alone.

❖ ❖ ❖

THINGS DID NOT fare well for Bub Meeks. In June 1897, Bub was suspected of helping rob the Guild Store in Fort Bridger and was captured by Deputy Calverly. He was recognized as a suspect in the Montpelier Bank robbery and transported to Idaho in September to face charges in the bank robbery. At the trial, in the county seat in Paris, Idaho, of the three eyewitnesses—Cashier Grover Gray, Bookkeeper Richard Groo, and Teller Bud Mcintosh—only Mcintosh could make a positive identification. Nineteen-year-old Mcintosh wore strong eyeglasses for his near-sightedness, but he had studied Meeks' face carefully during the robbery. Butch Cassidy was positively identified from his Wyoming prison mug shot by all three witnesses. Elzy Lay, who had been outside during most of the robbery, was not positively identified.[26]

On September 7, 1897, Bub was sentenced to thirty-five years in the Idaho State Penitentiary in Boise under his given name of Henry Meeks.[27] His sentence was later commuted to twelve years, but after an escape attempt it was doubled to twenty-four years. Bub made another escape attempt which resulted in him being shot in the leg, requiring amputation. He was later transferred to the Idaho Insane Asylum, where he made a successful escape.[28] He returned home to the Fort Bridger area of Wyoming and settled on his

Bub Meeks is identified with an "x" in this photograph taken at his trial. Also shown are the jury members. (*Courtesy of Max Lauridsen*)

ranch. He became paranoid as his mental health continued to decline. Idaho officials never chased him, possibly glad to be rid of the troublesome inmate. In his declining years, his own family had him committed to the Wyoming State Mental Hospital in Evanston where he passed away in 1912.

Some reports indicate that Butch planned to help Bub but nothing ever materialized.[29] Some say he planned to rob the Beckwith Bank in Evanston to fund the operation, but his plans were revealed.

◇ ◇ ◇

A NEWSPAPER LATER INTERVIEWED Butch's old friend Alice Stagner Burnaugh who lived near Lander, Wyoming, it reported Butch "hid in the Owl Creek foothills until about midnight when he came to the Burnaugh ranch home, awakened Mrs. Burnaugh (her husband was away at the time) and she fed him, helped him change horses and he left before daylight. He told Mrs. Burnaugh that he had robbed the Montpelier bank."[30]

◇ ◇ ◇

IN THE FALL OF 1896[31], Butch visited the Allen and Matilda Davis family near Vernal. Their daughter Maude had married Butch's good friend Elzy Lay.[32] Sheriff John T. Pope held a warrant for Butch and Elzy's arrest for the Montpelier robbery. When Pope received word that the outlaws were at the Davis ranch, he gathered a small posse and rode to the ranch after dark. Allen Davis demanded to know why the posse was on his property. Allen admitted the two outlaws had been at his home earlier, but said they had since left. Elzy was actually staying in a cabin in the back but was able to escape when his brother-in-law informed him the lawmen were there. The posse left and went back to Vernal, passing the Antler Saloon owned by Charlie Crouse and Aaron Overholt.[33] One posse member noticed the Davises' son Albert sitting on the steps of the saloon and that he quickly dashed inside when they passed. Butch was inside and was able to escape out the back to a waiting horse. Three weeks later, Pope received a postcard mailed from Arizona that read, "Pope, gawd damn you, lay off me. I don't want to kill you! Butch"[34]

Ann Bassett tells of a Thanksgiving dinner hosted by Butch and his friends in Brown's Park in the fall of 1895. However, if this was true it would have had to be in the fall of 1896, as Butch was still in the Wyoming prison in November 1895. Ann said the men "gave the Thanksgiving party for the Brown's Hole [Brown's Park] families together and did not spare expenses in putting over a grand spread of the best delicacies Rock Springs could supply. Butch was pouring coffee, poor Butch he could perform such minor jobs as robbing banks and holding up pay trains with out the flicker of an eye lash but serving coffee at a grand party that was something else. The blood curdling job almost floored him, he became panicky and showed that his nerve was completely shot to bits. He became frustrated and embarrassed over the blunder he had made when some of the other hosts better informed told him it was not good form to pour coffee from a big black coffee pot and reach from left to right across a guests plate, to grab a cup right under their noses.

"The boys went into a huddle in the kitchen and instructed Butch in the more formal art of filling coffee cups at the table. This just shows how etiquette can put fear into a brave mans heart."[35]

In January 1897, Butch essentially confessed to the Montpelier bank robbery. In mid-January he rode into the camp of a former deputy sheriff from Emery County, John Gitting. There he stayed the night at Gitting's camp which was on "the Big Hole on the Green River road." Gitting recognized Butch and assumed he was there to pump him for information. Gitting quickly turned the conversation to the Montpelier bank robbery and Butch "made no bones about his connection" to it. He laughingly responded that he was working on a much bigger haul. Gitting indicated that Butch likely had other friends nearby. Gitting was unarmed, but Butch carried two six-shooters and a Winchester. Gitting said Butch didn't seem nervous in the least, and he was off to Colorado the next morning.[36]

12. Castle Gate Robbery, 1897

BUTCH SPENT THE winter of 1896–97 in Robbers Roost on the lower Green River in Utah. Maude Davis Lay had been brought there by wagon to meet Elzy.[1] The two then led packhorses into the camp located in Horseshoe Canyon on Badman Trail and set up a fine camp with tents.[2] Another woman, possibly Etta Place,[3] joined Butch at a later date.[4] Maude confirmed it was Etta and later told her daughter of the walks she and the beautiful Etta took together.[5] Matt Warner later said the camp was called "Mary's Resort" and it included a cabin.[6] According to Pearl Baker, a cabin in the Roost had initials B.C. and E.P. along with E.L. and M.D. carved in the wooden mantle.[7]

Butch and Elzy planned to rob the Pleasant Valley Coal Company payroll in Castle Gate near Price, Utah, the following spring. The robbery has been called "one of the most daring affairs ever recorded."[8] Elzy and Butch had initially considered robbing the payroll the summer before, but knew it would require careful planning down to the smallest detail, so they took nearly a year in planning. The robbery had to be executed in broad daylight, in the midst of many people (miners waiting for their pay, some possibly armed), followed by a getaway down the narrow Price canyon—all elements of a bold and daring robbery.[9] They trained horses for their escape during their stay at Robbers Roost.[10]

When spring came, the outlaws left Robbers Roost. Butch returned to his old routine of working on local ranches. He moved to the Huntington area and worked on three different ranches owned by Joe Meeks, Jen Nielson, and Peter Murning.[11]

Some believe that during this time Butch made plans to rob the gold payroll that traveled from Salt Lake City to Fort Duchesne, Utah, via Nine Mile Canyon.[12] This gold was for the soldiers' payroll and the government allotment to Indians at Fort Duchesne. The gold traveled by train from Salt Lake

Robbers Roost near where Butch, Elzy, Maude Davis Lay, and perhaps Etta Place had their Winter Camp in 1896-1897. (*Author's photo*)

City to Price and then by cavalry escort through Nine Mile Canyon.[13] However this type of robbery was completely out of character for Butch; it would have required the killing of soldiers protecting the shipment. Possibly, Butch's efforts were a ruse to throw a monkey wrench into a robbery being planned by other outlaws.[14] Apparently word did leak about the potential robbery and additional soldiers were assigned to the escort. No robbery attempt was made.

In later years, Elzy revealed more about their horse training for the payroll robbery (which became known as the Castle Gate robbery) and told of one special horse—"Long Brown." Long Brown had been trained by Karl Neibauer, often called the "Dutchman,"[15] who lived near Helper, Utah, in Spring Canyon. He was a nobleman from Austria who had been a guard for Crown Prince Rudolf, which required him to be an excellent horseman.

When the Crown Prince and a forbidden lover both committed suicide in 1889, Karl fled Austria under suspicion of being an accomplice in a political plot resulting in the deaths. Butch and Elzy used Neibauer's place as the first relay point for the robbery.[16]

Another player in the robbery was Joe Walker. Joe showed up in Price, Utah, claiming he was a distant cousin of the prominent Whitmore family. He wanted his inheritance. The Whitmores did not recognize him as family. Consequently, Joe swore vengeance and over the next few years stole stock to cover his unrecognized inheritance. Joe was a friend of Butch's and was asked to help in the robbery.[17]

On March 6, 1897, Joe Walker stole some Whitmore horses with Gunplay Maxwell. Maxwell had a falling out with Joe and returned to Price where he informed the law of the stolen horses. Maxwell then participated in the posse that chased Joe. On March 26, Joe was surprised by the posse and shot and wounded Sheriff Tuttle in the hip. On April 5, formal charges were filed against Joe Walker for attempted murder.[18]

Butch and his partners spent time in the Price and Helper area further training their horses for racing and conditioning them to the loud train whistles and steam engines. The proposed getaway route wound four miles down the narrow Price canyon before it opened up, so the very best horse flesh available was crucial. On April 20, Butch bought four bottles of Old Crow whiskey at the local saloon and watched for the payroll train from Salt Lake. The train varied its arrival times to deter a possible robbery.

At about 12:40 P.M. on Wednesday April 21, 1897, the Rio Grande Western passenger train No. 2 arrived at the coal mine offices.[19] Butch and Elzy executed their plan with precision. E.L. Carpenter and two employees, Lewis and Phelps, carried the payroll from the train across the tracks to the mine office seventy-five yards away. The mine office was located on the top floor of a two-story rock building accessible by outside stairs. The main level housed the Wasatch Company store.[20] The payroll consisted of three or four sacks. One sack held $7,000 in gold. Reports differ on the amounts and contents of remaining sacks, though they held silver and possibly a smaller amount of gold and checks.[21]

As Carpenter, Lewis, and Phelps prepared to climb the outside stairs with the payroll sacks, a rough looking character, later identified as Butch Cassidy,

The Pleasant Valley Coal Company office was on the upper floor. (*Courtesy, Western Mining and Railroad Museum. All rights Reserved*)

stepped up and ordered, "Drop them sacks and hold up your hands," with his six-shooter pointing at them.[22] Astonished, E.L. Carpenter complied. Employee Phelps, who was young, ignored the commands and started up the stairs. Butch quickly hit him over the head with his revolver, which caused him to stagger backwards and drop his bag. The third man, Deputy Clerk T. W. Lewis, kept his sack of silver and made a run inside the store. Frank Caffey, who was inside the store reading a newspaper, stepped out to see what all the noise was about. Elzy who was still mounted on his horse, quickly pointed his revolver at Caffey and yelled, "Get back in there you son of a bitch or I'll fill your belly full of hot lead!" Caffey looked at Elzy's revolver, which he later said looked as big as a cannon, and ran back into the store.[23]

Butch reached down and grabbed Carpenter's sack of gold along with a handbag of checks and tossed them up to Elzy Lay who was still mounted.

E.L. Carpenter was the Pleasant Valley Coal Company paymaster. Sketch is from an early newspaper account. *(Author's collection)*

E. L. Carpenter, who was Held Up at Castle Gate.

For a moment Butch was in trouble as his horse pulled away from him. His heart probably pounded with the thought of being left behind with the crowd of over a hundred angry men who had gathered. However, Elzy used his own horse to crowd Butch's horse against a building, and Butch ran a few yards and threw himself onto his horse.

Butch rode off following Elzy with everyone standing around in amazement. Elzy fired his revolver in the air a few times. E.L. Carpenter shouted, "Robbers! Robbers! Stop those men, they have just robbed me!"[24] Three shots were fired from the offices, missing both of the bandits.

Authorities quickly commandeered the train to chase after the bandits as they galloped down the tracks, but the outlaws hid behind a section building as the train passed and then resumed their escape. Joe Walker had cut the telegraph wire to Price, which kept word from being sent to the outside. The bandits left behind a sack containing silver likely due to its weight, and they ditched the handbag of checks by the roadside about a mile from the robbery.[25]

Butch and Elzy rode through Spring Canyon just north of Helper and then cut south toward Robbers Roost. They changed horses north of Spring Creek at the Dutchman's place. Elzy had been riding Long Brown for his speed and endurance while Butch rode a little mare.[26] The next relay of horses, set by the Dutchman, were a gray and a bay.

Gang members cut the telegraph wire around two that afternoon on the Emery county road between Price and Cleveland, but it was too late as word had already been carried to Price and sent on. A mail carrier reported that he had met the two bandits near Cleveland, fourteen miles south of Price. Two separate posses were organized to chase the bandits—one posse from Huntington and the other from Castle Dale.[27] The two posses met near dusk and fired shots, each thinking the others were the bandits.

Some believe Elzy and Butch made their way to Robbers Roost, but not with the gold. The theory is they gave the gold to Joe Walker and possibly a lesser-known outlaw, Dave Fraughton, who rode toward Brown's Park. The two were likely instructed to bury the gold until things quieted down. According to Fraughton's family the gold was buried in Slab Canyon.[28] Others report it was delivered to Joe Walker's cabin in Chandler Canyon, a tributary of the Green River in Desolation Canyon.[29]

The relays of fresh horses allowed Butch and Elzy to quickly out-distance the posses. They rode horses without shoes so the tracks would mix with those of wild horses in the area. The outlaws went to Florence Creek to Jim McPherson's ranch located in the Book Cliffs. Florence Creek is another tributary of the Green River in Desolation Canyon. From the McPherson ranch the outlaws could access a trail through Chandler Canyon to the Uinta Basin and Brown's Park or they could ride southwesterly to Thompson.

McPherson had been friends with Butch for some time and supplied horses and grub when Butch needed them. McPherson operated a legitimate ranching business, but worked with the outlaws to survive since his ranch was so remote. He told his family that a lot of the outlaws were friendlier than the lawmen who chased them. In fact some years later, a posse shot at McPherson as they were looking for Joe Walker.[30]

McPherson was nervous upon seeing strangers at his ranch until he recognized Butch. McPherson asked Butch what he had been doing. Butch apparently reached in his pocket and took out a newspaper clipping instructing him to read all about it.[31] The bandits had picked up a newspaper in Woodside.

McPherson told his family that earlier the previous fall Butch had brought two horses, a black and a roan, to the ranch and asked that Jim look after them over the winter. After the robbery Butch asked Jim which of the two horses was best. McPherson replied the roan was a little better. Butch told Jim to keep the roan, and he would take the black.[32]

According to author Charles Kelly, Elzy Lay and a person named Fowler went to the Roost via a long route stopping in Torrey and Hanksville. Elzy stopped at a dance in Torrey while another man guarded the horses and

The Rio Grande Western railroad ran through a long narrow canyon called Castle Gate. Photo circa 1897. *(Author's collection)*

money.[33] In Hanksville, they stayed several days for rest and supplies. The money bags were said to be sitting out in plain sight.[34]

A newspaper described the event the following day: "The robbery was accomplished with so much bravado and daring that the suddenness of the act completely paralyzed the numbers of men who were lounging about near the scene, and there were nearly a hundred of them around and in the store who witnessed the whole affair."[35]

The bandits were described as one about twenty-five years old (Elzy) and the other middle-aged (Butch). "The younger wore a black hat, blue coat and goggles, while the man who held up Mr. Carpenter had on a light slouch hat, Denham overalls and brown coat. Both men were sunburned and appeared more like cowboys or common hobos than desperate highwaymen. One of the men rode a gray horse with only a bridle and no saddle. Each carried two six-shooters and were seen loitering around Caffey's saloon during Tuesday."[36]

The Pleasant Valley Coal Company offered a reward of $2,000 and doubled it the following day.

A newspaper report the next day identified Butch Cassidy and mentioned that he was also a suspect in Montpelier bank robbery.[37]

Sales agent E.L. Carpenter of the Pleasant Valley Coal Company positively identified Butch Cassidy as one of the two men who had robbed him. The identification was "readily" made from Butch's mug shot from the Wyoming penitentiary which was provided by Sheriff Davis of Rawlins. Carpenter remembered Butch's face well and gave a description of the second outlaw that closely "tallies the general appearance of Cassaday's side partner, whose wife lives in Vernal" (Lay). Sheriff Davis claimed a great deal of gold made its way into the Snake River country after the Castle Gate robbery.[38]

Bub Meeks may also have assisted in the robbery by manning a relay of horses. Dave Fraughton told his family he met up later with Butch and Elzy in the Lander, Wyoming, area.

On April 29, it was reported that "the daring Castlegate highwaymen are still at large and there is now not one lot of possibility that they will be captured."[39]

On May 6, it was reported that the chase had been abandoned since lawmen had lost the trail of the outlaws.[40] Later on May 24, it was reported that Secret Service officers were on the trail of the bandits.[41]

Sometime after the robbery, Butch returned to his pattern of finding work on a ranch and blending into the community. This time he found work on a small ranch near Sheridan, Wyoming, at the base of the Big Horn Mountains. The ranch, the Little Goose Ranch, was owned and operated by Dan Hilman. Dan needed help, but was apprehensive about hiring because of the additional expense, and he feared Butch was a typical cowboy who "just wanted to sit [on] a horse and ride herd."[42] Butch asked for a chance to prove himself and said all he needed was board and room and tobacco money.[43] Butch gave his name as LeRoy Parker.

Butch was the first one out of bed and had his team ready for plowing and his share of the milking done before anyone else. He wasn't afraid to work, including the dirty jobs. He proved to be Dan Hilman's best hand and soon endeared himself to the Hilmans. The Hilmans noted that Butch always kept a saddled horse nearby.

Dan's son Fred was thirteen and took a quick liking to Butch.[44] Butch asked Dan if it would be all right for him to teach Fred how to shoot a pistol. Dan agreed. Butch and Fred went up the hill and set up cans on the fence posts. Butch would ride his horse and shoot the cans off with alternating pistol shots, never missing. He told Fred to avoid using the pistol sights, but instead to point his thumb at what he wanted to hit. Soon Fred became a phenomenal shot.[45]

Fred recalled it was not uncommon to kill twenty rattlesnakes a day in the hayfield that summer. Fred was up on the overshot hay stacker when Butch yelled up, "Fred, I have something for you" and threw up a live rattlesnake. Fred said all hell broke loose but he was able to kill the snake. He said Butch laughed so hard he could hardly stand.

Butch asked for short leaves from the ranch to take care of other business. Each time the Hilmans thought that would be the last they would see of him, but he always returned in a few days. These leaves could have been trips to Powder Springs and Baggs.

Butch was reported to be staying at his cabin in the upper Powder Springs area in July 1897. Union Pacific officials became so nervous about rumors of his gang's presence in the area they brought in several lawmen to investigate. The officers indicated they had received reliable reports that Cassidy was planning a train robbery near Wamsutter. Armed guards were placed on the trains and engineers were told to be on the lookout for obstructions. If a robbery was actually being planned, the outlaws pulled back when increased officers appeared in the area.[46]

Butch and the bandits later decided to have some fun and spend part of the Castle Gate robbery money. They converged on the towns of Baggs and Dixon, Wyoming, on July 27, 1897. The newspaper reported the incident on August 7, 1897, stating "nine members of the notorious Cassidy gang spent three days in Baggs and Dixon gambling and drinking."[47] They drank and shot up the local bar, but left enough money behind to cover things. It was said they paid a silver dollar for every bullet hole they put in Jack Ryan's Bull Dog Saloon.[48] Ryan made enough money to open a first-rate bar in Rawlins.[49]

Butch continued to work at the Little Goose Ranch throughout the summer of 1897. One day in the fall he was gone but had left a note on a harness in the barn. The note stated, "Sorry to be leaving you. The author-ities are getting on to us. Best home I've ever had. LeRoy Parker." Along with the note was a revolver with another note stating "for Fred."[50]

Dan Hilman told his family they were not to talk about the man they knew as LeRoy Parker as it would bring trouble to them and to Parker.

Sometime after 1910, after Fred Hilman was married, he got a visit from an older man who looked familiar. Dan Hilman was out of town on a trip at the time. The man asked him if anyone had thrown a rattlesnake at him lately. Fred knew he was LeRoy Parker (Butch) as there was only one man who would have known about that experience from years earlier.[51]

13. WS Ranch and Wilcox Robbery, 1898~1900

IN THE SPRING OF 1898, the governors of Utah, Wyoming, and Colorado were concerned about the ongoing organized crimes in the intermountain area. In March, the three governors met in Salt Lake City to formulate plans to rid the area of the outlaws. They had met the prior year in Denver with some Wyoming Cattlemen to discuss and formulate plans.[1] They discussed offering large rewards and assembling "Texas Ranger" type lawmen to track down outlaws. The following month, Governor Heber M. Wells of Utah offered rewards totaling $4,500 for Butch and others from the Robbers Roost area.[2] Butch topped the list at $500.[3]

Uintah County (Utah) Sheriff William Preece wrote to Governor Wells and thanked him for his offer of assistance. Preece indicated that Cassidy and Lay were in the area, and he was watching Maude Davis Lay's home for Lay. He wrote that Cassidy had been visiting "a woman of questionable repute, who resides in Vernal." Preece explained that he did not "think it advisable to offer rewards or create any unnecessary excitement at present as these men are constantly on the alert and at the least sign of danger can elude us."[4] Other reports indicate Cassidy and Lay had already left the area by this time.

Previously in March 1897, Joe Walker had been involved in an altercation with Sheriff Tuttle. Tuttle was wounded by Walker's bullets. Walker later offered to pay for Tuttle's doctor bills.[5] The following month Walker participated in the Castle Gate robbery and became a wanted man. Walker should have heeded Butch's advice to leave the area after the robbery.

A posse led by Sheriff C.W. Allred located Walker's camp near the Book Cliffs on the morning of Friday, May 13, 1898.[6] The posse claimed they gave the camp proper warning to surrender, but the outlaws responded with gunfire. However, an examination showed bits of cloth from the bedding in Walker's bullet wounds suggesting they were shot while in their bedrolls.[7] Walker was shot though the heart. His partner, Johnny Herring,

General view of the W S ranch, western Socorro County, New Mexico. 1882. Loc
ranch

was also killed.[8] Johnny looked similar to Butch, and the posse thought they had killed the infamous outlaw. Two others were captured. One was believed to be Elzy Lay.

The *Salt Lake Tribune* ran a front page article announcing, "Bandit Leaders Killed" with Butch's mug shot sketch and a subheading "'Butch' Cassiday and Joe Walker Shot To Death By Officers."[9] Such news certainly would have broken his mother's heart back home in Circleville. The family continued to hear reports of Butch's demise only to hear later that he was alive.

An inquest was held to determine if one of the dead bandits was the famed outlaw Butch Cassidy. Probably out of greed for the reward, the body was incorrectly determined to be that of Butch Cassidy, however, the reward was never paid. Sheriff Ward of Evanston, Wyoming, volunteered to travel to Price and identify the body since he knew Cassidy well. The body was exhumed, and Ward signed an affidavit that the body was in fact *not* Butch Cassidy.[10]

Lula claimed Butch told his family later that he hid in a covered wagon to view his own funeral and that he was touched by the shedding of tears by

Keller Valley, on the San Francisco River. Bunkhouse and corrals at left; main ...t right.

the crowd. Likely Butch was feeling his oats at the time, and the incident was nothing more than a good story.

On June 5, 1898, the *Salt Lake Tribune* ran an article claiming to have intercepted a letter from Butch admitting he was alive and well.[11] The *Wyoming Press* in Evanston reported, "Butch Cassidy has come to life again, this time in the vicinity of Robbers Roost. Butch seems to have as many lives as the historical cat."[12]

As a result of the daring robberies in Montpelier and Castle Gate, Butch received a lot of press in the western newspapers throughout 1897 and 1898. "Butch Cassidy and his gang," as they were called, were blamed for many robberies, including a great number he was not involved in.

Butch attempted to make himself scarce. Once again Butch and Elzy looked for work on ranches and headed south in the fall of 1898.[13] (They may have received information about jobs from Will Carver.) They apparently landed jobs with the Erie Cattle Company in Cochise County, Arizona. Butch used the alias "Jim Lowe" and Elzy again used "William McGinnis," and the Erie superintendent Bob Johnson immediately hired them for a few weeks.[14] Erie Company was holding its final cattle roundup before being sold and dissolved. While working for the Erie Company, Butch and Elzy met the Ketchum brothers, Tom and Sam.[15] Butch was also reported to have worked for the Diamond A ranch around this time. Charles Siringo said the Pinkertons were unaware that Butch Cassidy and Jim Lowe were the same person.[16]

In New Mexico, William French was running the WS Ranch (Wilson and Stevens) near Alma in Catron County and was concerned about their losses to rustlers. The WS had been started in 1883 by Englishman Harold C. Wilson. French met with one of the owners and determined to hire new hands to help end the thefts. Butch and Elzy were part of this hiring[17] and arrived at the WS Ranch in February 1899.[18]

Butch and Elzy showed up with a man named Perry Tucker who had recently been recommended as foreman by French's outgoing foreman. Perry recommended that Jim Lowe be hired as his assistant, and McGinnis be hired to break broncos.

William French described Butch and Elzy: "The one, stoutly built man of middle height, was what they called in that country 'fair complected'. He had a habit of grinning and showing a very even row of small teeth when he spoke to you, and he answered to the name of Jim Lowe. The other was several years younger, much taller and darker—in fact, a quite good-looking young man, debonair, with a bit of a swagger. He seemed quite a cut above the ordinary cow hand and undoubtedly had more education. He owned up to the name of William McGinnis."[19]

Perry Tucker, the new foreman, cleaned up the "weak" employees and replaced them with new ones that he was able to find from an "unlimited supply, for new hands seemed to show up whenever he wanted them."

"Their zeal for everything in connection with the outfit was beyond all praise" as strays were brought in as part of the WS herd and there seemed to be no complaints from neighbors.[20]

Butch appeared to work well with Perry and was in charge of the herds on the trail, being the "trail boss." Elzy worked breaking horses for use on the ranch. French was impressed with Butch. He said, "It was then that the real genius of the former [Butch] came under my notice. The way he handled those poor cattle over that long and dusty trail of nearly 200 miles was a revelation. Frequently they had to go as much as seventy-five miles without water, but he never dropped a hoof, and there was no tail to this herd when he arrived at the road."[21]

French liked that Butch kept good control of the men when they went to town. He said, "There was no such thing as drinking, gambling or shooting up the town. Strict discipline was always maintained, and I was frequently congratulated by the merchants of Magdalena on having such a well-behaved outfit."

The only thing that puzzled French was the frequent turnover of hands. French explained, "They were all good hands and I hated to see them go, but it didn't seem to bother Jim [Butch] in the least. He seemed always able to replace them by others just as competent."

French said he "didn't quite understand" why the newcomers always acted as strangers to each other when French was around, but alone they acted "like long lost brothers."[22]

✧ ✧ ✧

IN JUNE 1899, a Union Pacific train was robbed near Wilcox, Wyoming. Butch was reported to be in Wyoming at the time. Butch often stayed at the horse camp some twenty miles from the WS Ranch headquarters and may have been able to leave for brief periods of time without raising suspicion.

At 2:18 A.M. on the rainy morning of June 2, 1899, engineer William J. "Grindstone" Jones aboard the Union Pacific Overland Flyer No.1 saw a warning light up ahead.[23] The train was westbound and was traveling about fifty miles an hour. Jones knew there had been recent work on the tracks in the area so decided to stop. The warning light consisted of two flashing lights, a red and white lantern which signified an emergency danger ahead.[24] The train consisted of three mail cars, a baggage car, an express car, and a tourist sleeper car under the direction of Conductor William Storey.

The train stopped about a mile past the Wilcox station, which was nine miles from Rock Creek and forty-three miles out of Laramie, Wyoming.[25]

The number of bandits involved in the robbery has been disputed for years. Some believe that six bandits were present while others claim there were only three bandits.

Quickly the masked men jumped up on the engine and ordered down Engineer Jones and his fireman John Walsh.[26]

The outlaws went to the mail car and hammered on the door. Robert Bruce and Len Dietrick, the clerks inside, quickly extinguished the lights and locked the doors. The outlaws then fired two shots into the mail car, and Bruce quickly unlocked the door. The outlaws searched the mail car, but indicated they were most interested in the express car.[27]

Traveling a few minutes behind this mail train was another train, sometimes called the "second section" of the train. The bandits inquired about the second train and were told that it had four cars of soldiers on it. The outlaws said they didn't care if the train carried forty cars of soldiers and went about their work.[28] Ironically, Douglas Preston, Butch's attorney, was one of the passengers on the second train.[29] One report says that Conductor Storey ran back and sent the second train, made up of mostly passenger cars, back to Rock Creek.[30]

The bandits gathered the crew onto the train and ordered the last two cars uncoupled. Dietrick, one of the mail clerks, boldly lifted the mask of one of the outlaws, who yelled, "You Son of a Bitch, you do that again and I'll pop you!"[31] The outlaws pistol-whipped Engineer Jones when he could not immediately move the train over a small bridge because the brakes were still set. The leader of the group stopped the whipping and said, "Hold there, we don't want any killing about this!"[32]

The final two cars were uncoupled and the remaining cars, including the express car, were moved forward across the small bridge. The bandits then dynamited the bridge, causing enough damage that it could not be crossed. The bridge was blown to prevent anyone from getting too close.

The engine pulled the express car down the tracks approximately two miles from the blown bridge. Express agent Ernest Charles Woodcock locked the door and yelled that he would shoot anyone who tried to enter. The bandits responded by throwing lit dynamite toward the car which blew out the express car wall and knocked Woodcock unconscious. The outlaws tried without success to revive him so he could open the safe. When he did not seem to be regaining consciousness, they used more dynamite to blow the safe but mistakenly used too much.[33] One report said, "The explosion completely wrecked the front end of the car, blowing off the roof and sides and demolishing most of the express matter. A hole about a foot in diameter was blown through the top of the safe and the door was blown off." Portions of the car were said to be blown 150 yards from the train. The bandits then gathered up most of the treasure that was not damaged and rode off.[34] It was reported that a half a ton of dynamite was used for the overall robbery

Left: The safe from the express car was manufactured by Hall's Safe company. (*Wyoming State Archives*)

Below: The express car and safe from the Wilcox robbery were severely damaged when outlaws used too much dynamite to blow the safe. (*Wyoming State Archives*)

and that the whole episode took about two hours. At this point, the engineer rushed the train into Medicine Bow and gave the alarm that they had been robbed.

The initial newspaper reports said $36,000 in currency and another $10,000 in diamonds had been stolen, with some of the currency being destroyed by the explosion. However, the Union Pacific refused to give exact numbers only saying it was a light run.[35] Another report gave more specifics stating, "The six bandits had gathered unsigned bank notes, cash, 19 scarf pins, 29 gold-plated cuff button pairs and four Elgin watches." The unsigned currency was described as "incomplete currency, $3,400 from the U.S. Treasury Department for First National Bank [of] Portland, Oregon."

The damage to the currency was described as "lower right hand corners all torn diagonally." Both the U.S. Marshal's office in Cheyenne and Pacific Express Company issued memos to agents, bankers, and merchants listing the currency denominations and bank numbers for the stolen currency. The damaged currency and residue from the dynamite made tracing the currency relatively easy.

Five years later in 1904, Union Pacific Superintendent W.L. Park wrote that the railroad had actually lost more than $50,000, some of it in gold.[36]

Who were the bandits? Butch Cassidy was immediately suspected and named in newspaper reports.[37] Engineer Jones swore that there were six bandits, giving descriptions of all six. Only three were chased by the posse heading north toward Casper and Hole-in-the-Wall. The posse met up with them at the Jumbo Water Hole where Converse County Sheriff Hazen was mortally wounded when shots were exchanged. The three bandits who went north were likely George Sutherland ("Flat Nose" Currie), Harvey Logan (Kid Curry), and Harry Longabaugh (the Sundance Kid). The three were later identified as George Currie and the "Roberts Brothers."[38] Reportedly Harvey Logan and Harry Longabaugh were sometimes known as the "Roberts Brothers."

Other reports included suspicious riders crossing the Sweetwater headed to Emory Burnaugh's ranch on the Muddy north of Lander and of riders headed to Brown's Park.[39]

The following day, newspaper reports around the country had front-page headings of "Bandits Dynamite U.P. Train!" According to researcher Elnora Fry, the first train robbery where bandits used dynamite was in Wilcox, Arizona, during the time of Butch's incarceration, and he had picked "Wilcox" to send a message to officials. (The Southern Pacific was robbed in January 1895 in Wilcox, Arizona, by five masked bandits who used dynamite.)

✧ ✧ ✧

SO AGAIN WE ASK: Who were the bandits at Wilcox? Butch's forte was bank robbery, although he likely helped in planning the train robbery and there *is* evidence that he was in Wyoming at this time. It appears that George Currie led the train robbing efforts as part of the "Wild Bunch," probably with the assistance of Harvey Logan. (Harvey Logan's first bank robbery was a bust in Belle Fourche, South Dakota, and landed him in jail for a month before he escaped.) The Wilcox train robbers were reported to be professionals as "they went about their work systematically" and "were prepared for any emergency."[40] E.C. Woodcock described the bandits as being "very gentlemanly in demeanor except for one man, the leader who was very rough and profane."

Engineer Jones described the six outlaws as follows:[41]

Leader: About 50 years old, 5 feet 7 or 8 inches tall; thin, round nose, large eyes with small eyeballs; wore slouch hat, light canvas coat; weight about 160 pounds. [This was likely George "Flat Nose" Currie since his nose was unique. The robbers were reported to be "under the leadership of one man and obeyed his orders without question."]

Second Outlaw: Dark complexion; black, wooly hair; wore slouch hat, dark suit; about 5 feet 9 or 10 inches tall; weight about 170 pounds. [This may have been another view of the leader since there are similarities.]

Third Outlaw: About 5 feet 9 or 10 inches tall; black suit; dark hair, weight about 160 or 170 pounds. [This was probably Harry Longabaugh.]

Fourth Outlaw: About 5 feet 6 inches tall; dark complexion; wore gray hat; pants inside boots; weight about 160 pounds. [This was most likely Harvey Logan.]

Fifth Outlaw: About 5 feet 6 inches tall; weight about 145 pounds; wore cowboy white hat with drooping brim; black leather shoes; canvas leggings, brown overalls or corduroy pants; light, medium length overcoat; spoke with Texas twang; carried carbine with long wood on barrel reaching to within five inches of end. [This was probably another description of the fourth outlaw.]

Sixth Outlaw: About 5 feet 8 inches tall; weight about 150 pounds;

stubby, sandy beard. [This was possibly another description of one of the previously described outlaws.]

There is no doubt that three outlaws headed toward Casper with a posse on their trail. Reportedly three other outlaws headed toward Lander, although no tracks were ever found. Engineer Jones speculated that they had possibly used a wagon. Burned out wagon remains were found in Rock Creek some time later.[42]

Jones later testified, "I saw all six robbers at one time or another I think I could probably identify three of them."[43] Jones's statement leaves room for doubt that there actually were six outlaws since he apparently did not see all six at the same time. E.C. Woodcock testified that he only saw three bandits. Union Pacific General Manager E. Dickerson told one newspaper, "I do not believe there were over three men in the hold-up."[44]

The newspaper reported that a posse of twenty men pursued the bandits. The Union Pacific sent a special train from Laramie, outfitted with a posse, horses, equipment, and food that arrived at the robbery site around nine o'clock the morning after the robbery. The Union Pacific offered a $1,000 reward for each of the bandits. The Pacific Express Company whose safe was robbed also offered $1,000 per bandit, and the U.S. Government added a $1,000 reward for each bandit. The Wyoming governor also dispatched Company C of the state militia. All of this resulted in nearly one hundred possemen.[45] The bandits were said to have about a five to seven hour headstart on the posse and were well mounted.[46]

As the three outlaws headed toward Casper, rain was falling and the North Platte River was flooding. The outlaws took two days to travel the 110 miles from the robbery site to Casper. They crossed between Casper Mountain and Muddy Mountain as a diversion to make it appear they were riding into Casper from Douglas.

On June 4, at 2 A.M., they rode across the bridge at Center Street in Casper. They were spotted, but the witnesses thought they were posse members and joked "there go the train robbers." The outlaws headed northwest from Casper. Al Hudspeth saw them at a cabin about six miles northwest of Casper and tried to ask them about some missing horses that he was searching for. They told him to "hit the road and hit it quick." Al reported this to the Natrona County sheriff and a posse was formed to check it out.

By Sunday the posse, including Converse County Sheriff Joe Hazen had spotted the outlaws from a distance. Natrona County Sheriff Hiestand lost his horse when an outlaw's slug spooked it as the posse got close to the outlaws. The posse continued to track the outlaws, losing their trail at times and exchanging shots from a distance. Early Monday morning in the heavy rain, the posse found the three outlaws' horses wandering about. Around noon, they moved near the Jumbo Water Hole to search for tracks. Joe Hazen shouted that he had found tracks. Shots rang out, hitting Hazen who died several days later. The outlaws then made their escape on foot down the draw to the west.

They waded through Castle Creek and then found a sheep camp at Sullivan Springs where they had breakfast with John DeVore. (A year later DeVore identified the body of Flat Nose George Currie who had been killed in Desolation Canyon near Price, Utah, by a posse. Currie was one of the three outlaws who joined him for breakfast.)

The three outlaws then walked into Kaycee, Wyoming, to John Nolen's ranch where they got fresh mounts. They gave Nolen and his friend Joe Gant watches from the robbery.

The posse followed the bandits trail over the Big Horn Mountains to the Big Horn Basin before they lost the trail in Big Horn Canyon and returned to Casper.[47]

WILL SIMPSON WROTE that he saw Butch shortly after the Wilcox robbery near Mail Camp, Wyoming. "The last time I saw George Cassidy was immediately after the Wilcox robbery of the Union Pacific, and I met him on the Muddy, between Fort Washakie and Thermopolis, Wyoming, and spent an hour with him. I told him he had been accused of being in the Wilcox robbery, that he had promised Governor Richards, Jesse Knight and myself that he was not to turn a trick in Wyoming, and he assured me that he was on his get-away that he had nothing whatever to do with the Wilcox robbery or the killing of Sheriff Hazen, and I know this to be true, because a few days later he turned over to Tom Skinner, in his saloon in Thermopolis, a considerable volume of gold coin. It is known that no gold was obtained from the Wilcox Robbery."

However, W.L. Park, of the Union Pacific, later admitted that the stolen loot at Wilcox robbery included some gold.

Author Charles Kelly wrote that A.G. Rupp of Welling, Wyoming, saw Butch in Wyoming at about the same time as Simpson did. Rupp operated a general store and had a wanted poster of Butch posted on the door. Several men rode up and used his corral one evening. One asked if he could have the wanted poster, and Rupp recognized him as the man whose picture was on the poster. Butch tore up the poster and stomped it into the mud. News of the Wilcox robbery arrived the following day.[48] According to Frederick Bechdolt, Butch Cassidy was present when the Wilcox loot was divided at a cabin at the crossing of the Little Muddy between Fort Washakie and Thermopolis[49]

Also witnessing Butch's presence in Wyoming at this time was the Emory Burnaugh family who lived on the Muddy Creek Road Ranch north of Lander. The Burnaughs recalled at least five outlaws, including Cassidy, coming to the ranch. The outlaws hid out in the sandstone cave-like overhangs at the ranch. Alice Stagner Burnaugh made sandwiches and had her two boys, Carl and Claude, deliver them in a lard pail. One of the outlaws reportedly was badly wounded, died, and was buried at the ranch. The identity of that outlaw is unknown.[50]

Although only three bandits may have been at the actual robbery, others were named as suspects. Harvey Logan's kid brother, Loney, was suspected, but probably was not involved other than being related to one who was. Loney did pass some of the bank notes from the robbery. He was killed by Pinkerton agents when he was in Kansas City visiting his Aunt Lee on February 28, 1900.[51]

Bob Lee, a cousin of Harvey and Loney Logan, was arrested, convicted, and sent to the Wyoming penitentiary for the Wilcox robbery. Lawman Frank Hadsell interviewed Bob Lee while he was in prison and said Lee only knew information about the robbery from hearsay. Lee also said he was aware of only three individuals involved in the robbery. He named Harvey Logan and a man named Frank Scramble who was later determined to be Harry Longabaugh. Later, Harvey Logan attempted to set the record straight and again indicated that only three men were involved in the robbery.[52]

Because of these two injustices to his family members, Harvey Logan became dangerously anti-social which further led him to be a violent killer.[53]

The currency from the Wilcox robbery would also create problems for others, such as Charlie Crouse and Charlie Gibbons, and led the Pinkertons to the WS Ranch in New Mexico. Author Charles Kelly wrote that Cassidy

Left: Harvey Logan, aka Kid Curry, was a participant in the Wilcox robbery. *(Author's collection)*
Right: George "Flat Nose" Sutherland Currie likely led the robbery of the Union Pacific near Wilcox. *(Hoofprints of the Past Museum, Kaycee, WY)*

paid Hanksville store owner Charlie Gibbons with a portion of the Wilcox currency. Gibbons and his wife went to Salt Lake City later for a shopping trip and used the currency. They were followed back to Richfield and held for questioning. Gibbons was able to convince lawmen he was not a member of the gang and they were let go.[54] Charlie Crouse was paid for horses that were used in the Winnemucca bank robbery with torn currency from the Wilcox robbery.[55]

If Butch was in Wyoming or present at Wilcox robbery, he soon returned to the WS Ranch.

Right: Frank Murray was the Pinkerton detective who went undercover to investigate Butch at the WS Ranch. *(Author's collection)*

Below: At left is Elzy Lay's mug shot from the New Mexico prison before his inmate processing was complete. On the right is his mug shot after his hair and mustache had been shaved and his prison uniform assigned. *(Used by permission, Utah State Historical Society, all rights reserved)*

14. Folsom Train Robbery, 1899

SOMETIME PRIOR TO July 1899, Elzy Lay quit the WS Ranch and joined the Ketchum gang, against the advice of Butch.[1] The gang made plans to rob a train near Folsom, New Mexico. Butch apparently did not like or trust the Ketchums, but he did respect Will Carver who was part of the Ketchum gang at times. William French, the WS boss, detested the Ketchums who had stolen and mistreated two of his best horses.[2]

The Ketchum gang had recently parted ways with their leader, Tom "Black Jack" Ketchum, because of his temper and sourness. The gang, or those involved in the train robbery, included Sam Ketchum, Elzy Lay and possibly Bruce "Red" Weaver. The identity of a fourth robber, known as G.W. Franks, is disputed. It's been speculated he was Harvey Logan, Will Carver, or George West Musgrave. It seems most likely he was Musgrave.[3]

The boys camped for a time before the robbery in their hideout in Turkey Creek Canyon near Cimarron, New Mexico. Today the hideout is located on the Philmont Boy Scout Ranch.[4]

The train robbery took place near Twin Mountains, seven miles south of Folsom, New Mexico, on the night of July 11, 1899. The plunder was somewhere in the range of $50,000 to $70,000. The outlaws escaped to their hideout on Turkey Creek, less Weaver who departed from the group just north of Springer.[5]

On July 16, a posse of five, led by U.S. Marshal Creighton Foraker of New Mexico and including Sheriff Edward J. Farr, located the outlaws in the evening around 5 P.M. using information from Perfecto Cordova who accompanied the posse.[6] A gunfight ensued. Elzy had gone with his canteen to retrieve water and was the first wounded. Elzy took two shots that knocked him down, and he was unconscious for a time. He later came to and crawled back to get his rifle during the commotion. He was able to get shots off and may have helped kill Sheriff Farr. Sam Ketchum was seriously wounded and taken out of the fight. Musgrave was able to obtain a hiding spot behind a split rock and with his smokeless ammunition the posse couldn't locate him. The posse's ammunition disadvantaged them because it gave off smoke after each shot, revealing their locations. Two other posse members were wounded. Henry Love later died on July 21 from blood poisoning resulting from a leg wound. F.H. Smith recovered from his wounds.[7]

The outlaws were able to escape in the cover of darkness and a heavy rainstorm. Sam Ketchum was so badly injured he told the others to go on without him. He was left at a nearby ranch in Ute Park, some twenty miles from the shootout site and was soon captured.[8] Sam died on July 24, 1899, from blood poisoning as a result of his wounds after refusing to have his arm amputated while in prison in Santa Fe. Elzy healed somewhat from the wounds to his left shoulder and back. Elzy was certainly tough as he put in over 700 miles in the saddle with several bullet wounds in his body.[9] Four weeks later, Elzy was captured by Cicero Stewart's posse at Lusk's cow camp outside of Carlsbad on August 15, 1899.

Elzy Lay and Musgrave had arrived at Lusk's camp claiming they were looking for stray horses. They rounded up one horse and said they would catch the others the next morning when they joined the camp for breakfast. Lusk sent his oldest son on a night ride to Carlsbad to alert Sheriff Stewart of two heavily armed cowboys in the area.

Stewart arrived at Lusk's camp at four that morning, laying in wait for the cowboys to come for breakfast. Elzy came alone as he and Musgrave had planned to take turns coming in for breakfast. As Elzy was wolfing down his breakfast, the posse moved in for his capture. Elzy, hearing footsteps, jumped into action calling out to Lusk, "Did you do this?" as he shot him in the wrist. Elzy then shot Deputy Rufe Thomas in the left arm and shoulder. Stewart's shot dropped Elzy as if he was dead. It had only stunned him, but this made it possible to capture him. He made one final attempt to reach for a gun but was pistol-whipped by Stewart. At this point Deputy Cantrell said, "Kill the belligerent sons a bitchin' outlaw." Stewart refused. Elzy was transported to Carlsbad. Musgrave had witnessed the capture from the hillside with binoculars and then rode off.

The local newspaper described Elzy as being six-feet tall, weighing 175 pounds with a short sandy beard and sandy complexion.[10] He was identified as William H. McGinnis by New Mexico merchant James K. Hunt.[11] Elzy was taken to Trinidad, Colorado, where Tom "Black Jack" Ketchum was being held after his recent capture. Both prisoners were photographed or "Kodacked."

Butch, at the time, was staying at the horse camp some twenty miles from the WS ranch headquarters. Tom Capehart, another hand from the WS Ranch, had joined Elzy and Musgrave sometime after the Turkey Creek fight. Tom rode a hard 400 miles in three days to the horse camp to inform Butch of Elzy's capture.[12] Capehart had not witnessed Elzy's arrest as he had gone for provisions and arrived at Lusk's camp hours later.

A few weeks later, Butch and Capehart went to the WS boss, French, to let him know that "Mac" was a prisoner and requested his help. They wanted French to put up bond for Mac. French believed that Elzy's charges were likely not bailable and worried that he would be suspected as an accomplice if he became too involved. He did agree to certify "Mac's" conduct during his employment at the WS. French suspected that Capehart had also participated in the train robbery and was the outlaw known as "Franks."[13]

Elzy was tried for the murder of Sheriff Farr in Raton beginning October 2. The jury rejected the first-degree murder charges and found him guilty of second degree murder after three hours of deliberation.[14] On October 10, 1899, he was sentenced to life imprisonment at the penitentiary in Santa Fe, New Mexico. Elzy entered prison as prisoner number 1348. His record listed him as 34 years old, 5 feet 9 ½ inches tall, 164 pounds, light hair and complexion, upper front tooth broken, bullet wounds in back and small scar on left of head.[15]

William French said that Pinkerton agent Frank Murray showed up a few months after Mac had been convicted to investigate a portion of the stolen money from the Wilcox train robbery. The money with forged signatures had shown up in a Silver City bank and was traced back to the store in Alma. Murray mentioned that the bills had been damaged in a corner from the explosion and were easy to detect. Murray, using the alias "Burns," came to Alma in early March 1900.[16]

The store in Alma said that they had received the money from a Johnny Ward of the WS Ranch. French reported that there were two Johnny Wards working on the ranch, one called "Big" and one called "Little." Big Johnny Ward had only been there a short time and was likely the one who had passed the bills. However, French happened to talk with Little Johnny Ward who was nearby, and he confessed that he has passed the bills, claiming he had gotten them from Clay McGonagill. French described McGonagill as "one of the transients who had worked with Jim [Lowe] on the trail for a couple of weeks or ten days."[17] However, Clay McGonagill was in fact an icon of the Southwest. He was a world champion roper and famous in early day rodeo history. He would later travel through Argentina with a rodeo troupe.[18] Big Johnny Ward was thought to be Ben Kilpatrick who was hired the fall of 1899.[19]

Murray showed French a photo of Butch Cassidy and asked if he recognized him. French explained that he didn't know the person in the photo as "Cassidy." French said, "I told him that all I knew about him was he was the best trail boss I had ever seen and one of the best men that the WS had in their employ since I had known them. I also said that he had great influence with his men, and that none of them ever got drunk or shot up the town or were guilty of any other foolishness while he was over them."[20]

Pinkerton Detective Charlie Siringo said Butch had a saloon in Alma while he was on the WS Ranch. Butch apparently took over the bartender job at the saloon attached to the Coats and Rowe store in Alma in the late summer or fall of 1899. Butch certainly had the personality to be a great bartender, and he may have owned a share of the saloon.[21]

Ironically Murray had become quite friendly with the local bartender, Jim Lowe, none other than Butch himself. Siringo said that Murray never suspected Jim Lowe was Butch Cassidy. However, French wrote that Murray had recognized Butch, but did not want to arrest him without a "regiment of cavalry."[22]

French told Butch of Murray's visit, and Butch apparently smiled, saying he was already suspicious of Murray's true identity. Siringo said that the gang had figured out Frank Murray (or "Rank" Curran as Siringo called him in his book) was a Pinkerton detective and the boys wanted to kill him. However, Butch helped him escape in the night.[23] Siringo claimed Murray admitted that he owed his life to Lowe.

Perry Tucker, the WS foreman, soon gave notice to French that he was quitting and recommended Jim Lowe as his replacement. French apparently considered it and talked with Butch asking him if he was in French's shoes would he hire himself, and Butch replied no "without the least hesitation." Butch made preparations to leave. French said, "Despite the bad character given him by the Pinkerton agent I was sorry to lose him."[24]

Butch left the area a short time later with Red Weaver. Author Jeffrey Burton says it was between March 15 and 20. As they were leaving they stole "every saddle horse" from neighbor N. M. Ashby who had been suspected of petty thievery from the WS Ranch for some time. Five other outlaws were in the area at the same time. Some historians believe they were Butch's associates who had also left the WS. Soon Butch and Weaver were only a day behind them. The identity of the five are unknown, but one lawman who pursued them named three as "Capehart, Black and Todd Carver." Some have suggested Harvey Logan, Ben Kilpatrick, and Will Carver, although the upcoming events seem out of character for these three. The local press called the five "the Smith Gang" and named four of the five as Smith brothers, Bill, Al, Floyd, and George.[25]

When Butch and Weaver approached the Springerville, Arizona, area, the other five outlaws had arrived there just a day ahead and aroused the suspicion of local sheriff Ed Beeler. Sheriff Beeler soon arrested Butch and Weaver as they left Springerville. Beeler did not arrest the other five outlaws because he was short-handed and the five were well armed. Beeler took Butch and Weaver to the Apache County Jail in St. Johns. Weaver gave him his real name while Butch identified himself as James Lowe and said that Captain William French of the WS would vouch for him. Jail records indicate that James Lowe and Bruce Weaver were received on March 27, 1900.[26]

The next day Beeler made an attempt to arrest the other five with a larger posse but relented after exchanging shots and killing two of the strangers' horses. A second group of pursuers was organized by local citizens. They followed behind Beeler, but were unaware that he had given up pursuit. The citizens group soon split up and all returned to town except two young Mormon cowboys, Andrew "Gus" Gibbons and Frank LeSueur. The five outlaws spotted the two cowboys and unmercifully ambushed and killed them. LeSueur had been shot five times, Gibbons six times, and both had head wounds. The outlaws then took their horses, weapons, money, and even their hats. Word reached town and the locals were outraged.[27]

Beeler vowed "to follow the outlaws and get them if it took all summer." The five later tussled with a posse led by George Scarborough, and Scarborough was killed.

Butch was released from the Apache County jail on March 31, 1900,[28] while Weaver was detained "on the ground of his suspicious appearance and his not being able to give a more definite account of himself." Butch claimed he had just recently picked up Weaver and did not know him. French said he heard later that Butch was glad to be rid of Weaver as he considered him a bluffer. French describes Butch's release, "how Jim had managed to arrange it was a masterpiece of diplomacy."[29] French said, "Even more amazing was that Butch was allowed to leave with all of the Ashby horses."

Weaver was released on April 8, to Socorro County, New Mexico, officials to face two charges of horse theft in that county.[30] Butch had apparently agreed to appear for the same charges. On April 27, both Weaver and Cassidy were no-billed on the first charge. The next day which was a Saturday, they both attended court in Socorro and pled not guilty. The trial was set for Friday, May 4. Butch apparently decided he was not going through another trial and disappeared. Weaver was granted bail at $1,000. However he was back in jail on June 14 for some irregularity. He was finally given liberty when his bond was secured on a later date.

Sometime later Butch was reported to be heading north with Will Carver to Brown's Park.[31] Charlie Siringo, however, said Butch hid out in Baggs and a Mrs. Nichols helped hide him.[32]

MEANWHILE, NEW MEXICO Governor Miguel Antonio Otero witnessed Elzy Lay's trial and felt he had not received a fair trial; he was anxious to see him pardoned early. Elzy's grandson, Harvey Murdock, said Otero was "very generous in his evaluation of the conduct and of the presence of mind and courage that McGinnis displayed during the trial."

Otero said that Elzy Lay told the court during the trial, "If the court please, I'm here on trial for murder. I understand there are charges against me for train robbery, another murder and for interfering with the U.S. Mail. I have been on trial, without being given a chance to procure many of my witnesses. I have no way to protect myself and I positively refuse to answer any questions except those asked by the prosecuting attorney, concerning the gunfight."[33]

Lay later received endorsements from prison officials for helping to quell a prison riot, which saved the life of the brother-in-law of the warden. He also helped break up an attempted prison escape by riding to town in the dark to get additional help.[34] Prison Superintendent Holm Olaf Bursum wrote to Governor Otero recommending Lay's release or commutation. Bursum stated Lay had been "a model prisoner in every sense of the word and during his entire imprisonment and not a single mark has been placed against him."[35] As a result, his sentence was commuted to ten years by Governor Otero on July 4, 1905, and with his good behavior he was released after six years on December 15, 1905.[36] Lay wrote a thank you letter to Governor Otero on July 5, 1905, telling him of his "joy and happiness" and gratitude for his confidence and kindness toward him. He assured the governor that he had "made no mistake" in granting Elzy's release and he planned "to become an honorable and useful citizen and one to whom you can point to with pride."[37]

At Elzy Lay's release he was the only individual who knew where the stolen loot from the Folsom train robbery was buried. He returned to Alma, New Mexico and stayed with Lewis and Walter Jones, the owners of the Alma store. Lewis Jones later recalled Elzy was a "goddamn nice lookin' fella, he wasn't a big man and he wasn't a little man. He wasn't blond, he was more a little dark complected and had kind of dark brown hair. Hell McGinnis stayed right here with us for six months, you know, and he told us every damn thing."[38]

Elzy left for three weeks to recover the remaining $58,000 of the train robbery loot.[39] He remained in Alma for two years. Elzy then drifted up into Baggs, Wyoming, with George Musgrave and married Mary Calvert in 1909. Mary's father was Kirk Calvert and had known Butch well.

Maude Davis, Elzy's first wife, married three more times after her marriage to Lay. Lay did get acquainted with his daughter with Maude Davis. He had two more children with Mary. His new father-in-law, Kirk Calvert, ironically was a deputy sheriff in Rawlins and later sheriff in Baggs.[40]

Lay dabbled in oil prospecting in Wyoming for a few years around 1916. He discovered a large gas field that is still in operation today but pulled out in discouragement before it was developed. He ran a bar in Shoshoni, Wyoming, for a time. He later moved to California and worked for the Imperial Valley Irrigation District. He also worked some in the motion picture business. He died in Los Angeles on November 10, 1934.[41]

Left: Attorney Orlando W. Powers was rumored to have met with Butch to discuss amnesty. *(Used by permission, Utah State Historical Society, all rights reserved)*

Below: Utah Governor Heber M. Wells essentially named Butch as "Utah Public Enemy Number One. *(Used by permission, Utah State Historical Society, all rights reserved)*

15. Amnesty Tales, 1900

THE TIME BUTCH spent at the WS Ranch had provided him some normalcy, and he hated to leave. He'd been able to associate with his criminal pals in secret, but still use his leadership talents in ranching. He, however, had lost his best friend, Elzy Lay, who was facing life in prison.

On April 17, 1900, "Flat Nose" George Currie was killed by a posse in Utah. Butch could see the writing on the wall and began to consider leaving the outlaw life behind permanently. Butch was not afraid of hard work on ranches, in fact most employers gave him praise, but each time he tried to live an honest life, the law seemed to catch up with him.

Stories began to circulate of Butch's plans to seek amnesty. There is little evidence that this was true. Rather Butch began to build a "nest egg" of loot from a number of robberies with plans to leave the U.S. and start over where no one knew him.

Matt Warner was released from the Utah State Pen on January 21, 1900. Matt had developed a relationship with then Utah Governor Heber M. Wells.

In Matt's memoirs he states that Governor Wells asked him to convince Butch to come in to see him, and Wells promised to do all in his powers to protect him from prosecution for crimes, if he promised to abandon the outlaw life as Matt had done.[1] Union Pacific files also suggest Matt Warner was working to help Butch obtain amnesty.

However, correspondence in Governor Well's files indicates that Matt was working for the Governor to provide information on his former outlaw friends and their locations.[2] Further, information from Sheriff William Preece indicates by this time that Butch may have no longer trusted Matt.[3]

Governor Wells at the time was troubled by the outlaws and extremely concerned over the recent murder of Moab's Sheriff Tyler on May 26, 1900. Butch Cassidy was named as a possible suspect in Tyler's killing, although he was not involved.

On June 29, 1900 a story broke in the *Deseret Evening News*: "Butch Cassidy To Surrender" with the Subtitle, "Famous Bandit Comes to Salt Lake City to Give Himself Up, Providing Gov. Wells Will Not Permit Him to be Extradited."[4]

Later investigation revealed that the story had been made up by an individual named Angus M. Cannon, Jr. and his friend who pretended to be Butch. They had duped a seasoned lawman, Salt Lake deputy Ben R. Harries. Harries was convinced that Butch had visited Salt Lake City.[5]

The Governor's office indicated that no one had approached his office on behalf of Butch Cassidy. Further they indicated that they could only offer, "the equal protection of the law and a fair trial" and could not promise to protect him from extradition to other states.[6]

Author Charles Kelly included stories of Butch's efforts to seek amnesty when he wrote his book *The Outlaw Trail*. He included information that he had obtained from Matt Warner. These stories included Butch visiting Salt Lake Attorney Orlando Powers and Governor Heber M. Wells. Kelly also included the story that Butch had turned in a revolver and rifle to Juab County Sheriff Parley P. Christison to show his desire to put his lawless past behind him. Christison also supposedly arranged for a meeting with Governor Wells, although a deal couldn't be made. Other authors have included similar stories, although there is no evidence these actually happened.

An article did run a short time later claiming they had interview Butch in southern Utah, and he had enjoyed reading about his supposed visit to Salt Lake City. Butch indicated he would be "willing to surrender if he would be allowed to make his own terms."[7]

Governor Wells continued to pursue avenues to catch those involved in the murder of Sheriff Tyler. Only a few days earlier Wells had offered $1,000 rewards for each of the killers of Sheriff Jesse Tyler and Sam Jenkins.[8] Two separate posses were organized and one headed north to Powder Springs and one south to Arizona. Harvey Logan was suspected as one of the killers of Sheriff Tyler.

Ironically, Sheriff Beeler of Arizona, who had months earlier arrested Butch, was in contact with Utah lawmen. Beeler was still on the trail of the five outlaws that had killed the two men in Arizona, Gibbons and LeSueur. Beeler believed the same outlaws who killed Tyler and Jenkins were also responsible for the deaths of Gibbons and LeSueur. Beeler traveled to Grand

Junction, Colorado in search of the suspected killers.[9] He sought information from the Utah posse about the suspected location of the killers of Tyler and Jenkins. It is highly unlikely that the killers of Gibbons and LeSueur were the same who had killed Tyler and Jenkins.[10] Beeler named three of five as Capehart, Black, and Todd Carver.[11] Tom Dilley was likely the one responsible for the murder of Tyler and Jenkins.

In the newspaper interview, Beeler mentioned that the five outlaws had included a sixth, "Low" who was captured in Arizona and then freed. Ironically, Beeler had no idea that he had in fact captured Butch Cassidy and certainly would not have released him had he known the prisoner's true identity.[12]

By June 8, the posses had lost the trail of the outlaws and relinquished their search.[13]

Later an idea of making Butch a guard on the Union Pacific railroad was hatched. As difficult as this may be to believe, evidence exists that the proposal was presented to the Utah and Wyoming governors at the time. A letter found in Governor Heber M. Wells files supports this idea.

The letter is from W.S. Seavey, general agent of the Thiel Detective Service, Denver Office to Governor Heber M. Wells, dated May 30, 1900, and states, "I desire to inform you that I have reliable information to the effect that if the authorities will let him alone and the U.P.R.R. officials will give him a job as a guard, the outlaw Butch Cassidy will lay down his arms, come in and give 'himself up,' go to work and be good peaceable citizen hereafter."[14]

A similar letter was also discovered in Wyoming Governor Richards' files.

A clandestine meeting was allegedly arranged between Butch and Union Pacific officials by Douglas Preston, but never came about due to bad weather. Butch waited all day at Lost Soldier pass in Wyoming for Preston and the officials who never appeared. Butch finally left. Later the officials arrived and discovered a note Butch had left under a rock stating, "Damn you Preston, you have double crossed me. I waited all day but you didn't show up. Tell the U.P. to go to hell. And you can go with them."[15]

Not long afterward, word was received that Butch was involved in a Union Pacific train robbery near Tipton, Wyoming and any arrangement was terminated. However, the proposal would not have helped Butch a great deal anyway as the Union Pacific could not grant him amnesty and other states would have soon searched him down.

Players in the Tipton Train robbery.
Top left: Ernest "Kid" Charter helped his brother with the horse relays. (*Courtesy Jack Stroud*)
Top right: Bert Charter helped with the horse relays. (*Courtesy Joe Charter*)
Bottom left: William "Bill" Cruzan was one of the robbers. (*Author's collection*)
Lower left: E.C. Woodcock was the expressman in both the Wilcox and the Tipton robberies. (*Union Pacific Museum*)

16. Tipton Train Robbery, 1900

AFTER BUTCH'S FAILED attempt for amnesty, he met with some of his co-conspirators in Denver in July 1900 to make final plans for two upcoming robberies to be executed within a few weeks of each other, although several hundred miles apart. The two robberies were a Union Pacific holdup near Tipton, Wyoming, and a bank robbery in Winnemucca, Nevada.[1] Butch was reportedly around Rawlins near the end of July and some feared that he was planning another robbery in the area.[2]

Jack Ryan[3] later told friends that he stayed at the Brown Palace Hotel in Denver to celebrate the Fourth of July with Butch Cassidy, Harry Longabaugh, and several others.[4] Ryan, a part time employee of the Union Pacific, may have supplied key information on the schedule of a gold shipment. However, Butch may have met with Frank Murray of the Denver Pinkerton office who could have been the source of inside information on the timing of the gold shipment. Murray may have felt obligated to Butch since Butch had saved his life in Alma, New Mexico, when Murray's cover was exposed and his life was in danger.[5]

According to Pinkerton records, Harry Longabaugh had originally planned to participate in the Tipton robbery but changed his mind at the last minute to assist Butch with the Winnemucca bank robbery. Longabaugh sent word to Harvey Logan via Jim Ferguson "that he could not keep his appointment."[6] As a result of this change, Harvey Logan was a man short for Tipton and recruited Will Cruzan at Jim Ferguson's ranch to help.

Will (or Bill) Cruzan hailed from Texas and had served time in the Colorado State Pen for grand larceny from March 22, 1895, to May 12, 1898. He was a skilled horse thief who knew the hidden canyons and where to hide a stolen herd. Pinkerton detective Charlie Siringo had trailed Cruzan and Harvey "Kid Curry" Logan for thousands of miles and could never catch up to them even when the pair had been burdened with a herd of stolen horses.[7]

Harry Longabaugh likely changed his mind because of Harvey's reputation for being psychotic. Compared to Logan's sociopathic tendencies,
Butch probably seemed like a calm and stable friend.

The names "Butch and Sundance" are well-know now, but when did they
forge their friendship? They may have known of each as cowboys earlier, but
it appears they became good friends in 1900. To Butch it was likely out of
necessity since his trusted friend, Elzy Lay, was serving a life sentence in New
Mexico. Exactly where and when they met remains mostly a mystery. Sundance started working for Al Reader's Stone Wall Ranch in early 1897 and
was tasked with establishing a winter camp near the Powder Springs hideout that Butch used at times.[8] They may have gotten to know each other
around this time. Researcher Jack Stroud believes that Bert Charter introduced Sundance to Butch in the fall of 1896 or the spring of 1897.

Similar to the Wilcox robbery, Butch Cassidy likely participated in the
planning, but not the execution of the Tipton train holdup due to the upcoming bank robbery in Nevada. His "promise" to Governor Richards to "not
turn a trick" in Wyoming may have also been a factor. The three outlaws who
conducted the robbery at Tipton were Harvey "Kid Curry" Logan, Ben "Tall
Texan" Kilpatrick, and William Cruzan with support from Bert and "Kid"
Charter and Jim Ferguson.[9] According to Pinkerton Detective Charlie
Siringo, Jim Ferguson confided to him undercover that the three robbers were
Logan, Kilpatrick, and Cruzan.[10]

On Wednesday August 29, 1900, at 8:30 P.M., train No. 3, known as the
Overland Limited and the fastest train on the Union Pacific,[11] was held up
between Rawlins and Rock Springs, Wyoming. After stopping for coal at Tipton, the westbound train continued toward Table Rock. As it was pulling up
a grade leaving Tipton, a masked man came over the tender car and stuck a
Colt .45 in the back of engineer Henry Wallenstein.[12]

The outlaw instructed him to stop the train when he saw a fire around
the bend. Then the outlaws ordered conductor E. J. Kerrigan to break the
train into two segments. He uncoupled the engine and the mail, express, and
baggage cars from the remainder of the train. The grade caused the loose back
cars to slip downhill, back toward Tipton.[13] The conductor had to set the

brake. The outlaws then ordered that the engine, mail, express, and baggage cars be pulled further ahead about a half-mile.

The bandits commanded the express agent to unlock the door and come out. E.C. Woodcock, who happened to be the same agent who had been working aboard the train robbed earlier at Wilcox, refused. Engineer Wallenstein convinced Woodcock to come out when he saw that the robbers intended to blow up the express car. Woodcock was successful in hiding two packages of money before he opened the door.

Three charges of dynamite were used to blow the "through safe,"[14] demolishing the express car and damaging the mail car. The outlaws gathered the loot, and the robbery was a success. The outlaws were on their horses by 10:30 P.M.

A posse, including lawmen Frank Hadsell and Joe LeFors, was sent to the robbery site in a special train car, which did not arrive at the scene until the following morning at 8:30. A total of three posses were eventually organized and sent on the outlaws' trail. The Robbers Roost Gang was immediately suspected.[15]

Once again, reports varied as to the number of bandits involved. One report indicated there were five masked thieves.[16] Only three were described as the others were at a distance:

First Robber: Height: 5 ft 10 in, smooth face, sandy complexion, grey eyes, and talks very fast.

Second Robber: Man about 5 ft 7 in, sandy complexion, talks very coarse, wore canvas coat, corduroy pants, shoes badly worn.

Third Robber: Man about 5 ft 9 in, dark complexion, wore flannel shirt, no coat.

Another man held the horses, but was too far away for description. Bert Charter's friend and local outlaw Billy Sawtelle, who helped supply the horses, was suspected of being the fourth robber.[17] Sawtelle had been involved in a gunfight in 1897 and killed one man and injured another. The Union Pacific offered $1,000 reward for each of the outlaws.

The outlaws escaped in a southern direction. They rode about eight miles to Delaney Springs on top of Delaney Rim, rested their horses, then rode southeast to Man and Boy Butte for a change of horses. A hideout and another relay of fresh horses were their goals as they rode to the Haystack Mountains near Baggs.

The posse from Green River, Wyoming, reported they "had followed the trail of the robbers around Haystack Mountain to the point where they had crossed the Snake River, some twenty miles below Baggs." The bandits ran into a bunch of range horses and used the old trick of herding the horses ahead of them for a distance and then allowing them to scatter. This made it almost impossible to discern which trail was left by the horses ridden by the robbers.

Marshal Joe Payne of Green River claimed the posse followed the trail for nearly seventy-five miles the first day. He said the outlaws had taken a southeasterly course and his posse had discovered burned papers and shells at two or three places where the outlaws camped. At one spot they found an abandoned, exhausted packhorse. A rainstorm washed out the trail from this point.[18]

Jim Ferguson supplied the outlaws with grub and horses, hiding them on Black Mountain near his ranch before and after the robbery. Ferguson's ranch was based at the northern foot of Black Mountain about one hundred miles south of the robbery site.[19] Pinkerton records indicate that the three robbers hid out at Ferguson's ranch from September 3 to September 22, 1900, when Ferguson was involved in a knife fight with a man named Cook and was forced by the locals to leave the area. The Pinkerton files specifically state that the "Brown Horse" ridden by Harvey Logan was supplied by Ferguson.[20]

Bert Charter and his younger brother, Kid, supplied packhorses needed for the heavy load at the relay points. Kid indicated the robbers separated near the Haystacks with Cruzan and Kilpatrick going east on the Overland Trail while Harvey Logan went west to Brown's Park. The Overland Trail passed nearby the north side of the Haystacks.[21] The plan was to meet in Fort Worth, Texas, after the Winnemucca bank robbery. All but Will Cruzan made the trip.

On September 5, 1900, U.S. Marshal Hadsell reported that the trail had been lost and there was "little likelihood of the posse finding it again." Also that same day, it was reported that two suspicious men were spotted near Grand Encampment.[22] This was likely Will Cruzan and Ben Kilpatrick.

Hesitant to reveal the worth of the valuables carried on their trains, railroad officials reported that only $50.40 had been stolen. Later reports indicate that the amount was much higher, nearing $55,000. Witnesses reported that the loot stolen "made a considerable showing in a gunny sack and the man who picked it up as they started off lifted it like the sack contained considerable weight."[23]

Top: The Union Pacific provided the Tipton posse with a special train car. Possemen above are 1) George Hiatt, 2) Timothy Keliher, 3) Joe LeFors, 4) H. Davis, 5) S. Funk, 6) Thomas Jefferson Carr. Some believe this was a publicity shot because of the men's attire, and some identify it as the Wilcox robbery posse. *Below:* These possemen are believed to be at the Tipton site, ready to ride. (*both photos from Wyoming State Archives*)

For years researchers believed that the loot stolen was in currency, but evidence later appeared that it included gold. The *Laramie Boomerang* newspaper reported on August 1, 1902, "Sacks Which Contained Gold Taken In the Tipton Hold-Up" found:

> Ed Rankin, eldest son of James G. Rankin, who is employed in one of the construction gangs of the Ferris-Haggarty tramway has found five sacks, which are presumed to have contained money, which was secured from the Express car by the five men who held up Train 101 at Tipton five years ago [actually it was only two years] in September, says [from] the markings, they must have contained between $40,000 and $50,000 in gold. A short time ago Ed and a companion were passing through the timber when they came across the five weather beaten and bleached canvass bags. Three bags were marked '$10,000 gold,' and the others '$5,000 gold.'" The bags also carried the letters, 'C.H.' indicating that they came from Chicago. All had been sealed with green wax and the seals were broken. Ed sent the bags to his father and Mr. Rankin forwarded them to General Manager Ed Dickinson at Omaha headquarters. It is the opinion of the authorities that there were five robbers implicated in the hold-up. They headed straight south from Tipton, and the posse headed by Sheriff Creed McDaniel of Carbon County, Sheriff Peter Swanson of Sweetwater County and United States Marshal Frank Hadsell followed the trail for a considerable distance until heavy rain came up and obliterated the Madre Range and this belief was strengthened by shepherds and miners, who reported that five heavily armed men had been seen in that section. There seems to be no doubt that the bandits met in the timber at the head of Cow Creek and there divided the plunder and then separated, and that the bags found were those that contained the stolen gold.

The gold was buried with plans for its retrieval.[24]

Jack Ryan, who had helped the outlaws, later became friends with Charlie Siringo while Siringo was undercover and unknowingly supplied information about the robbery and outlaws. Jack was eventually able to purchase the Club Saloon and Gambling Hall in Rawlins likely using his share of the loot.[25]

17. Winnemucca Bank Robbery, 1900

Butch, Sundance, and Will Carver took on the job of executing the bank robbery in Winnemucca while the other outlaws were involved in the Tipton train robbery and getaway.

The First National Bank of Winnemucca was founded in 1886 by George S. Nixon. At the time of the robbery, the *Silver State* newspaper advertised that the bank had $82,000 in capital on hand. It was certainly attractive to Butch and the gang.

In 1910, a Montana newspaper ran an article based on a supposed interview with Sundance regarding the Winnemucca robbery after he was in South America.[1] The source of interview has been questioned (some believe it came from Jim Duncan, a friend of the outlaws), yet it still provides some previously unknown details. The article quotes Sundance as referring to Butch as "Napoleon, the brainiest member of the bunch."[2]

Jim Duncan lived at Three Creek, Idaho. He originated in Texas. The 1870 census shows that the Duncan family were neighbors of Tom and Sam Ketchum in San Saba County. Tom and Sam became notorious outlaws who ran with Will Carver, Ben Kilpatrick, and Dave Atkins, and they had all grown up in Texas. Atkins later lived in Shoshone, Idaho, for a short time. Jim Duncan had a shady past and often used aliases such as John Porter and W.B. Tellis. He'd come to Three Creek with his brother Tap in the early 1890s, and when Tap moved in 1899, Jim bought his ranch. Through Jim's past associations he likely knew Will Carver well.[3]

The 1910 newspaper account said Sundance, Butch, and Carver had been hiding in Powder Springs. Sundance was sent to Winnemucca alone to scope out the bank and the escape route. Likely Jim Duncan helped plan the escape route since he was most familiar with the area. The interview said that Butch and Carver went to Twin Falls, Idaho, to buy horses. However, Twin Falls did not exist in 1900. It is likely that they rode the train to Shoshone, Idaho, and

The Charley Faraday Three Creek Store, near the Nevada-Idaho border, as it looked in 1888. Riders include members of the Rosevear family who lived at Three Creek. The man standing in back is 1888 store owner John Lewis. *(Photo and identification courtesy Donna Carnahan and Linda McDonald)*

purchased horses in the Rock Creek area before heading to Three Creek.[4]

The three outlaws met up in the Three Creek area near the Nevada–Idaho border. The 1910 Montana newspaper interview said they robbed a store owned by an elderly man and his wife to obtain supplies. Some historians have reported the store was owned by Jim Duncan, but Duncan's store didn't exist until nearly a year after the Winnemucca robbery. The store robbed on September 3, 1900, at Three Creek was owned and operated by twenty-six-year-old Charley Faraday who was still single then.[5]

A local newspaper reported that two masked men entered the store and ordered Faraday and a local dentist, the only two in the store at the time, to put up their hands. One outlaw held his gun on the locals while the other ransacked the safe and money drawer. Not finding much (only $10), he took some clothing and provisions, and they left on their horses. The use of masks implies that the robbers were known in the area and wanted to conceal their identities.[6] Another newspaper account said that the two bandits were known, suggesting the bandits were locals. It is highly likely that Jim Duncan was one of the bandits. The other bandit could have been Ira Brackett, a local man who was a friend of Jim Duncan.[7]

Another recent version of the Winnemucca bank robbery indicates that it was an inside job put up by bank owner, George Nixon, and executed by Tap and Jim Duncan with the involvement of other local Three Creek residents. However, this version offers little proof that they committed the robbery.

More likely Jim Duncan and Three Creek locals helped provide supplies and horses for the real outlaws.[8]

On the same night as the store robbery, four horses were stolen from the George Moore ranch. Three of the horses were owned by Moore, and the fourth was a prized white Arabian horse owned by the famous "Horse Queen of Idaho," Kittie Wilkins, whose brother was staying the night at Moore's ranch.[9] The prized horse, known as Powder Face, was never recovered. It is possible the four horses were saddled in the corral and provided to the outlaws with a promise of a share of the loot.[10]

Once the three outlaws arrived in the Winnemucca area on September 9, 1900, they set up camp about four miles from town near a haystack and water well near the CS Ranch owned by George D. Bliss. For ten days the outlaws made regular trips to town to case the bank and gain needed information. The ten days also allowed time for the local cowboys to leave their home ranches for the fall roundup. With most of the cowboys occupied elsewhere, it decreased those available for posses, and the outlaws' camp was more likely to go unnoticed.[11]

Butch soon made friends with a ten-year-old boy from the CS Ranch, Vic Button, whose father, Frank, was the foreman. Butch had a white horse young Button admired. Vic brought a different saddle horse to the camp each day to race Butch's horse; nothing could beat the white horse.

Vic said, "I had never seen such a horse. He could jump over a willow fence, high sagebrush, or anything." Vic told Butch there were over a hundred saddle horses at the CS Ranch but he was sure not one of them could ever beat the white horse. Butch responded, "You like that horse? Some day he will be yours."

Vic said the three men rode into town every few days and brought him back peppermint candy. They asked him all kinds of questions about the bank. Vic said he told them there were "three who worked there, Mr. Nixon, Mr. Lee and Fanny Harp." He said he knew all three of the men and that Mr. Lee was a "cranky guy." Vic said, "Butch had a big knife on the saddle he rode, and he said, 'Well I'd just as soon stick him [Mr. Lee] in the ribs.'" Vic also told the outlaws about the shortcut to Clover Valley through Soldier's Pass.[12]

In town, the three hung out near the livery stables located at Bridge Street and Second Street. Several boys came to throw rocks in the nearby Humboldt

The First National Bank in Winnemucca, Nevada, about 1905. (*Humboldt County Museum*)

River, and soon Butch was asking nine-year-old Lee Case about the town and the trails leading from town.[13]

ON WEDNESDAY, SEPTEMBER 19, 1900, the trio arrived in town just before noon and tied their horses in the alley behind the F.C. Robbins Merchandise Store, three buildings away from the bank. They then entered the bank through the front door on Bridge Street. The three outlaws did not wear masks.[14]

At noon the bank was nearly empty. The newspaper reported the occupants included Cashier Nixon, Assistant Cashier McBride, Bookkeeper Hill, Stenographer Calhoun, and W.S. Johnson, a horse buyer.[15] All were occupied with business when the three outlaws entered the bank. The leader, who was most likely Butch, shouted, "Gentlemen, throw up your hands; be quick about it and don't make any noise."[16]

The owner of the bank and cashier was George S. Nixon,[17] and he gave the following details:

> Just before the noon hour, with five of us in the office, three men entered the front door. As soon as they were inside, they pulled their guns, two with revolvers and the third with a Winchester, which he had covered in a blanket and demanded three clerks who were in the banking room to "put hands up." I was engaged in my private office with a client, the door between the banking room and private office being closed. As soon as the

clerks were made to understand the situation, one of the desperadoes walked to my private office door, threw it open, entered with a bound, presented a cocked revolver at my head and commanded the gentleman whom I was conversing with and myself to march out in the banking room. We did so. The robber then marched me into the vault and requested me to open the safes. I commenced to argue that the time lock was on and it was impossible for me to open up. He had his revolver at my head all this time. He then drew a murderous looking knife, placed it on my throat and informed me if I did not open the safe immediately, he would cut my throat. I realized that he meant what he said and opened both safes.[18]

Butch could certainly be convincing as a bandit when the time called for it. He threw three sacks of gold coin from the safe into an ore sack that he had brought. He also emptied all the gold from the money drawer, leaving the silver and bank notes.[19]

Nixon reported that the amount taken was $31,640, all in gold coin except $300 in currency.

The outlaws worked quietly enough that no one outside the bank was aware of what was going on inside.

Nixon described the bandit who came into his office. He said,

The man who entered my private office and marched me into the vault and who appeared to be the leader was perhaps about 5 ft 9 or 10 inches in height, light complexion, very skraggy light faded beard which stood out all around from his ears down.[20] Looked at first as though it was false, but I gave it close attention and satisfied myself that it was real. [He had] very small hands [which is a known trait of Butch Cassidy].[21] He bought a pair of gloves from one of our shopkeepers and he [the shopkeeper] informed us that the size was No. 7 or smaller. His hands were freckled. His nose was fairly long but thin, but not Roman. When he was emptying the money from the counter till into the sack he remarked that he was sorry he had to turn such a trick but that he was lame in his hip and could not work. I am, however, inclined to think that this was simply idle talk as I could not discern any lameness when he walked. In my opinion, he is an old hand at the business. He is also an expert horseman. He was about 35 years old and weight about 150 to 165 pounds. He has small veins which show quite distinctly on the globe of his cheek.[22]

✧ ✧ ✧

ONCE THE OUTLAWS had the gold, they escorted the five out the back door of the bank into the alley. The five were forced to face the wall with their hands up. Two of the outlaws jumped the fence with the gold while the third man held his Winchester on the hostages until the others reached the horses. He then jumped the fence. The hostages quickly ran back inside the bank. George Nixon grabbed a revolver and ran out on the street and gave an alarm by firing several shots into the air.

Nixon said the three robbers were two blocks away, riding fast, and shooting into the air. As they passed Bridge Street, several townspeople took shots at the robbers without hitting anyone.[23]

At the Cross Creek Bridge on Second Street, Butch accidentally dropped a sack of gold. He dismounted quickly to pick it up. Handing the sack to one of the others, he remounted and immediately continued the getaway out of town.[24] One report indicated that Butch's "horse dragged him for ten or fifteen feet by the bridle before he managed to stop the animal and regain his saddle."[25]

Nixon reported that the outlaws had been around town for two or three days before the robbery and the leader had been around Golconda (about fifteen miles from Winnemucca) for over a month. George Nixon said later that they had stolen three horses from his ranch the morning of the robbery. One of the horses he describes as being the best in a bunch of 125.[26]

The outlaws made a getaway along the river toward Golconda. Deputy Sheriff George Rose climbed a nearby windmill to see the escape route the outlaws took. Young Lee Case, anxious to see the excitement as school had just let out for lunch, followed behind the deputy. Deputy Rose took several shots at the outlaws without any effect. Rose then spotted the Southern Pacific switch engine at the nearby train station. He ran and commandeered the engine to chase the outlaws. After building enough steam the engine made it to the main line, which paralleled the road for several miles. The engine was able to nearly overtake the fleeing outlaws near the CS Ranch. Gunfire was exchanged again with no effect. The deputy claimed he wounded one of the horses.

According to news accounts, the outlaws had horses waiting in a field at the CS Ranch. They switched mounts and headed northeast over Soldier Pass of the Osgood Mountains. The pass led them to Clover Valley and to the next set of relay horses at the Silve Ranch.[27] When the outlaws' trail left

Vic Button in 1909
on Patsy, the horse Butch gave him.
Was this horse also the white Arabian
known as Powder Face?
(*Courtesy Lenore Conway*)

the railroad tracks, Deputy Rose left the train, secured horses, and followed with several men.[28] Another account indicates that the posse was formed in town before the chase was given with the train engine. This account indicates that the posse followed the bandits' trail into the river bottoms of a ranch owned by George Nixon. There the bandits' camp was found along with their spent horses, including "a fine big black stallion belonging to Mr. Nixon."[29] The posse included Indians known for their tracking skills.[30]

A telegraph was sent to Constable Colwell in Golconda, who also organized a posse. The Golconda posse headed to the CS Ranch and ended up falling behind the fleeing outlaws.[31] The two posses met up as they entered Soldier Pass.[32]

As the outlaws arrived at the Silve Ranch, they could see the pursuing posse in the distance. One of the men working at the ranch asked about the coming posse, and an outlaw shouted, "It's the Winnemucca Sheriff and a posse who are after us. We have robbed the Winnemucca bank!"[33] Earlier, while posing as cattle buyers, the outlaws had brought three saddle horses and a packhorse to the Silve Ranch and left them there. The white Arabian, Powder Face, was used to carry the heavy gold.

One account indicates that only three members of the pursuing posse caught up with the outlaws near the Silve Ranch. They were Jim McVey, Shorty Johnson, and Burns Colwell. The posse members quickly retreated when the outlaws said they would fight it out.

At the next change of horses in Clover Valley, Butch shouted to the approaching posse, "Give the white horse to the kid at the CS Ranch!" Powder Face had carried the gold well but was left with a section of her shoulder where the heavy gold had chaffed off the hair.[34]

The posse came back through Golconda, where Vic Button went to school, and brought him the white horse. He said the kids were eager to hear about the outlaws who had robbed the bank. And all he could say was, "You see what they gave me!" Vic named the horse Patsy and kept him for many years until the horse died when Vic was in college.

Vic reflected, "As I look back I remember these men were good to me. They seemed to have fun and joke among themselves. I can only say that for Butch to remember his promise to a kid when the posse was so close, he could not have been all bad."[35]

Another account by posse member Edward A. Ducker gave no mention of the white horse or any conversation with the outlaws. He stated, "None of the posse even came within shooting distance of the robbers except the Indian who had come from Golconda." When the outlaws saw the Indian getting too close, one outlaw "jumped to the ground and drew his rifle from his saddle scabbard. When the Indian saw this hostile maneuver he ducked down on the off side of his horse and described a wide, fast outward circle and back towards the posse." The bandit was then satisfied with the results and rejoined the other outlaws.

The bandits continued northeast toward Squaw Valley. With fresh horses they soon outdistanced all posses as the lawmen's horses tired.

At Squaw Valley, they stopped at an abandoned home, and "Whiskers" shaved his beard, leaving a note for the posse: "Here Boys, I will make you a present of these [shaved whiskers]." This account indicated the bandits used some intimidation as they left other notes along the way saying, "Don't get in a hurry boys, don't crowd us."[36] One report said that the bandits divided the money at the deserted home as money sacks were scattered about the place.[37]

It was later reported that the outlaws had relays of fresh horses every ten miles clear to the Idaho border.

A telegraph was sent to the mining town of Tuscarora, Nevada, requesting that they organize a posse. However, Tuscarora officials responded the following day saying they would do nothing unless expenses were paid. Too much time had elapsed, so they were advised to remain at home.

Word was later received that the outlaws were spotted twelve miles west of Tuscarora, headed north toward White Rock. The same newspaper also reported the outlaws were last seen headed toward the "Junipers by way of Squaw Valley." The Junipers were south of Silver City, Idaho. Another report indicated that the outlaws were twenty-five miles North of Tuscarora and that over twenty possemen were in pursuit.[38]

Lawmen traveled the area near Mountain City (south of Owyhee) and North Fork and determined the outlaws had taken another route.[39]

The escape route back to Three Creek, Idaho, ran north of Tuscarora and then south and east around the Jarbidge Mountains in order to avoid crossing the deep canyons of the Jarbidge River (or Bruneau River as it was known in 1900). The escape route was the longest in Butch's experience. One report from the Winnemucca posse indicated that they had followed the bandits' trail more than a hundred miles to the north into the Snake River Valley country in Idaho "but never came in contact with them" and that they found one of the outlaws' horses "in a deep box canyon in Jarbidge county [*sic*]." At Three Creek, the posse talked with George Moore, who owned the recovered horse. He told them four horses had been stolen from his ranch a month earlier. Moore eventually recovered his three horses, but the white Arabian named Powder Face was never found. Most likely Powder Face was the white horse given to Vic Button. The posse determined that the outlaws had "come down that way on their trip to Winnemucca and had carefully planned their line of retreat." The trail was lost at Three Creek, and the posse returned to Winnemucca.[40]

Sheriff McDeid of Humboldt County, Nevada, offered a $3,000 reward for the capture of the three outlaws. He described the three bandits:

> One about thirty five to forty years of age, about five feet eight or nine inches in height; weight about one hundred and fifty pounds; dark mustache, week's growth of beard; dark pants well worn, white hat.
>
> One smooth-faced; heavy set; about thirty years old; about five feet eight inches in height; dark hair; bluish grey suit, no vest, coat ripped under right arm; wore Congress shoes and white hat.
>
> One with full beard—scraggy, sandy brown; about five feet nine inches in height; weight about one hundred and fifty or sixty pounds; probably thirty years of age.

Sheriff McDeid sent telegrams to "Boise City [Idaho], Silver City [Idaho], Burns, Oregon, Vale, Oregon, Ontario, Oregon without any success as the outlaws eluded all pursuit.[41]

✧ ✧ ✧

INTERESTINGLY ENOUGH, George Nixon also stated that one of the abandoned horses in his field was branded M⌐, the Wyoming brand of Jay L. Torrey of Wyoming. Butch was apparently still getting his revenge on Torrey whom he felt had a part in his imprisonment in 1894-96.[42]

George S. Nixon and E.L. Carpenter, paymaster of the Pleasant Valley Coal Company, were friends. Nixon ironically had teased Carpenter about being robbed back in 1897. After he read the news account of the Winnemucca bank robbery, Carpenter was anxious to see his friend and return the favor.[43]

About a month after the robbery, three letters torn into strips were found at the outlaws' camp. They were given to George Nixon, who pasted them back together. The letters were correspondence with Butch's attorney, Douglas Preston, dealing with attempts to launder some damaged loot from a prior robbery.

Law Office
D.A. Preston
Rock Springs, Wyo.

Rock Springs, Wyo.

8/24/1900

My dear Sir—

Several influential parties are becoming interested and the chance of a sale are getting favorable.

Yours truly,

D.A. Preston

This letter and the second letter were both on blue paper and written by the same hand, but the second was without letterhead:

Send me at once a map of the country and describe as near as you can the place where you found that black stuff so I can go to it.

Tell me how you want it handled. You don't know it's value. If I can get hold of it first, I can fix a good many things favorable. Say nothing to any one about it.

P.

George Nixon, the owner of the Winnemucca bank, was determined to bring the outlaws to justice. He later became a U.S. Senator from Nevada. (*1909, Library of Congress*)

The third letter was on different paper:

Riverside, Wyo. Sept 1st, 1900.
C.E. Rowe,
Golconda, Nev.

Dear Friends—

Yours at hand this morning. We are glad to know you are getting along well. In regard to sale enclosed letters will explain everything. I am so glad that everything is favorable. We have left Baggs so write us at Encampment, Wyo. . . . Hoping to hear from you soon I am as ever,

Your friend

Mike

U.S. Marshal Frank A. Hadsell of Wyoming received information from Rawlins informants that the outlaws had exchanged "powder burned currency" and also had "a lot of gold coin that seemed to be blackened considerably."[44] The Union Pacific by then had admitted that some of the stolen loot from Wilcox included gold.

Douglas Preston was involved in laundering the damaged currency and continued to be suspected by the Pinkertons, but amazingly no charges or consequences ever came his way. Preston later even became the Attorney General for the State of Wyoming.

In the months that followed, George Nixon vacillated on whether or not it was Cassidy who had held him up. Cassidy's mug shot, sent to him by the Pinkertons, did not convince him. Nixon described the mug shot image as being "a man with a great deal squarer cut face and massive jaws, in fact somewhat of a bull dog appearance, while this man 'Whiskers' struck me as a face that, in case it was shaven, would have more of a coyote appearance."[45] The newspaper also reported that the leader of the robbers was a small man five-feet, seven-inches (two inches shorter than Butch was known to be).[46] It is possible that Will Carver was the man who held the knife to Nixon's neck or that Jim Duncan participated in the robbery, as some reports indicate that a fourth man was involved in the robbery.

After the robbery, Sundance and Butch visited Slater, Colorado, in the fall of 1900 before going to Fort Worth. Sundance had friends in the area, since he had worked on the A.R. Reader Ranch. Sundance was known in the area as Harry Alonzo. He introduced Butch as "Kennaday." Sundance told friends that he had helped rob a bank in Winnemucca. They boarded a train for Texas in Walcott, Colorado. Apparently they gave their horses and equipment to two cowboys, including Sundance's Model 1886 .40-82 caliber rifle.[47]

Sundance later sent a picture of himself and Etta Place taken in New York to friends in the Slater area. During his 1900 visit to Slater, Sundance revealed to friends that the outlaws were headed to South America, and the friends eventually received a letter from Sundance in South America.[48]

Later in the year, Harvey Logan and Will Carver traveled to Colorado and Idaho in the company of Annie Rogers and Lillie May Hunt (Carver and Hunt were on their honeymoon). The two outlaws left the women for a short time at the McFall House in Shoshone, Idaho, while they retrieved Will's share of the Winnemucca bank robbery proceeds. Lillie May Hunt testified that she saw six or seven sacks filled with twenty-dollar gold pieces.[49]

In 1901, George S. Nixon made an attempt to hire Tom Horn to bring in Cassidy, dead or alive.[50] For a time Nixon was even suspected of arranging the holdup to cover up missing funds. He was quickly cleared, mainly due to his diligence in trying to bring the bandits to justice.[51]

18. Fort Worth, 1900

I N NOVEMBER 1900, Butch met fellow outlaws in Fort Worth, Texas. Harvey Logan and Ben Kilpatrick had participated in the robbery of the Union Pacific near Tipton, Wyoming. Butch, Sundance, and Will Carver had just relieved the bank in Winnemucca of a tidy sum of gold. They had met in Brown's Park before meeting again in Fort Worth.[1] For some reason, Will Cruzan, who had participated in the Tipton robbery, did not make the trip south but remained in the intermountain region for an additional three years.

According to Pinkerton records, Will Carver married Lillie May Hunt in Tarrant County, Texas, on December 1, 1900.[2] Lillie used her real name, Callie May Hunt, and Carver used an alias, William Casey.[3] The idea behind the famous Fort Worth photograph of the five outlaws may have come from the new suits the gang had purchased for Carver's wedding.

Fanny Porter's whorehouse in San Antonio was a favorite stopping place for Butch and his cohorts. Fanny later revealed details about the men to the Pinkertons. She said Harry Longabaugh had a front gold tooth, which was later replaced with a white one.[4]

Butch may have chosen Fort Worth at the invitation of his mentor Mike Cassidy. In 1900, Fort Worth had a Mike Cassidy with a mysterious past living in the "Hell's Half Acre" section of town. This Mike was known locally as "Mikey Mike" and was originally from Ireland. There is no way to know if this was the Mike Cassidy from Butch's youth. If he was, he would have been a welcomed and friendly face for Butch who had been on the run for several years. Fort Worth's Mike had a criminal past and was in the saloon business. He had broken the local liquor laws and had a record. He lived with his wife and family at 1600 Calhoun, which was two streets east of Main.[5] Butch and Sundance were guests on more than one occasion at the Market Hotel at 12th and Calhoun.[6]

This studio portrait has become known as "The Fort Worth Five." It aided in the eventual downfall of the outlaws.
Standing: Will Carver and Harvey Logan (Kid Curry).
Seated: Harry Longabaugh (the Sundance Kid), Ben Kilpatrick, and Robert LeRoy Parker (Butch Cassidy).
(Courtesy Bob McCubbin)

Below: The studio imprint of Swartz in Fort Worth, TEX.

Butch may have arrived earlier in October to attend Buffalo Bill's Wild West show that was in town for two performances on October 10. The *Fort Worth Register* reported "there were many strangers in town" with more than 11,000 attendees.[7] Butch was known to enjoy these shows and later he attended a similar show in Buenos Aires, Argentina.

The Hell's Half Acre area of Fort Worth, with its seedy reputation, was an easy place to lay low. The outlaws apparently rented an apartment known as "Maddox Flats," managed by Kendall and Elizabeth Maddox. Later when Harvey Logan was in jail in Knoxville, Tennessee, he told the *Knoxville Sentinel*, "We rented an apartment and were living in style." According to the 1900 city directory, Maddox Flats was located at 1014½ Main Street. The "½" indicated that the apartment was upstairs.[8]

Nearby was Sheehan's Saloon located at 705 Main Street. The boys may have dropped in here for an occasional drink. Upstairs from Sheehan's Saloon was a portrait studio known as the John Swartz gallery.[9]

For some reason, maybe due to the liquor at Sheehan's, the boys decided to dress up and have their portrait taken by John Swartz. What better way to formalize their new identities than by capturing them in an image? John Swartz was from a family of well-known photographers in Fort Worth. John had partnered with his two brothers, David and Charles, in the previous years. The infamous photo, taken on November 21, 1900, has become one of the most recognized photos in American history and made John Swartz famous.[10]

Swartz was known as 'a master of studio portraits' and used the natural light from the upstairs studio to work his craft. At the time, he was running a special, twelve photos for only $1.75 (normally this could have been as high as $5).[11]

The men apparently purchased new clothes, including the popular bowler or derby hats, for their picture. Sundance was known to enjoy dressing in fancy clothes; ironically, he was the only one to wear unpolished shoes for the sitting. The group reportedly liked the photo so much they ordered a combined fifty prints and returned the next day for them.[12] Swartz also liked the photo and later displayed a copy in his waiting room.[13]

The outlaws spent at least two months in Fort Worth[14] and discussed plans to go to South America. Butch said later that he had been restless the previous two years in the U.S. and wanted to see more of the world.[15]

Fanny Porter operated a bawdyhouse in San Antonio that was popular with the outlaws. (*Courtesy Bob McCubbin*)

Ironically, the local police also used Swartz's studio to produce their mug shots. The man in charge of the department's "Rogue Gallery" was detective Charles R. Scott a twenty-one-year veteran of the Fort Worth Police Department. On a visit to the studio, Scott quickly recognized Harvey Logan as a familiar face in the department's "Rogue Gallery." Scott had been described by his boss as being able to recognize "by sight almost every professional thief in the Southwest."[16]

Scott took the photo of the group back to the department to check it against his files. He was thrilled and quickly wired the Denver Pinkerton office. They described the photo as being the "first real break" in tracking the outlaws.[17] The Pinkertons eventually made wanted posters using the photograph of the gang members with each member identified by name.[18] The Pinkerton Agency later distributed fifteen thousand circulars throughout the U.S. using the photograph.[19]

Lowell Spence spent a lot of time tracking Harvey Logan's activities and kept a record known as "Logan's Log" on stationery from the Menger Hotel in San Antonio. Spence later helped in identifying Harvey when he was captured in Knoxville and eventually identified his body in Colorado after the Parachute train robbery in 1904.[20]

Butch sent a copy of the group photo along with other photos[21] to Vic Button, the boy in Winnemucca to whom he had given the white horse. Vic

Annie Rogers and Harvey Logan had their photograph taken together in Denver. (*Courtesy Bob McCubbin*)

kept the photos locked away until 1914 when he gave the group photo to the local sheriff. Interestingly enough, an undated photograph of the Winnemucca sheriff's office taken sometime after the turn of the century shows a print of the "Fort Worth Five" photo prominently displayed on the wall. Later a framed copy of the Fort Worth Five ended up on the wall of the bank that had been robbed.[22] This occurrence evolved into a story that Butch had sent the photo to the bank with a note thanking them for their donation.

◆ ◆ ◆

AFTER THE Fort Worth stay, Carver and Logan left with Lillie May Hunt and Annie Rogers. They visited Denver and stayed at the Hotel Victor. Harvey had his picture taken with Annie Rogers.[23] Later they traveled to Shoshone, Idaho, and stayed at the McFall House. Lillie revealed to the Pinkertons later that the men had left for five days and when they returned Will had six or seven sacks filled with $20 gold pieces. He kept the sacks in a trunk along with a "big bundle of paper money."

Lillie also identified each of the outlaws in the Fort Worth photograph. She identified Will Carver as her husband Will Casey; Harvey Logan as "Bob Nevilles," and she knew Ben Kilpatrick as "Dan" and said that Dan was an expert bicycle rider and an athletic looking fellow, over six feet tall and 180 pounds. She identified Harry Longabaugh (Sundance) as "Harry" and Butch Cassidy as "Jim." She said that she had met both Jim and Harry at Fort Worth on her first visit to Maddox Flats. She described Jim as "light complected" and a little taller than Harvey Logan.[24]

Harry Longabaugh, "The Sundance Kid," and Etta Place had their photograph taken in New York on February 3, 1901, at DeYoung Photography Studio.

19. New York City, 1901

BUTCH, SUNDANCE AND Etta Place met in early 1901 in New York City,[1] checking into Mrs. Catherine Taylor's Boarding House located at 234 West Twelfth Street on February 1, 1901. Butch signed in as Jim Ryan while Sundance and Etta checked in as Mr. and Mrs. Harry E. Place.[2] They indicated that they were cattlemen from Wyoming. Butch posed as Etta's brother.

Not a lot is known of Etta Place and her true identity. The Pinkerton agents did find a hotel register where she had signed her name as Ethel Place. Place was Harry Longabaugh's mother's maiden name.

Rumors exist that she may have been Butch's girlfriend before she got together with Sundance.

Most believe that she came from Texas and was likely from one of the sporting houses, such as Fannie Porter's in San Antonio. It is also possible that she was a school teacher from Denver. She was certainly drawn to the exciting life that Butch and Sundance led.

Prior to meeting in New York, Etta and Sundance had visited Sundance's family in Pennsylvania, his first visit home in twenty years. He told his family that they were married. Both of Sundance's parents had passed away.[3] The two then traveled to Buffalo, New York, to Dr. Pierce's Invalid Hotel for undisclosed ailments. Sundance shared with his family he had a gunshot wound in his left leg.[4] Some have suspected he had a sexually transmitted disease. He was also treated by a Doctor Weinstein in New York City for still undisclosed ailments.[5] There exist several references to Sundance's poor health. The Pinkerton records indicate that he suffered from stomach trouble and ate Ralston Health Food whenever available.[6]

Much like in the movie *Butch Cassidy and the Sundance Kid*, the trio enjoyed what the city had to offer. When the Pinkertons discovered they had been just under their noses as "tourists in New York," the detectives were livid.[7]

On February 3, Sundance and Etta posed for a photograph together at the DeYoung Photography Studio located at 826 Broadway.[8] The photo was later found by the Pinkertons and used on wanted posters. The Pinkertons reported "the woman is said to be his wife and to be from Texas."[9]

On February 4, Butch purchased a watch for Etta at Tiffany's for $40.10.[10] Tiffany's jewelry store was located on the corner of Fifteen Street and Union Square. This may have been a wedding gift for her recent marriage to Sundance.

Why did Butch pick the alias "James Ryan?" He would again use this alias in South America. A James Ryan was one of two prospectors who discovered the Horn Silver Mine, a rich silver vein in Beaver County, Utah, in 1875.[11] Butch would have heard the name as a boy in Beaver as he was employed by Pat Ryan on his ranch near the mine. Perhaps it just sounded right to him. Butch may have stayed behind in New York, but likely all three, Butch, Sundance and Etta traveled to Argentina together.[12] Likely, they departed on February 20, 1901, on the British steamer *Herminius* for Buenos Aires, Argentine Republic, South America. The Pinkerton files indicate that only Sundance and Etta were on the ship.[13]

Butch and Sundance were determined to begin a new life as law-abiding citizens, planning to leave their outlaw days behind in the States. Butch's failed attempts for amnesty made him realize he could only begin a new life in another part of the world.

The following summer on July 3, 1901, the Great Northern Railroad was robbed of nearly $40,000, including several unsigned bills near Wagner, Montana, by Harvey "Kid Curry" Logan. Uncharacteristic of Cassidy's robberies, some reports indicated that passengers were also robbed. The unsigned bank notes were for the Bank of Helena, Montana, and were easily traceable. They led to the capture of Ben Kilpatrick and Harvey Logan.

Was Butch in Montana to help with the robbery and further shore up his nest egg for South America or had he already left for Argentina with Sundance and Etta? The Pinkerton files state that Cassidy was "suspected of complicity in the Great Northern Train robbery." The files indicate that Butch met with "Blake Graham" of Silver City, New Mexico, in May 1901 in Wilcox, Arizona.[14]

The Parker family received reports that Butch had been involved in the robbery of the Great Northern Railroad. However, other evidence suggests that Butch had relocated to Argentina in February and did not look back.

Reports of Butch's escapades were a continual embarrassment to the family. As news of the Great Northern robbery reached the Parker family they decided to stay home and "pull the blinds," foregoing Independence Day festivities in Circleville.

On December 15, 1901, Harvey "Kid Curry" Logan was arrested near Jefferson City, north of Knoxville, Tennessee. Logan was involved in an altercation with local toughs in Ike Jones's saloon on the evening of December 13. Two police officers beat Logan severely with their billy clubs as Logan tried to strangle a man named Luther Brady. Logan shot the two police officers and escaped out the back into a creek. In searching for Logan, police discovered a considerable number of bank notes from the Great Northern robbery in his hotel room. Logan was captured, later tried, and sentenced to a long-term prison sentence, but made a daring escape before he arrived at the federal prison.

According to Charlie Siringo, Harvey Logan was in Rawlins at Jack Ryan's saloon before he made the trip to Knoxville.[15] Harvey likely used Jack to help launder the unsigned bank notes through his saloon.

Siringo says that Joe LeFors mistakenly revealed Siringo's cover to Jack Ryan.[16] While undercover Siringo was pumping Ryan for information on the gang until LeFors made the slip up.

Right: Butch (Jim Ryan) and Sundance (Harry Place) registered this brand in Argentina. (Author's photograph)

Below: Butch, Sundance, and Etta Place established a ranch in an isolated area at the foot of the Andes.

20. Argentina, 1901~1905

AFTER JOURNEYING A MONTH from New York on the *Herminius*, the three (and likely there were three) arrived in Buenos Aires on March 23, 1901.[1] They found lodging in the Hotel Europa located near the harbor and stayed there for about a month.[2] The hotel was located at the corners of Calle 25 de Mayo and Calle Cangallo (today it is called Calle Peron).[3] The trio felt safer than they had in years, as they were literally on the other side of the world and no one knew their true identities.

Butch used the alias James "Santiago" P. Ryan and Sundance claimed the alias Harry "Enrique" A. Place.[4]

The Hotel Europa was only a few blocks from the banking district. Experimenting with a new concept, the two former outlaws actually *deposited* money in a bank. Sundance opened an account with $12,000 in gold notes. The bank, London and River Platte (Banco de Londres y Rio de la Plata), was located at Calle Reconquista.[5]

At the American Consulate in the 900 block of Calle Cordoba, a few blocks away, they inquired about obtaining land for a ranch. They met with Vice-Consul George Newbery, a former dentist from New York, who recommended the isolated area in southern Argentina known as Patagonia as he hoped to recruit other North Americans to the area for a new community, and he dealt in land development.[6] Further evidence indicates that Butch and Sundance already had plans to obtain land and raise stock in Patagonia before meeting Newbery.[7] Butch had apparently done his homework and knew of the land of opportunity in Patagonia.[8]

Newbery had followed his brother Ralph to Argentina in the 1870s. Both worked as dentists and invested in land and cattle. George acquired a ranch or "estancia" and had hired North American cowboys to work there, including Jarred (Augustus) Jones and John Commodore Perry of Texas who would have future connections to Butch and Sundance. Several of the migrant cowboys eventually started their own ranches, including Jones and Perry.

Leaving the U.S. was a wise move on the part of Butch and Sundance as several former outlaw friends had recently met their demise or capture. Will Carver was killed on April 2, 1901, while resisting arrest from Sheriff E.S. Bryant in Sonora, Texas. Also in 1901, Ben Kilpatrick and his girlfriend, Laura Bullion, were arrested for passing forged bank notes from the Great Northern Train robbery. By December, the notorious Harvey Logan was captured near Knoxville.

Butch, Sundance, and Etta set out for their journey to Patagonia on the western border of Argentina sometime in mid-1901. The area was desirable to them for its rich grass and abundant water and its isolation from populated areas. They took a train to Bahia Blanco where they stayed one night before changing trains to go to the city of Neuquén. At Neuquén, they purchased a team and wagon to travel the final four hundred miles to the valley of Cholila in the Chubut Province.

Much like today, the Cholila valley was somewhat remote, yet beautiful. Situated at the base of the Andes Mountains, it is close to the Chilean border. At the time, it was four hundred miles from the closest rail line.

The Pinkertons later described the trip to Cholila: "To reach it from Buenos Ayres would be by steamboat to Bahia Blanco, thence by smaller boat from Bahia Blanca to Rawson on the coast at the mouth of the Chubute River, from there on horse back to the '16 d'October.' Distance from Rawson to '16 d'October' two hundred miles, probably two weeks travel. Fare from New York to Buenos Ayres to Bahia Blanca and thence to Rawson $160 in gold. Steamers run twice a month. A horse at Rawson costs $50, wagon $200, and provisions for two weeks $100."[9]

One account indicated they hired Chilean Francisco Albornoz "as a guide for three days . . . until arriving at" Rio Negro. Albornoz was quoted as saying, "I found Enrique Place, Santiago Ryan and senora Etta . . . in a wagon."[10]

Another version indicated that young Scottish settler John Gardner met them on the road and took them to Cholila.[11]

Once they arrived in the valley, they lived in a canvas tent until a new four-room cabin and barns were built for their ranching operations[12] on the banks of Rio Blanco, a small river.[13] One account indicates that in October 1901 they were still living in a tent. Butch may have later built a separate cabin for himself near the four room cabin.[14] An early visitor who joined them at their campfire was Milton Roberts. Roberts was a twenty-one-year-old Welsh-Argentine. He served at that time as the Registrar of Brands under the function of the police. Butch and Sundance indicated their plan to hire hands for a ranch and talked of raising racehorses.[15] Roberts would become a trusted friend.

An Italian immigrant who later spent a night at the cabin described it: "The house was simply furnished and exhibited a certain painstaking tidiness, a geometric arrangement of things, pictures with cane frames, wallpaper made of clippings from North American magazines, and many beautiful weapons and lassos braided from horsehair. The men were tall, slim, laconic and nervous, with intense gazes. The lady who was reading, was well-dressed. I had a friendly dinner with them. Other neighbors recalled that she kept perfumed water in the house's wash basins, spoke some Spanish, and rode and shot like a man."[16]

One neighbor was impressed with the cabin and said that it had very good furniture for the time and was adorned with little things that were not common in houses in Cholila. The neighbor also noted that Etta was very pleasant and beautiful and wore pants and rode horses with a man's saddle and wore two pistols on her waist which she knew how to handle as she hunted small animals.[17]

Few pictures exist of Butch and Sundance at the Cholila ranch. One that appears to match the current cabin is often referred to as "Los Jinetes" or "The Riders." It shows Butch, Sundance, Etta, and some friends in front of the cabin with horses. I obtained a copy of this photo from Argentinian Regi Hammond during a visit to Cholila. Hammond's grandparents are also shown in the photo.

Another photo supposedly sent by Sundance to his sister Samanna is often referred to as "the tea party." The cabin in the background has subtle differences from the existing cabin and the "Riders" photo. The doors and windows appear different, making one wonder about the location. It is possible the photo was taken at the Jared Jones estancia since his cabin was very similar and may have been the model for the one Butch and Sundance built. The picture shows Butch, Sundance, and Etta with two pet dogs.

Butch and Sundance purchased sixteen colts for 855 pesos using funds from their bank account in Buenos Aires on June 17, 1901.[18] Interestingly, the man who helped them purchase the colts was Martin Sheffield. The

Lower photo: This photograph is known as "The Riders." The landscape and the cabin appear to be consistent with that at Butch and Sundance's ranch in Argentina. Those identified are: *Far left by horse:* Butch Cassidy. *Fifth man standing by woman:* George Hammond and his wife Ethel. *Second from right in front of horse:* Sundance. *Far right, almost out of photograph:* Etta Place. (*Courtesy Regi Hammond*)

Upper photo, page 176: An enlarged portion of the bottom photo, showing Butch Cassidy in Argentina. (*Courtesy Regi Hammond*)

Upper photo, this page: An enlarged portion of the bottom photo, showing Sundance and Etta Place with a Springer Spaniel and horse. (*Courtesy Regi Hammond*)

Known as the Tea Party Photo. *From left:* The Sundance Kid, Etta Place [Mr. and Mrs. Harry Place], and Butch Cassidy [Jim Ryan] with their Springer Spaniel and their black dog to the left of Butch. (*Courtesy Donna Ernst, copyright Paul D. Ernst*)

Sheffields had ties to Ben Kilpatrick back in the States. Martin Sheffield worked for a time for Jarred Jones.

Butch and Sundance registered a brand together plus individual brands on October 30, 1901, with the territorial government in Rawson.[19] The jointly-owned brand was a reverse P connected to a forward R to represent Place and Ryan. Butch's separate brand was a connected J and R for James Ryan.[20] Sundance's brand was a connected OK.[21] Near the year's end they purchased cattle and sheep for the ranch.[22] They eventually acquired stock of 1,300 sheep, 500 cattle, and 35 horses.

Sundance and Etta made at least one trip back to the United States. Cassidy traveled as far as Buenos Aires with them, but did not return to the U.S. On February 15, 1902, on their way to Buenos Aires, they signed the store register of Jarred Jones for supplies purchased in Nahuel Huapi.

On March 3, 1902, Sundance and Etta traveled to New York, arriving April 3, 1902, on the steamship *Soldier Prince*.[23] The two stayed in the States for several months. Sundance may have been seeking treatment for some health related issues as Pinkerton notes indicate he was treated in a hospital in May 1902.[24] Sundance visited his sister Samanna in Pennsylvania and his brother in New Jersey. They left New York on July 10, 1902, listed as crew members on the steamer *Harorius*.[25] Sundance was listed as "Purser" and Etta as "stewardess." They returned to Buenos Aires on August 9, 1902.[26] After Sundance returned, he filed a petition to purchase 2,500 hectares (about 6,175 acres) in the Cholila Valley while still in Buenos Aires.

According to Pinkerton records, Butch and Sundance were squatters on the land. They settled on "4 square leagues of Government land with Province of Chubut, district 16th October, near Cholilo,"[27] Obtaining title to lands in Argentina was (and still is) difficult and often took several years.

While Butch was in Buenos Aires during Sundance and Etta's U.S. trip, he visited George Newbery and looked into the steps necessary to obtain ownership of their original ranch. Butch filed on the land at the Colonial Land Department on April 2, 1902, filing on the first right to buy the land as they were settling and improving the land. When he returned to Cholila, Butch, along with several families, signed a joint land petition requesting 625 hectares of land (about 1,500 acres) from the government.[28] This was done on May 16, 1902, in an attempt to have their community recognized for future benefits.[29] Apparently this was the usual amount requested under the homestead laws of the time.[30]

Butch opened a small store on the ranch. He hired another North American, David Moore, to help run the store.[31] Butch with his affable personality probably enjoyed people coming into the store. Butch and Sundance hired several locals to work on the ranch including Alejandro Villagran as foreman.[32]

While alone in 1902, Butch wrote a letter to his good friend, Matilda Davis, Elzy Lay's former mother-in-law who lived near Vernal, Utah.

It is apparent that he trusted Matilda because he told her exactly where he could be found. One can sense Cassidy's loneliness in a far-away country.

On the top Butch had written his address, "Cholila, Ten Chubut, Argentine Republic, S. Am.," and the date, August 10, 1902.

My Dear friend,

I suppose you have thought long before this that I had forgotten you (Or was dead) but my Dear friend I am still alive. And when I think of my Old friends you are always the first to come to my mind It will probably surprise you to hear from me away down in this country but U.S. was to small for me. The last two years I was there, I was restless, I wanted to see more of the world. I had seen all of the U.S. that I thought was good, and a few months after I sent A—- over to see you, and get the Photo of the rope jumping (of which I have got here and often look at and wish I could see the originals, and I think I could liven some of the characters up a little for Maudie look very sad to me.) Another of my Uncles died and left $30,000, Thirty Thousand to our little family of 3 so I took my $10,000 and started to see a little more of the world. I visited the best Cities and best parts of the countrys of South A. till I got here, and this part of the country looks so good that I located, and I think for good. For I like the place better every day. I have 300 cattle, 1500 sheep, and 28 good saddle horses, 2 men to do my work, also good 4 room house, wearhouse stable, chicken house and some chickens.[33] The only thing lacking is a cook. For I am still living in Single Cussidness and I sometimes feel very lonely. for I am alone all day, and my neighbors don't amount to anything, besides the only language spoken in this country is Spanish, and I don't speak it well enough yet to converse on the latest scandles so dear to (?) the (?) hearts of all nations, and without which conversations are very stale. but the country is first class the only industry at present is stock raising (that is in this part) and it cant be beat for that purpose, for I never seen a finer grass country, and lots of it hundreds and hundreds of miles that is unsettled, and comparatively unknown, and where I am, it is a good agricultural country, all kind of small grain and vegetables grow without Irrigation. but I am at the foot of the Andes Mountains. and all the land east of here is prarie and Deserts, very good for stock, but for farming it would have to be Irrigated, but there is plenty of good land along the Mountain for all the people that will be here for the next hundred years, for I am a long way from Civilation it is 16 hundred miles to Buenos Aires the Capital of Argentine, and over 400 miles to the nearest RailRoad or Sea Port, in the Argentine Republic, but only about 150 miles to the Pacific Coast [to (corner torn off)] Chile but to get there we have to cross the Mountains. which was thought impossible till last summer when it was found that the Chilian

Matilda Davis (seated far right) and her family in Utah. Maude, who was married to Elzy Lay, is the tallest girl, standing in back. Matilda and Butch Cassidy corresponded by mail. (*Uintah, [Utah] County Library*)

> Gov. had cut a road almost across so that next summer we will be able to go to Port Mont [Puerto Montt], Chile, in about 4 days, where it use to take 2 months around the old trail and it will be a great benifit for us for Chile is our Beef Market and w can get our cattle there in 1/10 (?) the time and have them fat. And we can also [illegible] supplies in Chile for one third what they cost here. The climate is a great deal milder than Ashley Valley. The summers are beautiful, never as warm as there. And grass knee high every where. And lots of good cold mountain water. But the winters are very wet and disagreeable, for it rains most of the time, but sometimes we have lots of snow. But it don't last long. For it never gets cold enough to freeze much. I have never seen Ice one inch thick.[34]

The second page of the letter, which included Butch's signature, is missing; however, the handwriting matches closely with all known handwriting of Butch. Elzy Lay's grandson donated the letter to the Utah State Historical Society in his mother's name in the 1970s. His family possessed the second page for many years, but discovered it missing when they decided to donate the letter. His mother recalls the entire letter throughout her life as a valuable family possession and that it was, in fact, a letter from Butch. This was attested to her by both her mother (Maude Davis Lay) and her grandmother (Matilda Davis of Ashley) to whom the letter is addressed.[35]

When I visited Argentina in 2007, I found Butch's description of the ranch and surrounding area matches closely with what remains today. It is a beautiful setting at the base of the Andes Mountains, still fairly remote.

Butch tells Matilda of his plans to "settle here for good" confirming the idea that he planned to start over and go straight for the rest of his life. Butch and Sundance could have lived out their days peacefully on this ranch if the Pinkertons had left them alone.

George Newbery noted on August 15, 1902, Place and Ryan were "good fellows" and that they were "doing well" at their ranching operations and had "doubled their stock."[36]

In November 1902, the *Wyoming Press* newspaper in Evanston reported that Butch was no longer wanted in Wyoming for his crimes and that in fact he had an "understanding that if he did not return the old charges of train and bank robbery and cattle stealing would not be pushed against him." It further reported that "one officer has kept track of Cassidy and it is his opinion that the one time notorious outlaw has not turned a trick for many years and is now leading a good life, so far as criminal acts are concerned at least."[37]

In February 1903, former sheriff of Uintah County, Utah, John Pope told a Salt Lake newspaper that he was in close touch with Butch who had settled on a ranch, living a quiet life. Butch had further explained that he had given up the wild career and would lead a peaceful life if left alone.[38] Pope did not reveal the location of the ranch. Pope may have been in contact with Matilda Davis who had received the personal letter from Butch. This further supports the idea that Butch had every intention of going straight for good if he was left alone.

Butch was well liked by his new neighbors. He quickly made friends with his outgoing personality and ranching experience. Many of his neighbors were immigrants from Chile and he taught them the North American methods of raising stock and farming.[39] His neighbors were impressed with his talents with a pistol. Butch often repeated a trick in which he shot a small object while leaning with one hand against a wall and spinning his pistol in the other hand.[40]

The local police trusted Butch and Sundance. Friend and agent Milton Roberts used Sundance as a witness when registering the brand for a police horse. They also had a friendship with Sheriff Eduardo Humphreys and his brother Mauricio.[41]

Other friends included Daniel Gibbons, Jarred Jones, and George Hammond.

Daniel Gibbons was Butch's closest friend in Argentina, and he transacted business for the outlaws after they left the area. His son Mansel worked for Butch and Sundance. Mansel later became an outlaw himself and ran with North American bandits Wilson and Evans when they relocated to Patagonia. Dan Gibbons later spent time in jail because of his association with Butch and Sundance.

Jarred Jones owned a ranch next to George Newbery's ranch in Neuquén. During the winter of 1902, Butch traveled there to purchase horses and ended up staying for a month because of bad weather, playing poker and enjoying their company. Upon his departure he invited Jones to visit his ranch in Cholila.

Jones stayed later at Butch and Sundance's cabin in Cholila until he discovered a corral full of cattle with differing brands, he then kept his distance, but was still somewhat friendly. I visited with descendants of Jarred Jones in Argentina in 2007.

George Hammond was of Welsh decent and married Ethel Mair Roberts, the sister of police agent Milton Roberts.[42] George and Ethel Hammond visited Butch and Sundance's ranch often. They are present in the "The Riders" photo of Butch, Sundance, Etta, and friends in front of a the trio's cabin. George's wife, Ethel, was close to Etta Place and called her "Mae Rose." An Argentine Police report indicated that Etta was known locally as Ethel Place or Marie Place.[43]

Milton Roberts later attempted to arrest the two outlaws, however he was unsuccessful, as they had left the area. Roberts may actually have helped warn them of their impending arrest.

In my 2007 visit with George Hammond's grandson, Regi, he said that George had helped Butch and Sundance escape into Chile in 1905. Regi indicated that his family believed Butch had safely returned to the United States after 1908.

One of Butch's nearest neighbors was a former lawman John Commodore Perry. Perry had been the first sheriff of Crockett County, Texas, from 1891 to 1894.[44] It appears that Perry did not learn of his neighbors' backgrounds until years later.[45] He did arrive in the Cholila valley in 1903 somewhere near the time that the Pinkertons discovered Butch and Sundance's whereabouts.

The Pinkertons received word that the outlaws were living in Argentina by intercepting and reviewing Sundance's letters to his sister in Pennsylvania. On February 14, 1903, Robert A. Pinkerton wrote to the President of the Union Pacific soliciting funds to go to Argentina to capture "Longbaugh and Cassidy" and bring them to justice. He alluded that a deal was "about concluded" with the American Bankers' Association to arrest the outlaws and extradite them for the robbery of the First National Bank of Winnemucca. However, the bankers wished to delay in order to solicit additional help with the expenses.[46] The letters were simply wishful thinking on the part of the Pinkertons. The banks and railroads were content to leave the outlaws alone as long as they did not return to commit additional crimes. The Pinkertons were never successful in obtaining outside funding for the capture of Butch and Sundance.

The Pinkertons sent agent Frank Dimaio, who was finishing up an assignment in Brazil, to Buenos Aires in March 1903.[47] He interviewed George Newbery who identified Butch and Sundance as "Harry A. Place and wife and James Ryan . . . located at a sheep ranch at Cholilo." Newbery then "informed Detective Dimaio that, owing to geographical and climatical conditions it would be impossible to effect the arrest of these criminals [due to] the remote region where they had settled." "Cholilo . . . could only be reached from Puerto Madryn, a distance of 230 miles from Buenos Aires, or from there by a fifteen day journey on horseback through jungle country."[48] There are no jungles between Buenos Aries and the ranch. Likely Newbery was helping Butch and Sundance by buying them time. Newbery apparently agreed to lure Butch and Sundance to Buenos Aires for possible capture under the pretext that they could obtain title to their property in Cholila. However, nothing from this plan ever materialized.[49]

Dimaio then contacted authorities including Dr. Frank Beasley, the Chief of Police in Buenos Aires, to give him the outlaws' descriptions.[50] He had circulars printed with photos and descriptions of the three fugitives, which were "distributed to all police districts, banks, and shipping offices."[51] One of these wanted posters has survived in nearby Trevilin, Argentina.[52]

Also at this time, March 1903, Butch, Sundance, and Etta took a trip east across Argentina. They stayed in Gaiman at the hotel of Hugh Samuel Pugh. Hugh's daughter was impressed by the beauty and gun skills of Etta Place. When they left they gave the daughter a small horse as a gift. They then traveled to Trelew and stayed at the Hotel del Globo. They met North American Lincoln Haward who was manager of the Banco de la Nacion Argentina located near the hotel.[53]

On July 1, 1903, after Dimaio had returned to New York, Robert Pinkerton wrote to the Chief of Police in Buenos Aires. He indicated that they were planning to apprehend the outlaws when they returned to the United States. He provided detailed photos and descriptions of the outlaws along with information on Harvey Logan who had escaped from a Knoxville jail in June. He noted that a $500 reward for each outlaw would be paid upon their apprehension.[54]

On February 29, 1904, Butch wrote to his trusted friend Dan Gibbons. The forty-one-year-old friend and his family had settled in nearby Esquel in the 16 de Octubre colony in the 1890s.[55]

Cholila, Feb. 29, 1904

Mr. Dan Gibbons
16 de Octubre

Dear friend,

I have been laid up with a bad dose of the Town Disease and I dont know when I will be able to ride, but as soon as I am able I will be down. And I will want to buy some Rams, so please keep your ears open for we don't know where to look for them. If you hear of any one that want to sell please tell them about us. I have not been to Norquinco yet, so dont know what we will do there.

Kindest Regards to your Wife & Family.

Yours Most Truly,

Ryan

Look out for my horse.
P.S. Place starts for the Lake tomorrow to Buy Bulls.[56]

In 2007, the ranch that once belonged to Butch and Sundance was still remote and beautiful. This shows the cabin they built. (*Author's photograph*)

Butch must have enjoyed the local women and as a result was convalescing from a case of STD. The lake Butch refers to is likely Lake Nahuel Huapi, where their friend Jarred Jones lived.[57]

In March 1904, the Chubut Territorial Governor made a visit to Cholila. As indicated in Butch's letter, Sundance had left to purchase bulls on March 1, so he was not present for the governor's visit.

The governor and the chief of police together visited Butch and Etta at their Cholila cabin where Butch and Etta offered the dignitaries hospitality by inviting them to stay at their home.

Argentine author Marcello Gavirati writes, "It's hard to imagine the strange combination of sensations that had to go through the minds of Butch and Ethel [Etta], two fugitives in the United States, when they receive in their home the visit of the chief of police and the Governor of the Territory of Chubut. They offer their hospitality to the governor, and he accepts it by staying the night in the house of the trio."[58]

The next day, the settlers of the area threw a party for the governor to "show their respect and admiration to the Governor with food and games, followed by a dance (fiesta). . . . During the dance the Governor on guitar plays a Samba, that is danced by Santiago Ryan [Cassidy] and Rostia Solis, the daughter of the host."

The party continued until the first hours of the early morning and during this time the governor, astonished with the beauty and fine manners of Ethel (Etta), asks her for a dance. She accepts. Mrs. Place dances with the Governor of Chubut. Another version indicates that a display of shooting was held, and Etta demonstrated her shooting skills.[59]

The governor had traveled to the area because he had heard complaints about plans for a new colony there for North Americans being developed by George Newbery. The North Americans already in the area opposed the new growth. The day before the governor left he sent a telegraph to Buenos Aries halting authorization of the colony. In 1904 several additional North Americans settled in the Cholila Valley. These included several sheep farmers.

A few months later Butch and Sundance were the first to sign a new petition to the governor, along with several of their neighbors, requesting title to their land.[60] Obtaining title to the land was an ongoing effort and frustration. Argentine author Marcelo Gavirati, who has researched and written extensively on Butch and Sundance in Argentina, believes they were the first to claim the land in Cholila by the homestead law of Argentina. However, the first title to the property was not issued until 1941.[61]

During this time things started to turn against the idyllic life the trio had established in Cholila. On March 4, 1904, 5,000 pesos were stolen from a manager of the Argentine Lands of the South Company, of Leleque.[62] This occurred near Telsen, Argentina, approximately 230 miles east of Cholila.

Not long after, "Grice and Emil Hood," two teamsters working for Guillermo Imperiale, which was in charge of the company's shipments, were jailed as suspects in Norquinco.

It was soon learned that Grice had visited Butch and Sundance's cabin in Cholila on several occasions with another man, Ricardo Knight Perkins, who worked at Argentine Lands' company store in Leleque.[63]

Regi Hammond shows author Bill Betenson the Cholila Valley in 2007 where Butch, Sundance, and Etta Place settled in Argentina. (*Douglas Barnes Photography*)

Grice and Hood escaped from the Norquinco jail on April 21, 1904. Butch was accused of aiding in their escape and taken to Rawson, the Chubut capital, and held until the judge was convinced that "Santiago Ryan" was innocent. Ricardo Knight Perkins helped convince the judge of Butch's innocence.[64]

When Sundance returned from Nahuel Huapi, he and Etta went to Rawson to meet Butch. They then traveled to Puerto Madryn and then to Valparaiso before returning to Cholila. At the end of 1904, the three took another trip to Puerto Madryn and then took a ship to Buenos Aires. Butch and Sundance reportedly returned before Etta who did not return until near the end of January 1905.[65]

On December 30, 1904, Butch placed an order with a local settler, Richard Clarke, for merchandise that indicated he still planned to stay in Cholila. The merchandise included *bombillos* (metal straws for drinking mate, the local tea favored in Argentina), socks, slippers, a sweater, and handkerchiefs.[66]

For Butch, life on the Argentine ranch had been a fulfillment of a lifelong dream to settle as a rancher.

21. Rio Gallegos Robbery, 1905

O N FEBRUARY 14, 1905, a bank, the Banco de Londres y Tarapacá, some seven hundred miles away from Cholila was robbed of over 70,000 pesos in Rio Gallegos, near the Strait of Magellan by two English speaking bandits, who gave their names as Brady and Linden. They registered at the Hotel Argentino as "Herbert Linden and company." Brady was stout and the shorter of the two, easily engaging in conversation. Linden was more reserved and was a tall, thin man.[1] Butch and Sundance were immediately suspected as the robbery was conducted in a manner similar to their American robberies, including relays of fresh horses.[2]

There is proof, however, that Butch and Sundance were at their ranch in Cholila during the robbery as their signatures were included on an agricultural census survey for Cholila which took place in mid-February.[3] Dan Gibbons also testified that Butch and Sundance were in Cholila during the Rio Gallegos robbery, but he indicated that they may have had involvement because they began to sell off their possessions soon after the robbery.[4]

Brady and Linden were considered between the ages of 25 to 30. Butch and Sundance, at the time, were 39 and 38, respectively. Brady was described as having light brown hair, a dark brown to black beard, and green eyes; Linden was described with green eyes, blond hair, regular nose, skinny face, and when he spoke his upper lip lifted. Brady later revealed to officials that "he had belonged in North America to a gang that was headed by Tom Ketchum."[5]

Brady and Linden were likely two men known as "Hood and Grice."[6] Emilio (or Emil) Hood was identified by Cholila locals as a visitor to the ranch of Ryan and Place as early as 1904 and on into 1905. Another outlaw that appeared on the scene much later, Robert Evans told Dan Gibbon's son Cirilo that he had used the name Hood. However, Evans was described as crude, unfriendly, and illiterate, while Brady was fluent in Spanish, outgoing and cultured.[7]

Herbert Linden was thought to be an alias for a mysterious man known as "Grice who no one could capture." There is also evidence that Grice spent time at the Cholila ranch.[8] One begins to wonder if Butch helped plan the Rio Gallegos robbery or educated "Hood and Grice" on the finer points of robbery and escape with fresh relays of horses?

In Larry Pointer's recent book, *Grice Whom Nobody Could Catch*, he reports that Grice wrote that Sundance and Etta vacationed at Rio Gallegos so Sundance could case the bank and then gave Grice and "Tex" (Hood) the low down on the bank so they could rob it.

Herbert Grice was born in England on November 28, 1877, and immigrated to the U.S. in 1898. In 1900, he lived in Glasglow Valley, Montana. He married Pearl May Warren in Billings on October 19, 1909. Apparently he made many trips to Argentina while living in Montana. He spent time in the Montana State Prison in 1923 and eventually died on March 20, 1953, in Billings, Montana.[9]

The aliases get confusing, which, of course, was their purpose. But, succinctly, Brady and Linden seem to have been Hood and Grice. Grice can be traced to Montana. However, Brady/Hood may have both been aliases for the U.S. bandit George Musgrave. Brady confessed that he had belonged to a gang captained by "Black Jack Tom Ketchum" in New Mexico. Musgrave did not run with Tom Ketchum, but he did run with "Black Jack" Christian and the High Five gang in New Mexico.[10] (The two Black Jacks were often confused.) Musgrave did make his way to South America after the turn of the century. Musgrave and Brady shared many of the same character traits; each was described as "loquacious and sociable" and projecting himself well.

Years later two other bandits were suspected of the Rio Gallegos robbery, Wilson and Evans. Robert Evans and William Wilson were two North American bandits who appeared on the scene after Butch and Sundance's departure around 1907. Another North American bandit, Andrew Duffy, appeared in late 1907. Duffy reportedly knew Wilson and Evans earlier in Montana. Duffy's demise in August 1910 was rumored to have been at the hand of Evans. On December 29, 1909, Wilson and Evans robbed and murdered highly respected Arroyo Pescado merchant Llwyd Ap Iwan, which led to the formation of Mateo Gebhardt's ruthless and feared Frontier Police. Wilson and Evans were eventually killed by Frontier Police in a shootout near Rio Pico, Argentina, in December 1911.[11]

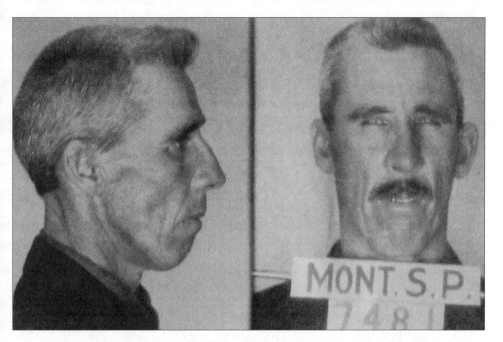

Herbert Grice made several trips from Montana to Argentina. This photograph was taken at the Montana State Prison. (*Courtesy Montana State Archives*)

Butch and Sundance got word that they were suspected of the Rio Gallegos robbery and made plans to depart.

One report has Territorial Governor Julio Lezana issuing an arrest warrant for Ryan and Place (Butch and Sundance). Another has the police chief of Buenos Aires issuing the warrant for their arrest. Authorities were influenced by the information received from the Pinkertons as the arrest warrant read in part, "their specialty is armed robbery of banks, trains and public holdings in broad daylight, and they were in the country, it is presumed they are the perpetrators."

Local Sheriff Eduardo Humphreys received word of the robbery and description of the bandits. On March 1, he sent a telegraph to police officials in Rawson saying he was sure the same bandits had robbed 5,000 pesos the previous year in Leleque, that they went by Grice and Hood, and their hideout was in Cholila at the ranch of the three North Americans. He added that the criminals carried good firearms and would not be taken alive.

The following day, Humphreys received a reply requesting he arrest the North Americans and bring them in for questioning. Humphreys responded that he was alone, without any horses, and that Cholila was outside his jurisdiction. Humphreys may have tipped off Butch and Sundance via Dan

Author Bill Betenson and Mauricio Sepulveda, who grew up in the cabin where Butch, Sundance, and Etta lived, shown inside the cabin in 2007. The photo, taken with a fisheye lens, shows the narrow width of the rooms. (*Douglas Barnes Photography*)

Gibbons. Humphreys resigned following accusations that he did not mount a pursuit of the suspects, and most particularly of his friends Ryan and Place. He later was re-instated by the governor.[12]

After Sheriff Humphreys resigned, his replacement, Inspector Espinosa, began looking for Butch and Sundance around the first of April, but they had fled into the mountains near Cholila.[13] Their friend George Hammond was responsible for keeping them hidden in the local mountains.[14]

Their close friend Dan Gibbons acted as their business manager. On April 19, 1905, Butch wrote a letter to Richard Clarke indicating he was wrapping up business and asking him to give the clothing he had ordered to Dan Gibbons:

> Mr. Richard Clarke
> Dear Friend
> Please let Dan Gibbons have the clothing I ordered with you and please collect what I owe you from Dan.
> Yours Truly,
> J.P. Ryan[15]

The cabin where the trio lived still stands in this 2007 photograph and has been restored recently by the town of Cholila, which now owns it. (*Author's photograph*)

On April 26, they settled their debts with the "company of Lands of the Englishmen" in Leleque.

Around this time their possessions were sold, which included their ranch buildings and the "right of possession of lands." Dan Gibbons later testified that Butch and Sundance sold their holdings to Thomas T. Austin for 20,000 pesos. Austin was an English settler and a manager of Chilean land company Compania Cochamo.[16]

On May 1, back at the home of Butch's mother, Annie passed away after a short illness without his knowledge. Butch wrote his last letter from Cholila to a nearby neighbor, John C. Perry. In his letter he asked that a debt be paid to his friend Dan Gibbons as they were leaving that very day:

> May 1, 1905
>
> John C. Perry
>
> Please pay to Dan Gibbon the amount due for us. I have received the amount from him $285.44. we are starting to day. Best regards
>
> Santiago Ryan[17]

As they left, the three likely felt badly at the loss of a lifestyle they enjoyed, peace and solitude in a beautiful valley with good friends and neighbors.

An Argentine Police report indicated that Butch changed his name to William Thompson and that Sundance and Etta had changed their names to Mr. and Mrs. Matthews.[18] The trio then left the area. One report said they crossed into Chile from Argentina near Corcovado. Today this route is a mountainous pass into Chile and remains somewhat remote.[19] Other reports indicate they fled north to San Carlos de Bariloche where they embarked on the Condor steamer across Lake Nahuel Huapi and into Chile.

A Patagonia police file contains a report that Butch and Sundance's Chilean ranch hand Wenceslao Solis claimed he accompanied the trio to Lake Nahuel Huapi on May 9, 1905, where they sailed across the lake from San Carlos de Bariloche to Chile. Solis stated he returned to Cholila with their saddles, and only later did he realize they were bandits.[20]

On June 28, 1905 Sundance wrote a letter to Dan Gibbons from Valparaiso, Chile.

> Dear Friend:
>
> We are writing to you to let you know that our business went well and we received your money. We arrived here today, and the day after tomorrow my wife and I leave for San Francisco. I'm very sorry. Dan, that we could not bring the brand R with us, but I hope that you will be able to fetch enough to pay you for the inconveniences.
>
> We want you to take care of Davy and his wife and see that they don't suffer in any way. And be kind to old Spaniel and give him pieces of meat once in a while and get rid of the black dog.
>
> I don't want to see Cholila ever again, but I will think of you and all of our friends often, and we want to assure you of our good wishes.
>
> Attached you will find the song "Sam Bass," which I promised to write down for you. As I have no more news, I will end by begging that you remember us to all our friends, without forgetting Juan and Vencylow, giving them our regards and good wishes, keeping a large portion for yourself and family.
>
> Remaining as always your true friend,
>
> H.A. Place[21]

Juan and Vencylow were likely their ranch hands, Juan Vidal and Wenceslao Solio, who eventually became involved with outlaws Evans and Wilson. Solio said he worked on the ranch for eight months as a peon.

The Hammond family were good friends of Butch, Sundance, and Etta. George Hammond, left, helped them hide in the mountains. (*Courtesy Regi Hammond*)

"Davy" may have been David Moore who ran Butch's store. The brand "R" may have referred to Butch's livestock brand.[22]

Sundance's brother Elwood lived in San Francisco, so one wonders if Sundance might have traveled up the Pacific coast from Chile to San Francisco. However, after March 1903, passenger ship records were required and no records have been found to support a visit to San Francisco. However, a "Mrs. E. Place" did sail on the ship *Seguranca* which arrived in New York City on July 29, 1905, indicating that possibly Etta went back to the states alone.[23]

According to the Pinkertons, a postal informant in Antofagasta, Chile, Frank D. Aller, said Sundance began using the alias Frank Boyd. Aller bailed Boyd out of a scrape with the Chilean government in 1905.[24]

With Cholila now behind them, Butch and Sundance headed north to look for further opportunities. They appear to have reverted to their old outlaw ways of building their "savings" through robbery.

Percy Seibert was Butch's friend and the manager of the mine where Butch and Sundance worked. He later investigated the killing of two bandits at San Vicente. Circa 1906. (*Bob Mc-Cubbin Collection*)

22. Back to a Life of Crime, 1905~1908

O N DECEMBER 19, 1905, four men robbed the Banco de la Nacion in Villa Mercedes of 12,000 pesos.[1] The bandits were described as "English ranchers." They had arrived in town a week before and stayed at a hotel two blocks from the bank. They frequently visited the café, candy store, and hotels. On the morning of the robbery, they were reportedly drinking whiskey two blocks from the bank. Three of the bandits went into the bank about 10:30 while one stayed with the horses. During the robbery, they exchanged shots with the bank manager, but were able to flee before the police responded.[2]

Villa Mercedes is located about four hundred miles west of the capital Buenos Aires and about seven hundred miles northeast of Butch and Sundance's Cholila ranch. Authorities suspected Ryan and Place as well as Grice and Hood. Both Butch and Sundance were reported to be in Rosario before the robbery, about three hundred miles from Villa Mercedes. Rosario locals described James Ryan (Cassidy) as "quite friendly, prudent and gentlemanly." They further indicated that the North Americans had studied the roads three months earlier and had "practiced target shooting three or four hours a day."[3]

The bandits were pursued closely by a posse headed by Chief of Police Belisario Olivera of Villa Mercedes.[4] Similar to planned escapes in the U.S., the bandits had relays of fresh mounts along the trail and peons to help provide supplies. They crossed the Pampas and eventually the Andes to safely reach Chile. Cassidy said later "in all his experience he had never been so closely trailed." At one of the change of relay horses, the bandits exchanged shots with the posse. One shot injured lawman Olivera's horse. One of the bandits was shot in the arm. One source indicates that it was Sundance.[5] The posse believed the outlaws had reinforcements and halted their pursuit, allowing the bandits to escape.[6]

The Concordia Tin Mine in central Bolivia where Butch and Sundance worked. (*Bob McCubbin Collection*)

The next day, December 20, the newspaper gave information on the chase and gunfight.

On December 25, the Buenos Aires newspaper ran a detailed article on the robbery and the getaway, along with photos of Butch, Sundance, Etta, and Harvey Logan supplied by the Pinkertons.[7] After the Pinkerton posters and photos were distributed, witnesses came forward saying they had seen the bandits, either along the escape route or prior to the robbery. Some reported a woman accompanied the outlaws. However, it's most likely Etta had already returned home to the United States.[8] It is unconfirmed that Harvey "Kid Curry" Logan was in South American in 1905 as he was reportedly killed after a bungled train robbery in Parachute, Colorado, in June 1904.

Later three North Americans were detained in Neuquén because of their likeness to Butch, Sundance, and Etta.[9] They were pulled from a train and held in a hotel. They gave their names as Jorge Hardee, his wife, Kemp L. Hwa, and Rufus May. Hardee was described as thirty-six-years old, regular thickness, white, blonde hair, bald, blue eyes, straight nose, upper lip thicker, and 5 feet 7 ½ inches tall. Hwa was described as twenty-three-years old, white, dark hair, a broken tooth, 5 feet 4 inches tall, light eyes, "sad glance."

May was described as twenty-nine-years old, 5 feet 11 inches tall, white, blonde hair and blue eyes.[10] They were later released without charges.

Back in the United States, the *New York Herald* ran a full page article on Sunday, September 23, 1906, headlined, "Yankee Desperadoes Are Holding Up the Argentine Republic." It described the outlaws' ranch and some of their alleged crimes, including the Villa Mercedes bank robbery.[11] The robbery was mistakenly dated March 1906. The Pinkertons provided information for the article, which named Butch, Sundance, Etta, and Harvey Logan.[12] Etta was described as being dressed as a man. Two or three other robberies in Argentina were mentioned in connection with the outlaws. The article detailed their travels from the States to their ranch in Cholila and concluded that their funds had run low forcing them to lawlessness once again. The ranch's description was exaggerated, claiming it was built on a high point allowing the bandits to see twenty miles in every direction.[13]

Wenceslao Solis reported that Sundance returned to Cholila with Emilio Hood in 1907 to sell two hundred sheep, which Dan Gibbons was tending, to John C. Perry.[14] He also hoped to sell thirty mares, but was unsuccessful. Solis said that Mansel Gibbons, son of Dan, arranged the sale and paid Sundance directly.[15]

Dan Gibbons also confirmed, after he was jailed for his known friendship with Butch and Sundance, that Sundance had returned with Hood.[16] But, he said, Butch never did return to Cholila after his departure in 1905. Dan said that Sundance stayed at the homes of Alejandro Villagran and Mansel Gibbons. Dan said no police were around at the time, but that he did advise Eduardo Humphreys of Sundance's return, but he apparently did nothing. Sundance had threatened to kill anyone who revealed his return to authorities.[17] Sundance told Gibbons that Etta was living in San Francisco and Butch could be found in northern Chile but had recently gone to Buenos Aires to see some North American friends who were in a rodeo at the Sports Coliseum. Gibbons also told authorities Ryan and Place left behind a box full of letters from friends in North America which they planned to retrieve at some point. However, no letters have been found or made public.[18]

From December 24, 1905, through January 1906, a rodeo troupe appeared at the Sportiva arena in Buenos Aires.[19] Texas rancher William "Bill" Connell, who worked with Butch on the WS Ranch and later had a ranch of his own in Argentina, claimed Butch had attended the rodeo performance in January 1906. Connell shared that Butch renewed his acquaintances and traded a white handled Colt .45 for a longer barreled Colt.[20]

Dan Gibbons, still in jail, was again interviewed several months later. Authorities inquired if he was satisfied with the information he had given earlier. Gibbons repled that he had signed the document of his statement "under threat of violence and after having been locked up for five days without food or water, and as a result he was not in a condition to understand what he had signed."[21] Gibbons continued to be jailed, but was never charged with any crimes.

Due to Dan Gibbon's friendship with the outlaws, he spent two years in jail and had a portion of his land confiscated. He drank heavily and wandered the streets of Esquel in his later years. He passed away in the 1940s.[22]

✧ ✧ ✧

Butch began using the alias James (Santiago) P. Maxwell and landed work with the Concordia Tin Mine in the Santa Vela Cruz range of the central Bolivian Andes. The mine was located at an elevation of 16,000 feet. Butch's experience with horses and mules got him a job with manager Clement Rolla Glass, hauling materials and purchasing livestock to provide meat for the workers. He was hired at $150 per month plus room and board.

Glass soon sent Butch, now known as Maxwell, to La Paz with three muleteers and $200 to purchase stock. He returned a week later with a herd of fine mules and $50 change. Glass found him trustworthy, capable of driving a hard bargain, and pleasant; he considered making him foreman. Soon Maxwell was carrying the mine's payroll remittances in excess of $100,000.[23]

✧ ✧ ✧

AFTER SUNDANCE SOLD the livestock in Cholila, he began using the alias H. A. "Enrique" Brown and hired on with contractor Roy Letson as muleteer for several months. Sundance drove mules from northern Argentina to a railroad construction camp near La Paz.[24] Once in La Paz, Sundance met up with Butch, and also gained employment at the mine.[25] Sundance started using the alias "Ingersoll."

At some point, Glass had discovered Butch's true identity but did not act upon it since Butch had been a trustworthy employee and the mining camp was full of unsavory men. Later Glass confronted Butch and Sundance when their plans for an upcoming robbery where overheard and reported to him. Butch admitted his identity, but assured Glass they never robbed their employers.

In December 1906, at a Christmas party at the Grand Hotel Guibert in La Paz, Bolivia, Butch and Sundance met American Percy Seibert, who was Glass's assistant.[26] He had recently returned from an extended trip in the United States. Later, Glass left Concordia, and Percy Seibert became the mine manager.

Percy Seibert and Butch became close friends. Seibert later admitted that he knew Butch and Sundance were outlaws, but said he "never had the slightest trouble getting along with them." Seibert stated, "Butch Cassidy was an agreeable and pleasant person. As soon as he arrived in a village he made friends. He allowed no other bandits to interfere with my camp. Cassidy purchased cattle and mules for us and always was scrupulously honest as far as we were concerned."[27]

He said Sundance was reserved, but he was quite fond of Butch. Both Butch and Sundance became regular guests at Sunday dinner with the Seibert family. Butch always secured his seat at the table with a good view of the valley and road leading up to Seibert's house.[28] Percy kept a scrapbook of his time in Bolivia. He kept several letters from Butch and some newspaper clippings.[29]

In late 1907, Butch still wanted to go straight and settle on a ranch like he had in Cholila. Butch was living near Santa Cruz, Bolivia.

Butch wrote a lengthy three-page letter to Percy and his friends back at the tin mine. He was excited to start fresh again:

Santa Cruz, Nov. 12, 1907

To The Boys at Concordia:

We arrived here about 3 weeks ago, after a very pleasant journey, and found just the place I have been looking for, for 20 years, and Ingersoll likes it better than I do, he says he won't try to live any where else. This is a Town of 18,000, and 14,000 are females and some of them are birds. This is the only place for old fellows like myself. One never gets to old if he has blue Eyes and a red face and looks capable of making a blue eyed Baby Boy.

Oh god if I could call back 20 years and have red hair with this complection of mine I would be happy. I have got into the 400 set as deep as I can go. The lady feeds me on fine wines, and she is the prettiest little thing I ever seen, but I am afraid Papa is going to tear my playhouse down for he is getting nasty, but there is plenty more. This place isn't what we expected at all there isn't any cattle here all the beef that is killed here come from Mojo a distance of 80 leagues, and are worth 80 to 100 Bs. but cattle do very well here the grass is good but water is scarce, there isn't any water in this town when there is a dry spell for a week

(Page 2) the people here in town have to buy water at 1.80 per barrel but they can get good water at 40 feet, but are to lazy to sink wells.

This is the last known photograph of Butch and Sundance in Bolivia. Sundance is in the center standing with the mule. Butch is to the left, mounted on the mule. (*Bob McCubbin Collection*)

land is cheap here and everything grows good that is planted, but there is damn little planted, everything is very high it costs us Bs 100 per head to feed our mules, 250 each for our selves. We Rented a house hired a good cook and are living like gentlemen.

Land is worth 10 cts per hectare 10 leagues from here and there is some good Estancias for sale, one 12 leagues from here of 4 leagues with plenty of water and good grass and some sugar cane for Bs 5,000, and others just as cheap, and if I don't fall down I will be living here before long.

It is pretty warm and some fever but the fever is caused by the food they eat, at least I am willing to chance it.

They are doing some work now building a R.R. from Port Suares, here and they claim it will be pushed right through, so now is the time to get started for land will go up before long.

It is 350 miles from here to Cochabamba and a hell of a road, just up one mountain and down the another all the way not a level spot on it big enough to whip a dog on, and most of

(Page 3) the way thick brush on both sides but there is people all along and lots of little towns in fact it is thickly settled. There is plenty of game on the road but it is safe for it is impossible to get it for brush I killed 1 turkey 1 Sand hill Crain and 1 Buzzard. We could hear the turkeys every day and seen some several times but I only got one shot, it won't do for

Reece to come over that road for he would Kill himself getting through the brush after birds we would of left here long ago, but we had a little trouble with the old mule Ingersoll hobbled her and tied her to a tree and wore a nice green pole out on her, but I didn't think he had done a good job so I worked a little while with rocks, between us we broke her jaw and we have been feeding her on mush ever since, but she can eat a little now and we will leave in a few days for a little trip south to see that country I am looking for the place Hutch wants, 8 leagues long, ½ league wide with a big river running through it from end to end

We expect to be back at Concordia in about 1 month.

Good luck to all you fellows.

J.P. Maxwell[30]

Butch was anxious to start a ranch. He told his friends he'd been looking for a place like this for twenty years. Butch was now forty-one years old. "Ingersoll" was, of course, a pseudonym for Sundance but who was the man he mentions as "Hutch?" Percy Seibert believed that Butch and Sundance went to work for James Hutcheon after leaving Concordia. Hutcheon operated a stage company in Bolivia.[31]

The last known letter written by Butch in South America was a letter to C.R. Glass, the mine manager of the Concordia mine, on February 16, 1908. The Percy Seibert scrapbook contained a third letter signed D.J. Myers in 1909, and some historians believe this might also be a letter written by Butch, however the handwriting does not match the other two letters (1907 and 1908).[32] Butch wrote the 1908 letter from the Concordia mine in Tres Cruces to Glass who was in La Paz at the time. At the top of the letter is written (in a different handwriting): Received 2-21-08:

Tres Curzes   Feb. 16, 1908

C.R. Glass,
    Dear Sir
Scarberry leaves here for Sicarica on the 18, he will be there the 20. I don't know how long he will be there but I will let you know when he leaves, every thing is OK here as far as I know.
    Yours Truly
        Gilles[33]

Butch's mother's maiden name was Gillies (with an *i*), so his choice of the alias "Gilles" likely came from that family connection. According to researcher Larry Pointer, George Scarbury was a mine manager near the Concordia mine. Butch apparently was keeping his former boss, Clement Rolla Glass, informed. At this point, Percy Seibert had taken over for Glass at the mine, making this short note curious. Interestingly, Glass died at his own hand a few months later in Buenos Aires, Argentina.[34]

Seibert studied the two outlaws. He further said, "Longabaugh was inclined to be distant, even sullen, and it was difficult to strike up a friendship with him. On the contrary, Cassidy was an exceptional pleasant and even cultured and charming man. He used good language and was never vulgar. Women, who met him, without knowing anything in his history, invariably liked him."[35]

Butch and Sundance quit their jobs at the Concordia Tin Mine in 1908 after Sundance had gotten drunk and bragged in public about their past crimes. Cassidy apparently did not want to bring shame to the Concordia, or they were afraid authorities would soon be after them, so they settled their accounts and left.[36] Author Arthur Chapman writes they robbed a mine remittance in Peru soon after this.

Seibert credited Butch and Sundance with a number of crimes in Bolivia. One, for example, was the robbery of a payroll in Eucalyptus of a railroad construction company. Apparently the express car was detached and transported a considerable distance. Another American, known as McVey, assisted the bandits.

Butch then went to work for another mine owned by a pair of wealthy Scotchmen to gain information prior to robbing them. According to Seibert, "They gave him a job as a night watchman, and told him they really needed no one, but wanted to give him a chance to make a little money. He told me after, that he had not the heart to hold up people who treated him so kindly."[37]

Butch also foiled an assassination plot made by other outlaws by giving warning. He rode two nights and one day to warn the manager of the Concordia mine when he heard of the assassination plans. Butch confided to his friend Percy that it was impossible for him to give up the bandit life and go straight because there was always an informer around to bring the law on him.

Percy said Butch quickly made friends with the Indians and children in the different villages, reportedly playing with them and keeping candy and sweets in his pockets for the children. Because of Seibert's fondness for Butch, he likely wondered how he could help Butch go straight.

Right: In the A.G. Francis article in *Wide World* magazine, this photograph was identified as Harvey "Kid Curry" Logan, one of the Aramayo Payroll bandits. It bears little resemblance to Logan and may have been the bandit known as "Madariga." (*Author's collection*)

Below: The inside two pages of a four-page wanted poster created by the Pinkerton Agency in their search for Butch, Sundance, and Etta. A photo of Harvey "Kid Curry" from the Fort Worth studio picture is on page four of the poster. (*Courtesy Marlyn Day*)

23. The Aramayo Payroll Robbery, 1908

IN AUGUST 1908, Butch and Sundance were reported to be in the Tupiza, Bolivia, area along with several other North American outlaws.[1] South American countries were attracting U.S. citizens on both sides of the law as a new land of opportunity.

On November 4, 1908, two well-armed bandits robbed the Aramayo and Francke Mining Company pack train led by Carlos Pero who was accompanied by his son Mariano and a hired hand, Gil Gonzales.

Discrepancy exists in the different descriptions of the two bandits and the details of the robbery. One account identified the outlaws as Americans; another account stated one was an American and the other a Chilean.

Two days later, two men, thought to be the Aramayo bandits, were killed in a gunfight in San Vicente, Bolivia.

The Aramayo Francke payroll robbery drew several varying accounts.

✧ ✧ ✧

CARLOS PERO'S ACCOUNT (1908). Carlos Pero, the mining payroll leader who was robbed, described the robbery in a report on the same day it occurred (November 4, 1908):

"At 9:30 in the morning, we encountered two well-armed Yankees, who awaited us with their faces covered by bandannas and their rifles ready, and they made us dismount and open the baggage, from which they took only the cash shipment. They also took from us a dark brown mule (called "Aramayo"), which is known to the stable hands in Tupiza, with a new hemp rope."

He stated: "The two Yankees are tall; one thin and the other—who carried a good pair of Hertz binoculars—heavyset."[2]

Carlos Pero further described the robbery and bandits:

. . . whose rifles were cocked and ready to fire at our slightest suspicious movement. In a very pleasant manner, they ordered my servant Gil

Gonzalez and my son Mariano to dismount, having found me following them on foot, and immediately ordered us to hand over the money we were carrying, to which I answered that they could search us and take whatever they wanted, as we were hardly in a position to offer any resistance. One of them quickly began to search our saddlebags and, not finding what he was looking for, demanded that we unload our baggage, specifying that they were not interested in our personal money nor in any articles that belonged to us, but only in the money that [we] were carrying for the company. They knew that I spoke English, in which language they asked me if we were not carrying eighty thousand *bolivianos*, to which I replied that the sum was not quite as large as they believed. And when I saw that there was no point in hiding anything, a search of the baggage having begun, and I informed them that it was only fifteen thousand. What I said caused great anguish, momentarily silencing the bandit nearest us. As soon as they saw the package containing the cash, which was beside another very similar package, the bandit conducting the search took it and passed it to his companion without bothering with the other packages nor searching any more of the baggage, which shows that they had clear knowledge of the package with the cash.[3]

Pero further said the bandits "wore new, dark-red thin-wale corduroy suites with narrow, soft brimmed hats. The brims turned down in such a way that, with the bandannas tied behind their ears, only their eyes could be seen. One of the bandits, the one who came closest to and talked with me, is thin and of normal stature, and the other, who always maintained a certain distance, is heavyset and taller. Both of them carried new carbines, which appeared to be of the Mauser-type, small caliber and thick barrel. But they were completely new, which is to say, they had never been used. The bandits also carried Colt revolvers, and I believe they also had very small Browning revolvers outside their cartridge belts, which were filled with rifle ammunition."[4]

Carlos Pero admitted that he never saw the faces of the bandits due to the bandannas, and he was not familiar with the two outlaws. Prior to the robbery two men in Tupiza had asked him for jobs whom he described as "looking like Austrians," but they were much taller and heavier-set than the bandits.[5]

After the robbery, Pero continued his journey to Guadalupe. He said they then ran into more bandits at Cotani. He described them as two North Americans, carrying saddlebags and a curious woman's saddle. They were also armed with rifles and pistols.

These two were later arrested in Salo on suspicion of the payroll robbery. The two fought violently before finally being captured. They identified themselves as a North American named Ray Walters and an Englishman named Frank Murray. Each had a rifle, two revolvers, and a dagger. The Buenos Aires newspaper reported that also in their possession were "ropes for tying the hands, acids suitable for drugging," five hundred *bolivianos*, and a pack mule (although not the one stolen from the Aramayo company).

Later after two other bandits were killed in San Vicente, Walters and Murray were released from custody.[6] Could the North American, Ray Walters possibly have been Butch or Sundance? Was Frank Murray truly an Englishman? The name Frank had been used before by Sundance (Frank Scramble, Frank Jones, and Frank Boyd). The mention of a woman's saddle brings to mind the possibility that it may have been Etta Place's saddle.

Carlos Pero's initial description of the payroll bandits is somewhat curious as he described the man some think was Butch as tall and thin. Butch was never considered a tall nor a thin man, but perhaps he was considered tall to a native Bolivian? Butch was considered stocky and more on the heavy side, rather than thin. Pero's description of Sundance as "heavyset" is peculiar as Sundance was typically known as tall and thin.

Business cards of "Enrique B. Hutcheon" were discovered later on the body of the dead bandit thought to be Butch. This has never been fully explained leaving open the possibility that the dead bandit may have been who the cards identified, Enrique B. Hutcheon, and not Butch Cassidy.

Who was Enrique B. Hutcheon? Was he the "Hutch" that Butch mentions earlier in correspondence? And was he any relation to James K. Hutcheon who ran a Bolivian Stage line? The Hutcheon stage line was suspected of involvement by Pero early in the investigations. In fact P. McPartland of the Hutcheon stage line wrote to Mr. Aramayo protesting the suspicion he had taken part in the robbery:

Senior Manuel Aramayo, Tupiza

Sir

I beg to draw your attention to the fact that Charles Pero of Qeuchisla has been indiscreet enough to express the opinion publicly to several persons that I am one of the individuals concerned in the robbery of certain moneys from him, as I am lead to believe that this took place on or about the 4th. Please note that I arrived at Potosi on the 3rd… with Mr Hutcheon's Coach and stayed at the Hotel Colon until the 5th… on the face of which you will see that it is impossible to connect me with this matter.

Trusting that you will contradict the said statement, as I do not wish to be talked about all over Bolivia and probably have to leave the country over it . . .

P. McPartland[7]

✧ ✧ ✧

NOVEMBER 4, 1908 TELEGRAM. A telegram following the incident indicated that one of bandits was a Chilean:

This morning Mr. Pero was robbed between Salo and Guadalupe by to two tall individuals, one slender and the other heavyset, a gringo and a Chilean; armed with rifles, they made Mr. Pero hand over the fifteen-thousand-boliviano remittance in cash, along with a dark brown mule, which they took with them. Ask the authorities to capture them . . . The heavyset man's name is said to be Madariaga.[8]

✧ ✧ ✧

JUAN FELIX ERAZO (1908). Juan Felix Erazo gave testimony of meeting the bandits before the robbery:

About a month ago Mr. (Edward) Graydon introduced me to a tall, blond, mustachioed, plump foreigner, whose name I don't remember. At that time we drank a few glasses of beer in Estarca in the home of Fortunato Valencia. They told me that they came from Esmorca and brought another foreigner, shorter than the other, and the three of them passed through Tomahuaico… On the sixth of November, I was in Cucho when, at seven in the morning, two gringos arrived, one was the same one Graydon introduced to me in Estarca; the other I don't remember having met. When I saw them in Tiburcio Bolivar's house, I went there, and they were at the door with their saddled mules, one solid black, and the other dark brown. Both carried revolvers and rifles on their saddles, but instead of revolvers, they apparently were pistols conveniently placed in their belts, and many bullets, which were displayed in their belts. I asked them where they were going, and they responded that they were going to inspect or study the wagon trail to San Vicente. I advised them to take a guide, then excused myself and left them. They went at seven-thirty in the morning.

(Bolivar) assured me that they had slept the previous night at the home of Narcisa, the widow of Burgos. Sunday night, the eighth of November, I learned that two gringos had been killed in San Vicente because they had stolen a cash shipment from Senor Pero, with the reports I have had from San Vicente, by the animals, weapons, and date upon which they left Cucho, I am convinced that they are exactly the same.[9]

These men certainly were reckless in their actions telling exactly where they were going and openly drinking and showing their arms. This certainly doesn't fit the pattern of the cautious Butch Cassidy. Also the description of a tall plump man doesn't seem to fit descriptions of either Butch or Sundance.

✧ ✧ ✧

A.G. FRANCIS'S ACCOUNT (1913). British mining engineer A.G. Francis wrote of meeting the bandits before the robbery. His account was published in May 1913 by *Wide World Magazine*.[10]

Francis said he met two American bandits in August 1908 calling themselves Frank Smith and George Low. Francis said he later learned their true identities were Harvey Logan (Smith) and Butch Cassidy (Low). Francis never does reveal his source of information or who identified the two as Logan and Cassidy, but it may have been Percy Seibert.

Francis's article was the first public report specifically naming Butch Cassidy in Bolivia and his possible death at San Vicente. A sketch of Butch's Wyoming mug shot accompanied the article along with a photograph claiming to be Harvey Logan. The supposed photo of Smith or Logan looked more like a heavy-set Poncho Villa.[11]

A.G. Francis[12] was supervising the transportation of a large gold-dredge on the San Juan del Ora River. Francis's camp was near the village of Verdugo, approximately fifteen miles south of Tupiza.

Francis tells that one evening he was eating dinner when his dogs started barking at the arrival of two Americans. He said one, who he described as Smith, " a burly, pleasant-looking man with a moustache, said cheerily: 'How do? We have seen Teddy'" (Teddy was Francis's friend in town) and "he told us you wouldn't object to having us stop here a while to rest our animals."

Some historians think that "Smith" was in fact Sundance. If this is the case then Francis's description doesn't match a typical description of Sundance who was known to be relatively tall and thin. Further, the photograph identified in the Francis article as Kid Curry looks nothing like Sundance.

Francis responded, "Get your saddles off, boys, and come right in." Francis said the other, "a rather slightly-built man of middle height, with a fair beard and moustache and eyes like gimlets was George Low."[13]

According to Francis, "Smith and Low proved very pleasant and amusing companions, and I was therefore not at all sorry when, as we were about to start on our trip to Esmoraca, they offered to accompany me." He claims Smith spent a good deal of time with him over the following few weeks, while Low made frequent trips into Tupiza.

One evening Smith showed his skill with a gun when an angry and drunk Chilean who worked for Francis rushed Smith with a knife during an evening dance. Smith fired two shots between the attackers feet to stop him. Francis's crew, or *carreros*, rushed to help the Chilean and Smith single-handily held them off while causing them to scatter with further shots.

On another trip, they ran into Argentine authorities who attempted to take Smith's pistol. He fled on horseback only to be followed later by Francis.

Sometime later Low returned and borrowed a big grey horse from Francis. He learned later that Low and Smith went to Tupiza where they stayed at the Hotel International.[14] The next morning, which was November 3, 1908, they watched the offices of the Aramayo Francke company. At about 10 a.m., they saw the manager and his son, along with two muleteers, ride out-of-town with several pack animals. Low and Smith soon left after getting a final drink. When asked where he was going, Low told the bartender that he was "going to get a nice little packet."

Francis said that same night (November 3) he was staying in Tomahuiaco[15] when his barking dogs awakened him around 1:00 a.m. Francis was sleeping in a hammock on the porch. He called out to see who was there and Low responded, "Don't you know your old horse in the dark, kid?"

Francis helped the two men unsaddle and noticed that Low appeared sick and immediately went to bed inside the building, while Smith ate a meal with Francis. Smith told Francis details of the Aramayo payroll robbery.

Smith revealed they planned to rob the National Bank in Tupiza, however, a cavalry regiment had arrived and was staying in barracks in the town square near the bank. They decided to wait for the cavalry to leave. With their funds getting low and no sign that the cavalry was leaving anytime soon, they changed their plans and decided to rob the Aramayo Francke payroll.

They learned that Aramayo Francke sent the payroll to their employees at the smelter and neighboring mines in the amount of 16,000 pounds once a month. They surprised the men transporting the funds, standing in the middle of the trail with Winchesters in hand and large handkerchiefs covering their faces.[16] The robbers ordered the payroll party to put their hands up. Smith held his guns on the company as Low transferred the contents from *petacas* (rawhide trunks) to his saddlebags. Low also confiscated one of the mules. Unfortunately the outlaws found the payroll to be much less than anticipated. In disappointment, Low questioned the chief of the party and found the larger payroll had passed a few days earlier.[17] Apparently the outlaws were expecting 80,000 *bolivianos*.[18]

Francis reported the outlaws instructed the party to continue their journey to the mines on "peril of being shot if they turned back." The bandits fled into the mountains to hide until nightfall when they made their way to Tomahuiaco and into the valley of the Rio San Juan to Francis's quarters.[19]

When they retired Francis thought deeply about the position he was in, having become an accessory in a serious crime. The next morning about 10 A.M., a friend came from Tupiza on a spent horse to warn the men. He exclaimed to the two outlaws, "You had better get out of this, boys; they are saddling up a hundred men to come after you."

The friend warned that a party of soldiers, accompanied by Indian trackers, had been out all night searching for traces of the outlaws. He had heard just before leaving Tupiza that they had found their tracks. He then rode off.

Smith then told Francis, "You might tell that boy of yours to get breakfast ready quickly, will you, kid? I suppose we had better be moving."

Francis explained that the two outlaws packed up, taking the stolen mule, but leaving the pack behind. He said "they displayed no nervousness or hurry in their proceedings, and, when breakfast was ready, we disposed of the meal in very good spirits and with considerable appetite."

Francis was surprised when Smith said, "Say, kid, you had better saddle up and come with us." They left with Low leading the stolen mule and Smith and Francis following behind.

Francis asked Smith, "Suppose the soldiers arrive, what are you going to do about it?" Smith calmly replied, "Why, we'll just sit down behind a rock and get to work." Francis said he put his best face forward, but feared he would be killed if the soldiers appeared. Smith told Francis they needed him to guide them up the narrow canyon to Estarca. Then they would make for Uyuni and the north where they would lie low until things blew over. Smith was confident, according to Francis, that they would not be caught.

Once they reached Estarca, they sent Francis ahead to see if it was safe. Francis said he found no one was talking of the holdup, and he waited for the two bandits in a room he had rented on previous trips. Low and Smith shared a bed in the corner, while Francis slept on a mattress on the floor. Smith said, "Good night, kid, I wish we could celebrate tonight, but in the circumstances it won't do."

They continued to make their journey to Uyuni the following morning without incident, parting from Francis once they understood which route to follow. Smith told Francis, "You don't want to come any further with us. If you meet those soldiers, tell them you passed us on the road to the Argentine." They may have been headed to Oruro to the Hotel Americano, which was Sundance's last known mailing address.[20]

Francis said that was the last he ever saw of the two outlaws. He went back to Tomahuiaco where he heard later that they had been killed in San Vicente.

In reviewing the Francis account, it is hard to believe that the cautious Butch Cassidy would act so nonchalant at the report of a hundred soldiers bearing down on his trail and then continue his journey on well-marked roads.

✧ ✧ ✧

How MANY DIFFERENT known outlaws were in Bolivia at this time using how many different aliases? Author James Horan mentions a young outlaw named Dey, Jack McVey was the foul-mouthed man who Butch evicted from Concordia, and Dick Clifford had come to Bolivia and joined the outlaw group headed by Harry Nation. Walters and Murray were the two men whom Carlos Pero met after the robbery. And what about the Chilean reported by the telegram?[21]

The cast of characters included many: Edward Graydon seen by Juan Felix Erazo at Estarca, P. McPartland of the Hutcheon Stage Line, and Smith and Low of A.G. Francis's account.[22]

And then there were the two who robbed Carlos Pero.

The main link to Cassidy being present in Tupiza, Bolivia, at the time of the robbery is from a hotel register listing "Santiago Lowe." Cassidy was known to use the alias Lowe in Arizona, but Lowe was not a prevalent alias for him in South America. Author James Horan noted that a missionary who had previously met Butch ran across him in the lobby of a hotel in Tupiza. "Why, Mr. Maxwell," he said, "How are you?" Cassidy gave him a cold stare and replied, "I'm fine, but my name is Lowe." And then he walked away.[23]

24. San Vicente, 1908

O N NOVEMBER 6, 1908, police killed two outlaws in San Vicente, Bolivia, just two days after the Aramayo payroll was stolen. The true identity of these two outlaws has been disputed for years. Some claim they were in fact Butch and Sundance. The earliest accounts did not identify the dead outlaws. The two bandits were buried with no names, *ningun nombre*.[1] Only years later would the outlaws in the graves become suspected of being Butch and Sundance; however, many questions remain. The American explorer Hiram Bingham indicated that he met two Americans some nine days after the San Vicente gun battle. One was an outlaw who had been chased out of the United States by the Pinkertons. Could this outlaw possibly have been Butch Cassidy?

Several different death accounts of the bandits exist, including some eyewitness testimonies.

REMIGIO SANCHEZ. Authorities convened an inquest, and the first eyewitness to testify was Remigio Sanchez, a miner from San Vicente. He said on the afternoon of November 6, at 3:30, a police commission composed of a captain, a police inspector, and two soldiers arrived in San Vicente. He went on:

> Later, at six-thirty, two mounted gringos came from the east, one on a dark brown mule and the other on a solid black mule. They went to the Corregidor's [town official's] house to ask for lodging. He referred them to Bonifacio Cassasola and noticed that each one was armed with a rifle and a revolver. They told the Corregidor[2] that they came from La Quiaca and were going to Santa Catalina. After this, the Corregidor left and went to notify the commission. The police inspector, with two soldiers and the Corrigidor, immediately came to look and find out who the men were. Once they had passed through to the patio and were about four steps from the door of the room, one of the gringos—the smaller one—appeared

and fired one shot and then another from his revolver at the soldier, who ran screaming to the house of Julian Sainz, where he died in moments.

Sanchez said the Corregidor then rounded up people to help, including Sanchez himself. He said:

> They immediately posted us to watch the roof and the back of the house, because the captain feared that they [the outlaws] might make a hole in the wall and escape, as they were no longer firing. We remained all night until, at dawn, the captain ordered the owner of the house to go inside. The captain entered with a soldier, and then all of us entered and found the smaller gringo stretched out on the floor, dead, one bullet wound in the temple and another in the arm. The taller one was hugging a large ceramic jug. He was dead, also, with a bullet wound in the forehead and several in the arm.

Sanchez called an official to investigate and he found: "a homespun cotton package stitched up with the bills inside it, eighty pounds in the pocket of the tallest and forty-six pounds in the pocket of the other one. This is what I was told, but I didn't see it. They also took from the pocket of the tall one a handful of one-boliviano bills and some nickel coin. Upon finishing this operation, we went to lunch. In the afternoon, after Delfin Rivera identified them, we interred them."

Sanchez gave a description though some of it was based on hearsay: "The tall gringo was dressed in a light-brown cashmere suit, a grey hat, red gaiters, a belt with about twenty-eight bullets, a gold watch, a dagger (so I was told), and a silk handkerchief. The smaller one wore a yellow suit, apparently cashmere, red gaiter, a grey hat. He had a silver watch, a blue silk handkerchief, a cartridge belt with about thirty bullets. The pair had bullets in all their pockets. Both were unshaven blonds, with somewhat turned up noses, the smaller one a bit ugly and the larger one good-looking."[3]

This description of the dead bandits' clothing does not match Pero's description of what the robbers wore at the scene of the robbery, raising the question, were they the same men?

✧ ✧ ✧

Cleto Bellot. Corregidor Cleto Bellot gave further details of the bandits in his testimony. He says on arriving the men unsaddled their mounts, left their rifles and saddles outside, and came inside where they chatted.

Bellot then withdrew and notified the commission of the bandits. After the firing began, he was asked to gather additional men. He stated, "It should be mentioned that, while rounding up the men, I heard three screams of desperation. After the guards were posted, no more shots were heard, except that the inspector fired one shot at about midnight."

OFFICIALS THEN INVENTORIED the bodies and the possessions, however, "no detailed description of the individual bandits' physical features, nor scars and wound marks" were made.[4]

The inventories of the two dead bandits were as follows:[5]

SMALLER OUTLAW:
- One leather purse containing a paper on which the address of a La Paz postoffice box was written.
- One six-shot Colt revolver with holster, belt and 30 cartridges
- One silver pocket watch with silver chain
- Two notebooks with several notations
- 16 pounds sterling
- Two half-pound sterling notes
- One silver coin with five cents
- One unusable pocket mirror
- Two removable buttons
- One metal comb
- Seven cards inscribed Enrique B. Hutcheon
- Seven cards inscribed Edward Graydon
- One linen handkerchief
- One black pencil

THE HEAVY-SET TALLER OUTLAW:
- One 18 karat gold watch, number 93,220, without crystal
- One leather and metal lasso
- Bills and coins in various denominations from Bolivian banks, totaling 93 *bolivianos* and five cents.
- One nickel penknife
- One English dictionary
- Two linen handkerchiefs
- One ordinary pocket mirror

- Nine removable shirt buttons
- Two cuff links
- Eight small wooden or bone buttons
- One waterproof cloak
- 121 Winchester cartridges
- One new modified Winchester carbine

In their baggage:

- Two saddle blankets
- One cotton blanket
- One Bolivian poncho
- One plain English saddle
- One pair of iron spurs
- One triangular file (in the saddlebags)
- One pair of leather saddlebags
- Two unusable silk handkerchiefs
- One pair of chamois gloves
- One pair of wool socks
- One used towel
- One map of Bolivia
- 88 pounds of sterling
- 14,400 *bolivianos* total (The Aramayo payroll was 15,000.)
- Cartridges for Colt revolvers & Mauser & Winchester carbines
- One used bridle
- One saddle skin
- One cinch
- One Mauser carbine and scabbard
- One pair of binoculars
- Three cotton handkerchiefs
- One saddle blanket
- One set of reins
- One whip

No additional clothing was reported found, yet the clothing of the dead bandits (light brown and yellow cashmere suits) does not match the description of the bandits given by the victim of the robbery, Carlos Pero, who said they wore red and thin-wale corduroy suits. Further, 600 *bolivianos* from the robbery was not accounted for. Interestingly enough, the two bandits who were first arrested after the Aramayo robbery, Walters and Murray, who were armed to the teeth and put up a great resistance, were reported to have 500 *bolivianos* on them when they were captured. It is possible that Walters and Murray wore the red and thin-wale corduroy suits and were the actual bandits who robbed the payroll?

If indeed the two dead bandits were North American why would they need to carry an English dictionary? Could one of them have been a Chilean, as reported in one account, who needed a dictionary?

Hiram Bingham Account (1911): Hiram Bingham III, an American explorer, wrote the earliest English account of the death of the two bandits in Bolivia in his book, *Across South America*, published in 1911.

Bingham mentions two American outlaws he met some nine days after the San Vicente gunfight. Bingham explains before he arrived in Tupiza, he was in La Quiaca on November 15, 1908, and was called upon by "two rough-looking Anglo-Saxons who told us hair-raising stories of the dangers of the Bolivian roads where highway robbers driven out of the United States by the force of law and order [are] hounded to death all over the world by Pinkerton detectives." They "had found a pleasant resting-place in which to pursue their chosen occupation without let or hindrance. We found out afterwards that one of our informants was one of this same gang of robbers."[6]

Bingham went on to say, "He put the case quite emphatically to us that it was necessary for them to make a living, that they were not allowed to do so peaceably in the States, that they desired only to be let alone and had no intention of troubling travelers except those that sought to get information against them." The outlaw further explained that they relied entirely on being able to overcome armed escorts carrying the mine payrolls for their support. He said the only ones who suffered were those who put up a resistance. He talked of "how famous had been their crimes, at the same time assuring us that they were all very decent fellows and quite pleasant companions."[7]

One wonders if this bandit could have been Butch Cassidy? If so, he was very much alive nine days after the gun battle in San Vicente. The bandit's claim that he could never be left alone by the Pinkertons was the same story that Butch shared with Percy Seibert and Rolla Glass.

Bingham states he arrived in Tupiza, Bolivia, on November 16, 1908. He said prior to his arrival, two bandits, one of whom had been chased out of Arizona by Pinkerton detectives, held up a $20,000 mine payroll. The mine owners offered a large reward for the capture of the bandits, dead or alive. A party of fifty Bolivian soldiers was organized to pursue the bandits who were overtaken while having lunch in an Indian hut. The outlaws had carelessly left their rifles and ammunition yards away from the building. In a fight between bandits and soldiers, three or four soldiers were killed and many more were wounded. The soldiers set the hut on fire, forcing the bandits into the open where they were killed. The bandits were not named. Their mules were sold to Don Santiago Hutcheon who turned one over to Bingham for his use.[8] Don Santiago Hutcheon was probably the same James K. "Santiago" Hutcheon who ran a Bolivian Stage line.

Don Santiago Hutcheon confirmed to Bingham that he had carried hundreds of thousands of dollars in cash and had never been molested because he neither carried arms nor spread information of the bandit's doings. It is interesting that one of the dead bandits' bodies had seven business cards inscribed Enrique B. Hutcheon on him. Was there a relationship between these two men named Hutcheon or with the "Hutch" Butch mentions in correspondence?

Neither Butch nor Sundance were wanted in Arizona, however other outlaws were, for example, the High Five Gang split up after the death of their leader Black Jack Will Christian. Two members of that gang disappeared (Bob Christian and Sid Moore) and a third member, George West Musgrave, fled to South America. Is there a chance Christian or Moore were in South America also and were killed after the payroll robbery?

✧ ✧ ✧

FRANK ALLER (1909). On July 31, 1909, the U.S. vice-consulate in Antofagasta, Chile, Frank Aller, whom Sundance had sought out in the past for help as "Frank Boyd," wrote the U.S. legation in La Paz, Bolivia, saying he understood that Frank Boyd and his companion Maxwell were killed in San Vicente. He requested an investigation and consequential death certificates. In early 1911, he received a report and death certificates from the Bolivian government for the two gringos, whose names were unknown.[9]

✧ ✧ ✧

A.G. FRANCIS'S ACCOUNT (1913): British Mining engineer A. G Francis's lengthy account from *Wide World Magazine* continued. He further wrote that the next day after he left the two outlaws whom he had identified as Kid Curry (Harvey Logan) and Butch Cassidy, he was told that two white men had been killed the previous evening at San Vicente. He then rode to San Vicente for further details, but did not make mention of seeing their bodies.

Once at San Vicente, Francis had learned that when the outlaws arrived in town, they demanded lodging and were shown ironically to the Indian Justice of the Peace's home where they ordered a bottle of beer. Their animals were put in the corral, and the mule was identified as belonging to Messrs. Aramayo Francke and Cia. Soldiers were quickly notified.

The soldiers sent one comrade to investigate. When he entered the room, Low shot him twice in the throat before he had time to "enunciate a word." He staggered out of the room and died.

The rest of the troop was alarmed by the shots and "instantly commenced a siege." The two outlaws were trapped with their only escape route going out the door that the attackers were firing into.

Francis continued, "For some hours the bandits' shots answered those of the besiegers, but at last all was silent within." Both bandits were found dead. Low was found near the door, a pile of empty cartridges by his side with five bullets in his body. The man Francis identified as Kid Curry was on the floor in a corner, leaning against a wall with two bullet holes in the wall near his head and one bullet in his brain. The bullet was supposedly extracted and found to correspond to Low's revolver, a Colt .45. It was concluded that, "finding escape impossible and being too badly wounded to live," Kid Curry had requested Low put a bullet through his head. After three attempts, Low was finally successful in killing Curry. Low then ended his own life by putting a bullet into his own brain. Francis wrote, "Both men were buried in San Vicente, in unconsecrated ground."[10]

A few problems with Francis's account (divided between this chapter and the previous one) include his description of the bandits using horses, specifically Low borrowing a horse from Francis. It was accepted as fact that the San Vicente bandits rode mules as they were better conditioned for the high altitude of the area. The illustrations that accompanied the article included horses.

Francis's failure to mention seeing the bodies of the bandits is even more curious, but perhaps they had already been buried?

Francis said the bandits were Butch and Kid Curry. Kid Curry (Harvey Logan) likely died in Parachute, Colorado, in June 1904, showing Francis was mixed up about the true identities of the bandits. Francis's description of the two outlaws does not appear to be an accurate description for Butch and particularly Sundance, and the photograph of Kid Curry accompanying the article resembles neither Kid Curry nor Sundance. An earlier 1910 *Wide World Magazine* article detailed Kid Curry's career in South America and included the same photo along with the mug shot from his 1897 capture near Lavina, Montana.[11] Could this individual, mistakenly identified as Kid Curry, be a known Chilean outlaw named "Madariaga" who was mentioned in November 4 telegram?

If the outlaw Low was truly Butch Cassidy, he acted much like an amateur outlaw and not the seasoned outlaw that Cassidy was. The Aramayo Robbery was bungled from the beginning to the end of the chase, much different than Butch's well-planned and executed strikes. Aside from the absence of planning, he acted without a care when it was reported up to one hundred soldiers were converging on their trail. Further they traveled the main roads. Later when they stopped at San Vicente and knew that soldiers were searching for them, they ventured into town together, left their rifles and additional ammunition outside and entered a courtyard with a single entrance/exit without realizing their pursuers were staying in the same area.[12]

At the San Vicente gunfight the bandit thought to be Cassidy demonstrated complete panic by firing on the first soldier before anything was spoken. The body was known to contain only flesh wounds and not the 5 bullet holes reported. Why would a man commit suicide based on flesh wounds? Cassidy had been successful in getting out of jail both in St. Johns, Arizona, and earlier in Argentina.

Back in the United States word of Francis's *Wide World Magazine* article reached Wyoming. On May 16, 1913, it was reported in newspapers:

> Butch Cassidy, for many years the pet outlaw of Fremont county [Wyoming], is reported to have been killed the past winter in South America. Cassiday was a bank robber and a horse thief on a big scale. Pursuit finally became so close that he left the country and went to South America.
>
> According to the report Cassidy and another bank robber named Kid Curry, had joined forces in the Argentine Republic. They held up a pack train and were wounded in the fight which followed, and unable to get away Cassidy killed his companion and then himself.[13]

❖ ❖ ❖

THE PINKERTON FILES (1914). The Pinkerton files indicate that they did not know what had become of Butch Cassidy. They kept copies of different reports for several years. In 1914, they received information that Cassidy was being held in a prison in Antofagasta, Chile, after being captured following a bank robbery. The reports indicated that Sundance and Cassidy had parted ways after a drunken fight between them. Cassidy later attempted to rob a bank with an American woman. He killed the mayor, but, during Butch's escape his horse stumbled and Butch's leg was broken, allowing him to be captured. The Pinkertons wrote to the officials asking for a photo of the prisoner. No further information was filed in the report.[14]

❖ ❖ ❖

FREDERICK BECHDOLT'S ACCOUNT (1924). In 1924, Frederick R. Bechdolt published a book titled *Tales of the Old-Timers* and told of Butch's death in Argentina in 1906 based on information supposedly obtained from Will Simpson and former Wyoming Governor W.A. Richards. After "Lonabaugh" was killed, Cassidy held out as long as he could against a detachment of soldiers until his ammunition ran low and then committed suicide with his Colt .45 revolver.[15]

❖ ❖ ❖

BILLY SAWTELLE'S REPORT. To further confuse the deaths of Butch and Sundance, two other American outlaws, William Wilson and Robert Evans, where killed on December 11, 1911, by authorities near Rio Pico, Argentina. Many were confused that Wilson and Evans were Butch and Sundance, and newspapers reported that Butch and Sundance had been killed in Argentina.[16]

Friends of the outlaws paid the expenses for Billy Sawtelle to travel to Argentina in 1912 to investigate rumors that Butch and Sundance had been killed. The rumors they investigated were not of the San Vicente bandits, but the deaths of Wilson and Evans.

Sawtelle returned and related the killing of the bandits, thought to be Butch and Sundance, to Bert Charter who in turn told Will Simpson of their deaths.

❖ ❖ ❖

ARTHUR CHAPMAN'S ACCOUNT (1930). Perhaps the most popular and well-known account was published in April 1930 in the *Elks Magazine*. The article entitled, "'Butch' Cassidy" was written by Arthur Chapman and based

Left: San Vicente, Bolivia, as it looks today. (*Author's collection*)

Below: This photo shows the courtyard and buildings where the gunfight took place in San Vicente where two outlaws were killed. Some say this shows a government commission. (*Bob McCubbin Collection*)

on information he had received from Percy Seibert.[17] Chapman's prose helped to create the legend that was later made into the 1969 Hollywood movie. According to Chapman's account, the two outlaws killed at San Vicente were Butch and Sundance. Although Seibert had never personally identified the bodies in San Vicente, he identified the two deceased outlaws as Butch and Sundance throughout the article. Seibert maintained a scrapbook that included two Buenos Aires newspaper articles of the Aramayo robbery and gunfight at San Vicente. Lula Betenson later said her brother Butch explained that Seibert identified the bodies as Butch and Sundance to give him a chance at a new start.[18]

The Chapman article states that Butch transferred his operations of banditry to South America and ran it successfully for several years. Then word came that he and Sundance had been killed: "various stories of the slaying of these bandit leaders came out of the wild interior of South America, but authentic details were lacking." The article claimed the true details of Butch's demise only came from "inquiries painstakingly pursued by men who had known him as a sociable, trustworthy fellow, who was on the square," specifically, Percy A. Seibert. Chapman wrote the San Vicente shootout happened a few weeks after the Aramayo robbery in early 1909. Chapman said Butch and Sundance returned to Tupiza after the robbery and landed jobs with a transportation outfit. The two then hurried to Uyuni upon hearing they were wanted for the robbery. During the entire time, they kept the Aramayo mule that was recognized by police in San Vicente. When a police captain walked into the courtyard demanding their surrender, Cassidy answered with shots, killing the policeman.

A company of cavalry staying outside of town was called in to help in the capture. Chapman described the event much like the Hollywood blockbuster. The two outlaws had left behind their rifles and ammunition.

> Soldiers were firing through the open gate and from all other vantage points outside the wall. Longabaugh got halfway across the courtyard and fell, desperately wounded, but not before he had effectively emptied his six-shooter.
>
> When Cassidy saw his partner fall, he rushed into the courtyard. Bullets rained about him as he ran to Longabaugh's side. Some of the shots found their mark, but Cassidy, though wounded, managed to pick up Longabaugh and stagger back to the house with his heavy burden.

Cassidy saw Longabaugh was mortally wounded. Furthermore, it was going to be impossible to carry on the battle much longer unless the rifles and ammunition could be reached. Cassidy made several attempts to cross the courtyard. At each attempt he was wounded and driven back.

The battle now settled into a siege. Night came on, and men fired at the red flashes from the weapons. He had only a few cartridges left. Longabaugh's cartridge belt was empty as was the dead Bolivian captain's.

The soldiers, about 9 or 10 o'clock in the evening, heard two shots fired in the bullet-ridden station. Then no more shots came. The soldiers continued firing through the night.

Around noon an officer and a detachment of soldiers rushed into the station. They found Longabaugh and Cassidy dead. Cassidy had fired a bullet into Longabaugh's head and had used his last cartridge to kill himself.

Chapman's article spawned the idea of the final demise of Butch Cassidy and the Sundance Kid. The account has tones of Hollywood embellishment. For example we know from the inventory after the death that the dead bandits still possessed 150 rounds of ammunition.

A slug was reportedly found in the skull of the dead bandit. The bullet from a frontier Colt .45 shot at close range would certainly not be left in the skull. It would have exited. It is possible that the two outlaws were executed by the soldiers.[19]

Chapman mentions "Dey" who helped Butch and Sundance with an Argentine robbery and later moved into Bolivia and became acquainted with Seibert in May 1906.[20]

✧ ✧ ✧

DAN BUCK AND ANNE MEADOWS'S RESEARCH. Buck and Meadows started researching the demise of the two outlaws in about 1985 and added some corrections to previous accounts. However, there still remains a lack of conclusive evidence that the two dead bandits were, in fact, Butch and Sundance. Harry Longabaugh had been corresponding with his sister Samanna back in Pennsylvania, and one source indicates that after the 1908 gun battle the correspondence ceased, suggesting that Longabaugh was one of the two bandits killed. However, the same source also indicated that the correspondence had actually ceased sometime around 1905, some three years before the 1908 gun battle. Even more confusing is another Longabaugh source which indicates that Samanna possibly received correspondence as late as 1915, suggesting that Longabaugh may have been alive after the gun battle.[21]

✧ ✧ ✧

FOR SOME THE STORY of Butch Cassidy ends here. But for others, additional research is required before a conclusion can be made.

In December 1991 a team of scientists and researchers exhumed the graves believed to be those of the two dead bandits in San Vicente. Those involved were certain they had at least located the body of the Sundance Kid. Anne Meadows writes in her book *Digging Up Butch and Sundance*, "After X-rays of the skull revealed a few tiny metal fragments embedded in the cranial vault, supporting Clyde's [Clyde Snow, a forensic expert] belief that a gunshot wound in the lower forehead was the cause of death, he gave the skull to Dr. Lewis Sadler, who pioneered a technique in which digitized photographs of people are superimposed over video images of the skulls to see whether they match at certain critical points. In his laboratory at the Department of Biomedical Visualization at the University of Illinois at Chicago, Sadler placed tissue-depth markers on the San Vicente skull to show what the outline of the head would have been when the skull had flesh on it. He then aligned a video image of the skull with a photograph of the Sundance Kid. The orbits of the eyes fell into place, and the contour of the skull matched. Eric (Stover) witnessed the procedure and telephoned us to say, 'We've got him!'"[22]

Larry Pointer who was involved in the PBS documentary which covered the exhumation and DNA analysis wrote:

> In 1992 . . . the burial [sites] located by Dan Buck were excavated. Anthropologists Eric Stover and Clyde Snow were called in. Snow is best known for his work in helping close the mystery of the final fate of Nazi butcher Dr. Josef Mengele. The remains of two Caucasian adult males were retrieved from the burial site at San Vicente. Both had sustained damage to the skulls consistent with gunshot wounds described in Arthur Chapman's magazine article.[23] Traces of lead were verified on the edges of skull fragments.
>
> An incomplete skull was all that remained of the one body. A nearly complete skeleton was reconstructed for the other. Several physical attributes of this second skeleton were consistent with those of the Sundance Kid.
>
> Superimposition of the skull with Pinkerton Agency photos of Sundance yielded high correlations. Yet when DNA samples extracted from nucleated cells from each Bolivian skeleton were compared to DNA from

living relatives of both outlaws, there *was not* [emphasis added] a positive match with either of the San Vicente outlaws.

Prior to the DNA results, the team spoke to the media indicating that they had "almost certainly" found the bones of Butch and Sundance.[24] Reports indicated that they had at least obtained the remains of Sundance.[25]

Once the DNA results were final, Larry Pointer indicated that, "the NOVA [a TV documentary being made] ending was redone to state that instead, they had unearthed a German miner who had been killed by a dynamite explosion. The bullet wounds were problematical to this new 'spin.'"

Pointer states, "Dr. Snow, of Norman, Oklahoma, is a prestigious forensic expert. His data, which he personally discussed with me, should be available as primary source citations in verifying that, indeed, the investigation had unearthed the two perpetrators of the Aramayo, Francke and Company mine payroll robbery on November 4, 1908. They just did not happen to be the two outlaws — Butch Cassidy and the Sundance Kid — that [the team] had so badly wanted them to be. The official Bolivian documentation left the two bandits as John Does whose "names remain unknown."[26]

Larry further explains, "The more complete skeleton did provide enough evidence to identify that this person was one of the bandits who was killed. He had an American belt buckle, American buttons, gold dental work that was state-of-the-art 1900 midwest American dental work, as well as less sophisticated South American dental filling materials in the jaw and skull. Importantly, he had a healed bullet wound on the left tibia, complete with lead fragments. And [he had] lead around the bullet hole in his head, as did the other partial skull exhumed adjacent to the first skeleton by Dr. Eric Stover during the NOVA expedition of the early 1990s."[27]

Others believe that the wrong remains were exhumed. They believe that Butch Cassidy and the Sundance Kid remain buried in the San Vicente cemetery in unmarked graves.

❖ ❖ ❖

SO THE ANSWER TO THE QUESTION of whether Butch and/or Sundance were killed at San Vicente and buried in the local cemetery continues to be elusive.

Above: Maximilian Parker, Butch's father, with his daughters in 1933. Blanch, Lula, Jen, Maxi, Knell, and Leona. (*Author's collection*)
Below: Maximilian Parker and his sons, in Circleville, Utah, in 1933. Dan, Bill, Maxi, Joe, Carl (a son-in-law), Eb, Mark. (*Author's collection*)

25. Back Home, 1925

BY 1925, THE FAMILY of Robert LeRoy Parker, alias Butch Cassidy, in Circleville, Utah, had decreased in size. Annie Parker had passed away in 1905 leaving Maximilian a widower. Most of the thirteen Parker children had married and moved away. The three youngest sons, Eb, Mark, and Joe Rawlins remained bachelors and ranchers on the Parker ranch near Circleville. Lula Parker had married Circleville farmer Joseph Betenson in 1907, and they were raising their children in town.[1] Lula kept a watchful eye on her aging father and her three single brothers, often cooking and cleaning for them.

Near the turn of the century, the family had bought a two-story red brick home and moved into town.[2] In 1925, Maximilian and his three sons lived in the home but continued to work the old Parker ranch.

One day in the early fall, Mark Parker was at the ranch fixing fence when a new black Ford touring car pulled up and a man got out. At first Mark thought the man was his cousin Fred Levi. But as the man got closer, "his face broke into a characteristic Parker grin."[3] Mark was puzzled. Mark "studied the face and suddenly realized it could be but one person—Bob Parker."[4] After a brief visit the two men drove into Circleville to the Parker home. Robert LeRoy Parker, aka Butch Cassidy, had come home. He didn't know the family had moved into town, and he had returned to the cabin he had left some forty-one years before.

Maximilian was then eighty-one-years old. He was sitting on the step by the kitchen door on the west side of the house. The fancy car pulled up, and Mark and another man got out.

"Bob's face for once was solemn; perhaps he wondered how he would be accepted. The screen door to the kitchen was open behind Dad's back. Bob took off his hat and twirled it through the door. It landed squarely on the post of the rocking chair inside. Dad knew him. No one could ever describe that meeting after all the years of uncertainty and separation—forty-one years. That reunion proved the strength of Dad's heart; he survived it."[5]

> Mark Parker ran up to Lula's house to get her and to ask her to her fix dinner for a guest, but he didn't tell her who was there. Lula and her husband Joseph, or "Jose" as he was called, went to the Parker home. Lula wrote: "We walked in the front gate and around to the kitchen door. I glanced at the unfamiliar car and wondered who it was this time. As we stepped into the kitchen, put down the food, and went into the living room, the conversation stopped. The stranger stood up as I stepped into the room, and I studied his face in the awkward silence. He wasn't a stranger, not really, and yet he was. Why did he look so familiar?[6]
>
> Dad smiled. 'I'll bet you don't know who this is.' I was puzzled. By his features, he had to be family. 'Lula, this is LeRoy!' Dad announced.
>
> My jaw dropped. Even though I was sure he was alive and somewhere in the country, I had never anticipated this meeting. Bob grinned. My knees felt like rubber, and my insides turned upside down. Any resentment I had harbored toward my outlaw brother melted.[7] [Lula said she always felt like their mother's early death was caused by a broken heart over her oldest son's outlaw life.]

Lula fixed a large feast for the prodigal son's return. They visited into the early morning. Lula continued:

> He was surprised at all our nicknames and often wondered whom we were talking about. Intensely interested in talking about Mother, he expressed his deep sorrow for having caused her so much heartache. He knew he had broken her heart. Realization of the sorrow and humiliation he had caused the family had kept him from coming home long before.
>
> Bob said he had never forgotten how Mother looked that morning he left in 1884. Repeatedly he steered the conversations back to Mother. He couldn't hear enough of her. He asked about every member of the family—what they were doing, what their children were like.[8]

Butch emphasized that he and Sundance really intended to go straight in South America, but he said, "When a man gets down, they won't let him up. He never quits paying the price." Lula said that Butch didn't want to "talk about his past or his escapades and did so only as we asked questions."[9]

The big question was what had happened in Bolivia that resulted in the reports of his death? Butch said that he and Sundance had planned to meet at a certain time and place to go back to the States, but Butch's leg had become badly swollen from what was possibly a scorpion bite, and he had missed the planned meeting. He told of how an Indian woman had nursed him back to health, and he had traveled around with her young son for a time, using him as "a blind" as he said the authorities were after him.[10] He drifted up into Mexico by himself. He said he had run into Sundance and Etta in Mexico City later and that was the last he had seen of them.[11]

When asked about San Vicente, he said he wasn't there, and he didn't know what had happened exactly, but he had heard that the bodies had been identified as him and Sundance by Percy Seibert.[12] We now know this to be incorrect as Percy did not personally travel to San Vicente, but he did give information later that essentially identified the two dead outlaws as Butch and Sundance.[13]

Butch stayed with his dad for two days, then went up on Circleville Mountain to Dog Valley with his brothers for about a week. Lula's son Mark Betenson was eleven at the time and was sent home from Dog Valley. He was quite put out. Later his uncle Eb told him who the stranger was. He then confided to his mother that he knew about Butch's visit, and they talked about it often.[14]

Butch stayed another day or two with his father and then left, never to return.

Maximilian had tried to get Butch to stay in Circleville, but he refused. He had things to see about and old friends to look up. He asked that his visit be kept a secret.

Lula said that Maximilian said to the family, "'This is our secret. You are never to mention it to anyone. If you want a secret kept, never tell it.' And we never did. Even other members of our own family didn't know for years."[15] Maximilian was well loved and respected by his children, and they obeyed his request. Lula was the last surviving member of her immediate family and the last member who was present for Butch's visit.

Lula said, "Occasionally Dad had a letter from him, but his letters were always carefully destroyed to protect Bob. We worried about what trouble it might cause him if they fell into the wrong hands. One day Dad received a letter from one of Bob's friends, reporting that Bob had died of pneumonia. The letter assured Dad that his son was laid away very nicely. It was simply signed "Jeff."[16]

Lula said, "Robert LeRoy Parker died in the Northwest in the fall of 1937, a year before Dad died. He was not the man known as William Phillips, reported to be Butch Cassidy."[17] Lula said that she thought Bob was using the alias Bob Parks when he visited the family.

Lula refused to name his burial location and stated, "Where he is buried and under what name is still our secret." She said her father, Maximilian, said, "All his life he was chased. Now he has a chance to rest in peace, and that's the way it must be."[18] Lula further said, "If I were to reveal his burial place, someone would be sure to disturb it under some pretext, and my brother is entitled to rest in peace."[19]

LULA BETENSON'S ACCOUNT of Robert LeRoy Parker's return to his family home is just one of many personal accounts from people who say they saw Butch in the United States after 1908. Some of these people knew Butch well; his family certainly did. Some are people who were well-respected, and most have nothing to gain from a fabrication.

There are reports from people who say Butch and Sundance died in Bolivia, and there are accounts of individuals who say they saw him in the United States after that. Eyewitness accounts exist in both cases.

Butch died several deaths in his lifetime, which one of the death reports should we believe? Butch was first reported to have been killed near Price, Utah, in 1898, and the courts even ruled the body was his. However, that was a case of mistaken identity. Is it not possibly that reports of Butch's death at San Vicente were also mistaken identity?

SOME OF THE MORE interesting accounts are from people who knew Butch and either wrote or were interviewed about his return to the West.

JOSIE BASSETT. Josie Bassett had known Butch well from his early days in Brown's Park. She said that both Butch and Elzy Lay visited her on two different occasions after 1908. The first time was in 1929 in Rock Springs when she was managing a boarding house for Tom Vernon. Tom joined them for drinks on this occasion. He said later, "Killed in South America—hell!" Butch Cassidy came by . . . and stayed with me for two days. There is no mistake."

Butch and Elzy visited Josie again in 1932 in Baggs, Wyoming.[20] Josie confirmed this to Elzy's grandson Harvey "Harv" Murdock in the early 1960s during a visit he had with Josie at her home on Cub Creek, near Jensen, Utah. Harv is adamant to this day that Josie spoke the truth.[21]

Josie stated, "I saw Butch Cassidy when he came back from South America." She said that both Butch and Elzy Lay, "were out of condition, and carried too much weight. . . ."[22]

✧ ✧ ✧

Bert CHARTER. Butch's old friend Bert Charter, who had helped out with horses on a number of the robberies, retired to the Jackson Hole, Wyoming, area. Charter was convinced that Butch had not died in South America because Butch had visited the Charter ranch in Jackson Hole in 1925, long after his supposed demise.

Charter later told his neighbor and author Struthers Burt about Cassidy. Burt in his book *Powder River* wrote, "But there is one famous member of the Hole in the Wall Gang who I, for one, am sure is still alive. There are too many people who ought to know who are equally certain; including a most trustworthy neighbor of mine, a prosperous and highly respected cattleman."[23]

✧ ✧ ✧

JOHN TAYLOR. A car dealer in Rock Springs John Taylor, said, "One day in 1922 Butch Cassidy drove into the shop in a Model T to get some work done on the car. He was pulling a two-wheel trailer loaded with camping gear. "He asked me a lot of questions about old-timers around Rock Springs. He didn't tell me who he was, but I recognized him. . . ."[24]

✧ ✧ ✧

TOM WELCH. Tom Welch, an associate of Butch and his friends was asked in 1959 if Cassidy had died in South America. Welch responded, "Well, if he did, then I met and shook hands with a dead man in Lander in 1930!"

In another interview, Welch said, "If Butch Cassidy was killed in South America . . . I had a couple of drinks of whisky with a mighty lively ghost."[25]

Welch said in 1924, Cassidy had stopped at Welch's ranch on Henry's Fork, "He was driving an old Model T with a little trailer on behind, and he had it stacked with camping gear, grub and all kinds of things. He said, 'Tom, B'gawd, I come back to visit my old friends. You hop in with me and we're goin' to make all the rounds!'" Welch said they toured Lander, South Pass, Rock Springs, Vernal, and Brown's Park.[26]

Fred Hilman. Fred Hilman was the boy on the ranch outside of Sheridan, Wyoming, where Butch worked shortly after the Castle Gate robbery. Butch endeared himself to the family by taking time to teach young Fred how to shoot a revolver. Fred was on the receiving end of a rattlesnake Butch tossed up on a hay stacker as a practical joke.

According to Fred Hilman, Butch returned sometime around 1910, after Fred was married. He asked Fred if anyone had thrown a rattlesnake at him lately? Fred quickly recognized Butch and knew he was the only one who knew the story as the Hilmans had kept his identity secret. In October 2009, Fred's son Zane confirmed the account.[27]

Clifford McMullin. The McMullins were cousins to the Parkers. Maximilian Parker's sister Ada had married Brigham Young McMullin. Clifford McMullin, a grandson to B.Y. McMullin, said in 1925 he ran into Cassidy when he stopped in a boat for gas on the Colorado River. Clifford knew Cassidy from when he had come to hide out at Brig's house in Leeds, and Clifford recognized Butch but didn't say anything to give him away. Cassidy asked Clifford, "How's uncle Brig and aunt Ada?"[28]

Ada Calvert Piper. Ada, who had grown up in the Baggs, Wyoming, area, knew Butch Cassidy well as he had come to her father Kirk Calvert's general store and ranch. Ada's sister Mary Calvert married Elzy Lay after he got out of prison. Ada was convinced Butch had returned from South America.[29] In a 1963 letter she stated that Harry Alonzo (Longabaugh) had been killed in South America, but "Butch Cassidy was not killed in S.A. He was here in 1930 and I visited with him and he told several of us he escaped."[30]

⬦ ⬦ ⬦

Otto Schnauber. At a Butch Cassidy Symposium in Rock Springs a few years ago, I met a couple of older folks who introduced themselves as grandchildren of Otto Schnauber who was a Rock Springs butcher in the 1890s. They told of a time in the 1930s when they were living with their grandfather, Otto. A stranger came to visit and they were asked to go outside and play. They thought this was somewhat strange since they had always been allowed to stay inside when visitors came. The stranger was an older man who seemed

Rock Springs butcher Otto Schnauber whose children say they remember Butch visiting in the 1930s. (*Courtesy Schnauber family*)

to be a good friend of Otto's. Their grandparents later told the children that the stranger was Butch Cassidy, and he had worked with Otto years before. The grandchildren had come to the event specifically to tell me of the incident because they wanted me to know Butch was alive long after the 1908 gunfight in Bolivia.[31]

✧ ✧ ✧

ELLNOR PARKER. Dan Parker's daughter-in-law Ellnor said that Butch visited his brother Dan in Milford, Utah, in late 1930 or early 1931.[32] Butch's father, Maximilian, and two brothers were also present. Ellnor was taking care of Dan who at the time was suffering from bad health. Dan lived in a room above the Drug Store in Milford. Ellnor said she was very excited to meet Butch since she'd heard so much about him. They talked for three or four hours. Butch was "really taken by my baby," Ellnor said. Butch cradled her oldest son who was born in September 1930 and sang to him a little song she had never heard before.[33] The song went:

> *Tony Ivans has gone away,*
> *Gone to Mexico to stay.*
> *No more taters, nor more corn . . . .*

Ellnor said that Butch had visited Dan on an earlier occasion in 1929.[34] She thought Butch had died and was buried in Spokane.[35] It has been further reported that Dan Parker corresponded with Butch, and Butch sent Dan money until he died in 1937. Ellnor mentioned that she had read many of Butch's letters to the family.

✧ ✧ ✧

WALLACE OTT. An old rancher in Southern Utah, Wallace Ott claimed he met Butch Cassidy as a boy in Henrieville, Utah, in April 1936. Cassidy was visiting Ott's neighbor Elijah "Lige" Moore. Moore and Cassidy were friends from earlier years. Wallace was close to Lige, who invited him over to meet Cassidy.[36]

✧ ✧ ✧

JOYCE WARNER. Matt Warner's daughter Joyce claimed that a man visited her in 1939 in Price, Utah, looking for Matt. Unfortunately Matt had passed away in December 1938. The stranger confided that he was Cassidy. Matt had written to Charles Kelly in 1937 telling him that Butch had died in South America.[37] Matt may have been protecting the identity of his friend. Steve Lacy who knew Joyce claimed that the man who had visited Joyce died in 1943 as "Frank Irvin" in Tonopah, Nevada, after retiring from the railroad.[38]

✧ ✧ ✧

MERRILL JOHNSON. Utah State patrolman Merrill Johnson pulled over an old man near Kanab, Utah, in July 1941 for failing to obey a stop sign. He gave the man a warning ticket. Later, Merrill returned to Kanab to find the same old man at the home of his in-laws, the Kitchens. He was introduced to the old man as an old friend of the Kitchens, Bob Parker—Butch Cassidy. Parker was on his way to Fredonia, Arizona, to visit his brother Bill Parker. Johnson listened to the two men reminisce about their youth. Johnson remembered Parker saying he had been in Bolivia and later had been in a car accident and spent time in a hospital. The next day Johnson drove him to Fredonia. Johnson was later shown pictures of Cassidy and confirmed that was who had visited. Johnson's wife confirmed the incident and said her father had been a close friend of Cassidy's.[39]

✧ ✧ ✧

AGATHA APPLEGATE NAY. During Butch's visit to his family in 1925, a young twelve-year-old Circleville girl, Agatha Applegate, stopped at the Parker home to collect money for a magazine subscription. It was getting late and she needed to get home. Agatha specifically remembered meeting a stranger named Bob who "had piercing eyes and grinned when he spoke." She said Bob knew her family and was sincerely interested in what she had to say. Bob asked how the Applegates were doing and wanted to know all about them. She later found he was Maximilian's son, known to the world as Butch Cassidy.[40]

✧ ✧ ✧

JOHN ROLFE BURROUGHS. Well-respected historian Burroughs, who was a graduate of the University of Arizona and Harvard University, wrote the book *Where the Old West Stayed Young*, published in 1962, and many other books. Burroughs accepted that Sundance had died in Bolivia but wrote " . . . considerable doubt exists relative to the identity of the man killed with Longabaugh. . . . I am positive that Butch Cassidy returned to the United States, where he lived to be an old man. Just who was killed along with Harry Longabaugh remains open to speculation. It very well could have been a character by the name of Tom Dilley. . . . *But it was not Butch Cassidy*." [Emphasis in original quotation.]

Burroughs went on to explain that he had interviewed several individuals during research for his book and was convinced Butch had returned. Burroughs had interviewed Tom Vernon, Tom Welch, John Taylor, and Josephine Bassett Morris, among others.[41]

✧ ✧ ✧

ART DAVIDSON. Old prospector Art Davidson met a cousin to Butch Cassidy, Robert McMullin, in the 1930s. McMullin claimed he was Cassidy. He told Art many tales of his outlaw life, and Art wrote a manuscript of the tales but passed away before it could be published. A friend later published the manuscript under the title *Sometimes Cassidy*. The book tells of two Robert LeRoy Parkers who each were known as "Butch Cassidy." They were half-brothers through two different polygamist wives of Robert Parker. However research of the two wives of Robert Parker show he only had children with his first wife. The two Cassidys supposedly died in Johnnie, Nevada, in the early 1940s and are buried near each other.[42]

✧ ✧ ✧

WILL SIMPSON. Will Simpson, who had prosecuted Cassidy in the 1890s, was not convinced that Butch had returned from South America. He stated in a 1937 letter to Harry Logue, "I do not believe that Cassidy ever returned from South America, notwithstanding a number of Lander people have told me personally that they had talked to him. I know of two men who went to South America to determine whether or not he was dead. One of them is living now, and I understand that he went to the place where Cassidy was killed and buried and satisfied himself of Cassidy's death.[43] I have in my mind the man who represented himself to be Cassidy was Ed McClellan better known as Big Ed."[44]

✧ ✧ ✧

DAVID LOVE. Dr. David Love, world-renowned geologist and historian, tells a story to author John McPhee in *Rising from the Plains*. During a summer vacation from his college studies at Yale, Love visited the office of his long-time family doctor, Francis Smith, M.D., in Lander in about 1923. Doc Smith told Love that one of his recent office visitors had been Robert LeRoy Parker himself.

Smith related that Cassidy had appeared in his doorway and when Smith didn't immediately recognize him: "The patient remarked that his face had been altered by a surgeon in Paris. Then he lifted his shirt, exposing the deep crease of a repaired bullet wound—craftsmanship that Doc Smith recognized precisely as his own."[45]

✧ ✧ ✧

WILLIAM T. PHILLIPS. One of the more curious episodes of the Butch Cassidy story involves William T. Phillips. Until recently some people believed that Butch returned under the assumed alias of William T. Phillips. Historian Larry Pointer recently discovered the true identity of Phillips whose early days had been elusive. He was William T. Wilcox.[46] Wilcox was in prison at the same time as Butch in the 1890s and may have known Butch well.

Phillips or Wilcox lived in the Spokane, Washington, area and told those close to him that he was the outlaw Butch Cassidy. Phillips made several trips to Wyoming in search of Butch's outlaw caches and to visit old friends, some of whom said he knew things that he could have known only if he *was* Cassidy. Phillips looked similar to Butch in some of his later photos; others were less convincing. Comparison of Wilcox's mug shot and the older Phillips's studio photo show convincingly that they were the same person. (Some believe Wilcox assumed the name of his cousin, the real William T. Phillips, who died at a young age.) Lula Parker Betenson had steadfastly maintained that Phillips *was not* her brother.

William T. Phillips was apparently an alias for William Wilcox who was in the Wyoming prison at the same time as Butch Cassidy. The mug shot of Wilcox is shown on page 90 of this book. (*Courtesy Larry Pointer*)

One of the most compelling parts of the Phillips's story is the number of Cassidy's close Wyoming friends he visited and convinced that he was truly Cassidy, including Charlie Stough, Leonard Short, Harry Logue, Orson Grimmett, Hank Boedeker, Eugene Amoretti, Jr.,[47] and Ed Farlow. Farlow said he knew Phillips was Cassidy because he related an incident that only Cassidy and one other knew about and the other had passed away.[48] Logue indicated that Cassidy also visited John Chapman in the 1930s in Lander.[49] Chapman had helped arrest Butch in 1892.

Some of the reports of Phillips's visits indicate that there was another man traveling with him. Who was this mystery man?

Deputy Sheriff Harry R. Logue stated, "He [George Parker, aka Butch] was supposed to have been killed in South America some years ago, but [I] want to say that George was in Lander hunting up his old haunts and friends in the summer of 1929."[50]

Phillips corresponded with one of Cassidy's Wyoming girlfriends, Mary Boyd, and gave her an opal ring inscribed "Geo C. to Mary B."

During Phillips's later years he wrote a manuscript called *The Bandit Invincible* detailing the outlaw career of Butch Cassidy.

However, not all old-timers agreed that Phillips was Cassidy. Wyoming pioneer rancher Jim Reagan maintained that Butch Cassidy and William T. Phillips were both outlaws who had worked together.

A 1946 newspaper article stated, "Mr. Reagan is one of the pioneers of Wyoming who recalls vividly the stirring events of the early days. When the associate of Butch Cassiday appeared here a few years ago representing himself as the real Butch, Reagan recognized him as Phillips. He [the man] was able to deceive a number of Lander men who knew Butch well. Reagan says that Cassiday and Phillips were holed up in a little log cabin in a canyon over the end of the Big Horn Mountains hiding out from officers after one of their bank raids. The two outlaws would come to Reagan's sheep camp for grub and he would feed them and fill their needs out of his supply."[51]

James Regan said he, " . . . knew Phillips well at Lost Cabin when he ran a poker game during shearing time. He was a tall man, 5 foot 11 inches, weighing 210 to 215, much larger than Butch who scaled about 150 to 160."[52]

W.T. "Billy" Jones, who was mayor of Lander in 1942, knew Cassidy well in the 1890s when Jones was a butcher. Jones said of Cassidy, "He was not a large man and did not tally with the size and build of this man Phillips."[53]

Phillips married and had one adopted son. He owned and operated a machine shop in Spokane, but died in 1937 of rectal cancer and his ashes were spread over the Spokane River.

Recently an original, more detailed version of the Phillips manuscript was located which contains much unpublished information.[54] The manuscript contains errors, but also some details known by one close to Cassidy. Larry Pointer and a team of historians are reviewing the manuscript in detail and plan to release their findings soon after 2012.

Some have surmised that Butch may have become reacquainted with Phillips and used Phillips as an alias. We do have evidence they spent time together in Wyoming from Jim Reagan's testimony. Is there a possibility that Cassidy and Phillips visited Wyoming friends together? Did Cassidy work with Phillips on the manuscript *Bandit Invincible*?

❖ ❖ ❖

IRS, Arthur Reed Reynolds. Even the Internal Revenue Service began to seek out Butch. In the 1920-1930s, Arthur Reed Reynolds who worked as a tax collector for the IRS, was sent to Southern Utah to look for Butch Cassidy. The IRS had heard stories of Cassidy being in the area and sent Reynolds to follow up. It appears Reynolds did not find Cassidy during his search.[55]

❖ ❖ ❖

NO CONCLUSIVE EVIDENCE proves that Butch Cassidy died in the shootout at San Vicente. Some of the original documents related to the deaths of the outlaws in Bolivia have never been made public beyond authors Dan Buck and Anne Meadows. These documents need to be made available so that they can be examined and researched by others.

On one hand we have circumstantial evidence that the two bandits may have been Butch and Sundance, but the two graves dug up revealed that neither contained Butch Cassidy's body. Yet one of the exhumed skeletal heads contained lead tracings around a bullet hole supporting the idea that it may have been one of the San Vicente bandits.

On the other hand, we have many reports from eyewitnesses who say they saw Butch in the U.S. after the San Vicente shootout.

Some have speculated that if Lula Betenson had been a middle-aged man in a business suit rather than a spry ninety-one-year-old woman, her book would have gotten more respect, especially with her background as a Utah state legislator and a church and community leader.

Lula was correct in her assessment of William Phillips. Time has shown that William T. Phillips was not Butch Cassidy, just as Lula said.

Time has also shown that if she had revealed her brother's gravesite it probably would have been dug up for DNA testing, just as Lula feared.

Beyond the eyewitness accounts of Butch's return to the United States, little documented evidence places him in the U.S. after 1908. But when dozens of people testify that Butch returned and they personally saw him, I believe their accounts should be given credence, especially since no real proof exists to the contrary. Why should we disregard them?

I have spent much of my life trailing down every piece of information I can about Robert LeRoy Parker, aka Butch Cassidy, examining it with an open mind, and sharing it with others for their ideas and insights.

Lula Parker Betenson was my great grandmother, and I knew her well. I believe and support her account of the return of her brother in 1925.

Dan Parker later in life with his daughters. (*Author's collection*)

A. Dan Parker

D AN PARKER LOST part of two fingers on his right hand. Like many episodes in the lives of the Parker boys, several versions of what happened next are told. One version is that young Dan and his brother Bob, later to be known as Butch Cassidy, were chopping wood. Dan held the wood and Butch worked the axe. Dan unknowingly got his hand too close and Bob accidentally chopped off part of Dan's index and middle fingers.[1]

In another version, Dan was holding the getaway horses in a robbery and a bullet hit his right hand and took off parts of two fingers.[2] Still another version claims that it happened while Dan was in prison.[3]

However it happened, Dan wasn't anxious to talk about it or much of anything else from his past. He responded to a neighbor's question about how he had lost his fingers by gruffly saying, "Just by poking my nose in other people's business, like you're doing now!"

Dan Parker arrived back in his home state of Utah after being released from a Detroit prison in December 1897 where he'd been incarcerated for his involvement in a stage holdup. Four years after getting out of prison, on December 11, 1901, Dan married Annice Ann McMullin in the St. George Mormon Temple, in St. George, Utah.[4] Annice Ann McMullin, whose nickname was "Nan," was Dan's first cousin. Nan's mother and Dan's father were brother and sister. The newlyweds lived for a time in Leeds, Utah, where Nan's family lived. Dan's mother, Annie, was happy to see her prodigal son return, marry, and settle down.

Dan and Nan later settled in the southern Utah town of Parowan. Dan and Nan had 11 children. The first child was a stillborn, but they raised ten children, five boys and five girls. Dan's daughter said that their mother would not allow Dan to talk to the children about his outlaw days because she didn't want the other children at school to tease them and call them "little out-laws."[5] One of Dan's daughters remembered that her mother showed her Dan's pardon when she was a teenager.[6]

Dan's daughter said that her father and mother didn't get along at times and as a result Dan was gone from home often. However, Dan was kind to his children, and they were always delighted to see him. Dan's daughter said, "He would take me up town [Parowan] to buy me candy because he said I was so pretty. My mother would curl my hair and put a big bow in it. People would stop and say, 'You mean you are the father of this beautiful girl?' and he would respond with a cuss word." Like most of Dan's children, she felt like she was his favorite.[7]

Dan traveled around looking for work. The Pinkerton Detective Agency kept tabs on him because his brother was Butch Cassidy. One file states that he was working in a coal mine near Fay, Lincoln County, Nevada.[8] Dan's brother-in-law Joseph Betenson wrote in his journal that he went to work in the mining town of Kimberly, Utah, with Dan and several others, including Dan's brothers Eb and Joe Rawlins in the summer of 1905. They chopped cordwood for the mill and power plant at a dollar per cord.[9]

In 1907, Dan Parker moved his family from Parowan to Circle Valley by team and wagon to run the Parker ranch for his father for one year. Nan would not go without her sewing machine, so Dan loaded it up with the family.[10]

Dan's niece said that Dan and his siblings were very close. She remembers, as a child growing up in Circleville, that Dan would come to visit her mother often in the summertime. On one of his visits, he and her mother were peeling peaches in the kitchen and were "just laughing their heads off" as they visited together.[11]

At some point in Dan's life he developed severe stomach problems, which later led to his death. A number of family members, who remember Dan, say that he took baking soda by the handful to try to settle his stomach and relieve his stomach pains.[12]

The Parker family loved to give each other nicknames. Dan's nickname was "Snip," possibly referring to his two snipped fingers.

Dan was known for his unique personality. He was often colorfully blunt. Once Dan was working on a haying crew, and, as part of their room and board, the crew ate meals with the farm family. At the first meal, Dan was having a second cup of coffee when the farmwife noticed and asked, "What do you think of my coffee, Mr. Parker?" Dan responded, "It's thin, Ma'am, mighty thin."[13]

The Mormon communities of southern Utah often combined their livestock herds into what they called "co-ops." Dan was lambing for one of three co-op sheep herds near Parowan. He requested the use of a rifle from the church bishop, who was the local leader, because of problems with coyotes. The bishop proudly brought him a small Winchester 1892 .25-20 a couple of days later. The bishop said, "Nice little rifle, Dan. Yes, yes, nice little rifle, costs less to shoot and easier to carry. Yes, yes, easier to carry!" About three days later, the bishop returned and asked Dan, "How do you like that rifle, Dan, how do you like it?" Without hesitating, Dan responded, "I don't; I'd just as well have a pocketful of rocks!"[14]

Dan was known to use "colorful" language at times, but was always careful around women. When with men, his language was slightly different. Dan was at the local saloon one night, and the stories were coming "close and tall." A stranger came over to confront Dan. He had five dollars in his hand and said to Dan, "Stranger, I have said for a number of years that if I ever listened to a man who swore more than I do in the course of an ordinary conversation, I would give him five dollars." Dan looked at him and said, "What do we do, have a contest?" The man handed him the five and said, "No contest—the money is yours."[15]

Everyone knew deer hunting was important to Dan. Other things were important too. The local men gathered at a Ray Adams's gas station to gossip and pass the time. It was mid-October and Ray asked him if he was going. He said, 'No, I can't afford it. I would have to have a license, a box of cartridges, a bottle of whiskey, and at least one loaf of bread. No, I'm not going."[16]

Vern Mortensen told a story about Dan. "I worked at the Parowan Mercantile for several years. One morning Dan came in with his three younger boys. He talked to Art Joseph [the owner] for a few minutes then Art called me over and said, 'You take Dan and fix him up with what he needs. Then bring the bill to me.' When we got to the clothing department Dan said, 'We are going to Circleville to a funeral. My father died last night.' I said, 'Well that's too bad, I'm sorry.' Dan looked me right in the eyes and said, 'G— D—, it ain't too bad. He's 94 years old. He'd ought to be dead.' When Dan's needs were filled I made the entries on a regular charge book. He asked to sign it and did. Then [he] left with shoes, pants, and shirts. I took the book to Art and said, 'That's a pretty good-sized bill. I wonder how he's going to pay it.' Art said, 'I do too, but he'll find a way. Dan Parker is an honorable man.'"[17]

Later on in his life, Dan developed a raspy voice that could sound frightening. Dan's nephew, Scott Parker Betenson, tells of a time when he and his brother, Mark, were playing at the Parker home in Circleville and were making a lot of noise. Dan, in his raspy voice, said, "You little sons of bitches, if you don't quiet down, I'll grab you by the windpipe and run with you!" Scott was scared to death and said that he will remember that as long as he lives.[18]

In 1926, Dan knew he had unique insight into law enforcement, so he applied to be city marshal for the town of Parowan. But he was passed over for another applicant who probably had less experience in the field.[19]

In the late 1920s and early 1930s, Dan worked in the mines west of Milford, Utah, and stayed in a room at the Horn Silver Hotel.[20] In 1930 his father and two of his brothers (most likely Eb and Rawlins) brought someone to the hotel for a visit. According to a recorded interview with Dan's oldest son, Max, that "someone" was Butch Cassidy.[21] Dan's daughter said that this did in fact occur, and that Maximilian and Dan swore Max's wife to secrecy because she was also at the hotel at the time of Butch's visit.[22]

During the Great Depression, Dan participated in the government's Works Program Administration (W.P.A.) participating in community projects in order to supplement his income. One project was a rock fence around the Parowan cemetery.[23]

In the 1930s, the movies came calling. Representatives from a Southern California motion picture company approached Dan about making a movie of the lives of him and his brother Butch Cassidy. Dan postponed the idea and died before anything came of it. However, Dan started to write the story of his life and Butch's in a manuscript that he submitted to a publisher for consideration. Dan became so frustrated with the publisher one evening, because the company wanted to romanticize it, that he threw the entire manuscript into the fire.[24]

During World War II, in 1942, Dan was employed as a guard at the Yankee Reservoir in Parowan Canyon. While camping there, he became ill with his continuing stomach problems. After two or three days, he was brought out of the canyon to his home. When he refused to go to a doctor, Nan called Dan's two brothers, Eb and Joe Rawlins, to come because she was worried. They took Dan to the hospital in Cedar City, but it was too late.

On August 5, 1942, at 2:30 P.M., after being ill for ten days, Daniel Sinclair Parker passed away at the age of seventy-four from a bleeding ulcer in the Iron County Hospital in Cedar City. His obituary stated "digestive disorders."[25] The newspaper reported, "Well-known resident of this community for the past thirty-four years died." "Impressive funeral services" were held August 10, 1942, in Parowan, in a Mormon church filled to capacity with many friends and relatives, many from out of state. Dan's body was buried in the Parowan cemetery with the grave dedicated by his brother-in-law Joseph Betenson. His pallbearers were his two brothers, Eb and Joe Rawlins, a son-in-law, and three sons.[26]

Daniel Sinclair Parker left behind many things, including the outlaw past that he had left behind many years before. Dan, like his brother Butch, was a product of his time. Young people sought out excitement where it was available. Often times their lives ended in tragedy. Dan was fortunate to have a strong family. With the love of his family, he was able to overcome his early reckless ways and begin a new life. Dan also left behind a great posterity of individuals who are successful in the world and in their communities.

Lula Parker Betenson with her oldest daughter. (*Author's collection*)

APPENDIX

B. Lula Parker Betenson

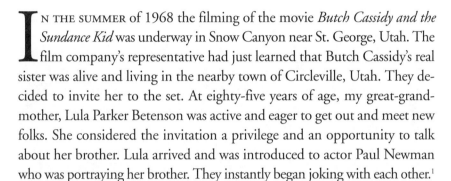

I N THE SUMMER of 1968 the filming of the movie *Butch Cassidy and the Sundance Kid* was underway in Snow Canyon near St. George, Utah. The film company's representative had just learned that Butch Cassidy's real sister was alive and living in the nearby town of Circleville, Utah. They decided to invite her to the set. At eighty-five years of age, my great-grandmother, Lula Parker Betenson was active and eager to get out and meet new folks. She considered the invitation a privilege and an opportunity to talk about her brother. Lula arrived and was introduced to actor Paul Newman who was portraying her brother. They instantly began joking with each other.[1]

Lula and Robert Redford, who played the Sundance Kid, also became friends, especially after his involvement in riding the Outlaw Trail, which was made into a documentary and a book a few years later. Bob Redford later gave Lula a tape recorder for a birthday present so she could record information about her brother. She, in turn, knitted baby blankets for his children. They seemed to have a genuine respect for each other.

Lula was born Lula Christine Parker on April 5, 1884, in the tiny southern Utah town of Spry.[2] Her mother was working on the Marshall Ranch at the time, which was considered part of the town of Spry. She was the ninth of thirteen children and just a baby when her older brother left home in 1884. But she got to know him through his letters sent home and stories from her parents and older siblings. She later met him when he returned home in 1925.

Lula grew up on the Parker Ranch in Circle Valley, which is still located three miles south of the town of Circleville, Utah.

The Parkers loved family, and horses were considered part of it. Lula recalled that as a child she and her sister Nina and brother Mark had gone into town in their homemade sleigh pulled by Old Jack, a favorite horse. On the way home, a terrible blizzard hit. The drifting snow was so dense, they could not see where they were going. Lula said that "being girl-like," she and Nina started to cry. Mark told them, "Don't worry. Old Jack knows the way. He'll get us home." So Mark gave Old Jack his head and, sure enough, he finally pulled the three kids into the yard. Lula said, "We were cold and frightened but home safe at last. There was no place like home, believe me!"[3]

From an early age, Lula was outgoing, social, and loved to perform. She sang in glee clubs and for local community programs. One of her favorite solos was, "Where the Silver Colorado Wends Its Way." Lula said that on the Fourth of July, groups of people would wake up at dawn, load into the wagons, and then ride from house to house singing patriotic songs.

As a young lady, she joined the Walter's Theatrical Stock Company and traveled with them throughout Utah and Idaho. The company traveled by horse and buggy from one community to another, playing three- or five-night stands, performing a different play each night. Lula said she especially remembered presenting "Jack O' Diamonds" in which she had an excellent part.[4]

Lula also spent many years as drama director in auxiliaries of the Church of Jesus Christ of Latter Day Saints.

Lula enjoyed performing so much she found it difficult to leave the theater. She said, "I had a very happy young life and wasn't anxious to settle down." However, she met the man of her dreams who was also from Circleville. Lula said, "When Joseph Betenson asked me to marry him, I knew I couldn't find a better man in the whole world."[5] Lula married Joseph Adelbert Betenson on New Year's Eve, December 31, 1907.[6] Lula and Jose ("Jose" rhymes with close) settled in Circleville and lovingly raised their children, three boys and two girls: Pauline, Mark, Scott, John and Barbara.

After forty years of marriage, Jose died unexpectedly of a heart attack on July 8, 1948.[7] Lula described his death as the "greatest loss in my life." Jose had made many friends in his life and at his funeral, a neighbor told Lula that, "We have come to mourn the richest man in town – not in money, but in respect of his fellowmen and in friends."[8]

After her husband's death, Lula kept busy with church and community service. Lula was patriotic and was active in politics. She served as a messenger in the Utah House of Representatives for two terms[9] and was the democratic chairwoman in Piute County, Utah, for 28 years.[10] She enjoyed a heated political debate even into her later years.

Paul Newman, Lula Betenson, and Robert Redford on the location of the movie
Butch Cassidy and the Sundance Kid. (*Author's collection*)

In 1962, Governor George D. Clyde appointed Lula as the Piute County representative to the Utah Legislature upon a vacancy. As a representative, Lula fought hard for better schools, local control, better roads, and employment and education projects for Utah's rural counties.[11]

Lula was the only one of her sisters to raise her young family in her hometown.[12] Maximilian was a widower for thirty-three years and only two of Lula's brothers, Dan and Bill, married. Three brothers lived with their father in Circleville, Eb, Mark, and Joe Rawlins; so Lula "mothered" her father and three brothers along with her own children.

Interest in Butch Cassidy seemed to explode with the release of the 1969 movie *Butch Cassidy and the Sundance Kid,* and Lula began to correspond with many people throughout the world about her brother Butch. She grew tired of the outrageous stories and total untruths that were written in newspapers and books about him.

Several years before the movie was released, Lula had started writing a book about Butch to set the record straight. Certain family members opposed the book about Butch because his reputation had been a great family embarrassment for many years. In fact, a family pact had been made between Maximilian and his children about Butch's final years. Although discussions about Butch came up, the family did not openly discuss his outlaw days until the 1950s. After many years Lula finally published *Butch Cassidy, My Brother* in 1975 at the age of ninety-one.

Lula kept many things secret about her brother because of promises she had made to her father and family many years earlier. However, most significantly, in her book she revealed that Butch Cassidy was not killed in South America, but had returned to Circleville to visit the family in 1925. Lula knew where Butch died and where he was buried, but she swore she would never reveal where he was buried. She feared that if she told, his remains would be disturbed. In the early 1970s for example, the graves of outlaws Joe Walker and Johnny Herring were exhumed in Price, Utah. This bothered Lula greatly. She said that Butch had been chased his whole life, and she wanted his remains to rest in peace.

Lula traveled extensively in her later years. She went to New York City for a book signing of her book and to Harvard University in Connecticut for the world premier of *Butch Cassidy and the Sundance Kid*[13] and appeared on radio and television programs. She also traveled throughout the West to autograph her book and attend conventions of outlaw-lawman associations.

She chose not to write about Dan Parker's outlaw days to protect his large family. Butch did not have direct descendants.

Like her brother Butch Cassidy, Lula empathized with the underdog and fought for their causes. She was a classy lady with a lot of spirit and zest for life, even into her nineties.

On May 5, 1980, Lula passed away in the Panguitch, Utah, hospital at the age of ninety-six after suffering a paralyzing stroke.[14] Her twelve brothers and sisters preceded Lula in death.

Lula was survived by her five children, Mark Betenson and John Betenson both of Circleville, Scott Betenson and Pauline Betenson (Applegate), both of Kanab, Utah, and Barbara Betenson (Carlson) of Salt Lake City. At the time, Lula had seven grandchildren, seventeen great grandchildren, and two great-great grandchildren.

Funeral services were held on a cold, overcast spring afternoon, on Friday May 9, 1980, at the Circleville LDS second ward chapel.[15] I had the privilege of being one of her pallbearers. Lula was buried in the Circleville cemetery.

I'll always remember what a great and kind lady Lula was. She had a contagious personality and a twinkle in her brown eyes, which made people around her feel good. Lula was a dainty lady who always tried to look her best. She treated her friends and family with respect and kindness.

Soon after Lula's death, a local historian appeared on the Salt Lake television news claiming that Lula had confirmed to him from her hospital bed where Butch was buried. He further claimed that Lula asked him to not reveal the story until after her death. The news program took the so-called historian and their cameras by helicopter to Johnnie, Nevada, where a pile of rocks was identified as Butch's grave. The sad part of the whole fiasco was that Lula was paralyzed on one side of her body and could not speak. I know this from my own personal visits to the hospital, and family members confirm it.

Some have criticized Lula's book and story since her death, mainly because she would not reveal where Butch was buried. Still others claim she was not telling the truth based on interviews with other family members, specifically a niece. These claims are unfounded as this niece and her family was not in Circleville in 1925 and did not witness the visit of Butch. Some writers seem to twist the facts to support their theories.

I've tried to stay abreast of what has been written, although a lot has been written over the years. No definitive proof has been given to disprove Lula's claims that Butch came back in 1925. I see no reason to discount her story.

This letter to Matilda Davis, written by Butch Cassidy from Argentina in 1902, assures his friend Matilda that he is alive and well. The complete text of the letter can be found on pages 180–181. *(Courtesy Harvey Murdock)*

Notes

CHAPTER 2: BUTCH'S HERITAGE (PAGES 17–28)

1. Family Group Sheet. All Mormon family group sheets referenced can be found at the Church of Jesus Christ of Latter Day Saints History and Archives Library, Salt Lake City, UT.

2. The 1841 U.K. Census shows that he was a "warper" and was living in Chatburn, Whalley, Clitheroe, Lancashire. A warper operates a cotton loom during the early stages in the weaving process. The 1851 census lists Robert, Ann, Maximilian, Martha Alice, and Arthur living at Water Flatts, Accrington, Lancashire. Courtesy of Mike Bell.

3. Family Group Sheet.

4. Family Group Sheet.

5. Robert Parker had a younger brother William who also joined the Mormon Church and immigrated to Utah in 1852. A younger sister, Martha, immigrated to Utah in 1854.

6. The correct spelling of Maxi's full name is Maximilian with one "L." His name has been misspelled many different ways, including with two "L"s and as two words (Maxi Million), but his signature and grave marker indicate the correct spelling.

7. Griffiths, *Life Sketch of Ann Hartley Parker*. Lula Parker Betenson, *My Brother, Butch Cassidy,* 5.

8. Mormon handcart pioneer Josiah Rogerson described the handcarts. *Handcarts to Zion* quotes him: "The open handcart was made of Iowa hickory or oak. It was surrounded by a small wagon box three or four feet long with side and end pieces about eight inches high. Two persons were assigned to the pulling of each open cart, but in many instances, the father had to pull the covered cart along."

9. Records of the Museum of Church History and Art, Salt Lake City, Utah.

10. Berrett, *Sacred Places: Iowa and Nebraska,*180-181.

11. Judd, *Treasures of Pioneer History*, Vol. 5, 240-242.

12. Betenson, *Butch Cassidy, My Brother*, 15-18.

13. Hafen, *Handcarts to Zion*, 61.

14. Griffiths, *Life Sketch of Ann Hartley Parker.*

15. The pioneer journal of Archie Walters.

16. Griffiths, *Life Sketch of Ann Hartley Parker.*

17. *Piute County News*, May 28, 1937.

18. *Deseret News*, August 9, 1865.

19. *Deseret News,* January 2, 1878.

20. *Deseret News*, July 17, 1878.

21. Betenson, *Butch Cassidy, My Brother*, 15-18.

22. *Deseret News*, July 17, 1878.

23. *Deseret News*, Oct. 11, 1882 and July 8, 1885.

24. *Deseret News*, June 6, 1883.

25. *Salt Lake Tribune,* April 20, 1881.

26. Records of the Church of Jesus Christ of Latter Day Saints. However, there is no record of any children with his second wife. The book *Sometimes Cassidy* is based on the premise that Robert Parker had a child named Robert LeRoy Parker with his second wife, and he also became a wanted outlaw named Butch Cassidy. The name of the wife on the Church records is Jensenie Hansmire Madsen with a birth year of 1824. Another report indicates that Robert had three polygamist wives, but fails to provide evidence (Source: Kerry Ross Boren).

27. *Deseret News*, Salt Lake City, October 5, 1887; *The Southern Utonian*, October 7, 1887.

28. *Ogden Standard*, October 2, 1887.

29. *U. S. v. Robert Parker,* District of Utah, Case File 1931, year 1887.

30. Larson, *The Red Hills of November*, 292-293.

31. *Deseret News*, Salt Lake City, March 7, 1888; Larson, *The Red Hills of November*, 246.

32. *Salt Lake Tribune*, September 17, 1889 and April 8, 1891. Second District Court records indicate he was indicted on Dec 9, 1887, and May 18, 1888, or possibly 1887.

33. *U. S. v. Robert Parker,* District of Utah, Case File 1822, 1888, and Case File 47, 1889.

34. *Salt Lake Tribune*, April 8, 1891.

35. Utah Department of Corrections, Inmate Services Prison Commitment Registers, Utah State Archives.

36. Washington City cemetery, Parker headstone.

37. Betenson, *Butch Cassidy, My Brother*, 19.

38. *Piute County News*, August 5, 1938. Maxi and Annie were married by Daniel McAllister in the "old Salt Lake endowment house" which was a predecessor of the LDS Salt Lake Temple.

39. Betenson, *Butch Cassidy, My Brother, 32.*

40. Family records, Naturalization papers for Maximilian Parker.

41. Betenson, *Butch Cassidy, My Brother,* 20.

42. *Piute County News*, May 28, 1937.

43. *Piute County News*, June 10, 1938.

44. Family Group Sheet, Church of Jesus Christ of Latter Day Saints. *Piute County News*, August 5, 1938.

45. Family Group Record, Church of Jesus Christ of Latter Day Saints. The 1880 U.S. Census confirms that her birth was in England and that her parents were both born in Scotland.

46. Historian Mike Bell's research found Ann Gillies was born in Brandling Village at 49 South Front Street. He provided a copy of the 1851 U.K. census that shows the Gillies family.

47. Ironically, Ann's headstone in Circleville, Utah, indicates she was born in Scotland. Ann was proud of her Scottish heritage. Lula also stated in a 1979 interview that Annie was born in Scotland and the family moved to England shortly thereafter.

48. *Samuel Curling Ship* Passenger List on LDS.org.

49. Olsen, *The Price We Paid*, 225.

50. Olsen, *The Price We Paid*, 221-222.

51. Olsen, *The Price We Paid*, 224.

52. Olsen, *The Price We Paid*, 227.

53. Robert and John Gillies records in the Pioneer Overland Travel information on LDS.org.

54. Olsen, *The Price We Paid*, 401.

55. Martin's Cove Visitor Center, Wyoming.

56. Pioneer Overland Travel – Company Detail, "Jesse B. Martin Company" on LDS.org.

58. Martin, Jesse Bigler, Journal, 1853-1857, fd. 3, 76-118..

59. Martin, Jesse Bigler, Journal, 1853-1857, fd. 3, 76-118.

60. Betenson, *Butch Cassidy, My Brother*, 30.

61. Betenson, *Butch Cassidy, My Brother*, 30.

62. Betenson, *Butch Cassidy, My Brother*, 30

63. *Southern Utonian*, April 20, 1888, Beaver, Utah.

64. Conversation with Jacquie Tobin at the Parker reunion in September, 2007.

65. *Deseret Evening News*, February 15, 1900. The article mentions that Dan Gillies moved with several others from Circleville to Green River. Dan purchased a farm and had gone to work plowing and preparing for spring crops. I visited the ranch. Green River tends to have very mild winters and plowing in February would not be unusual.

CHAPTER 3: GROWING UP (PAGES 29–34)

1. Betenson, *Butch Cassidy, My Brother*, 7. His name is shown on LDS Church records and the 1880 U.S. Census as Robert. Butch signed his court records as "George" Cassidy.

2. Betenson, "My Brother, Butch Cassidy," 22, an unpublished manuscript that Lula Parker Betenson and Pearl Baker completed. It should not be confused

with the book with a similar title that Lula later wrote with Dora Flack titled *Butch Cassidy, My Brother*.

3. Pinkerton Files, Criminal File of George Parker, alias "Butch" Cassidy.

4. Affidavit concerning service in the Indian Wars within the State of Utah and Service, 1909; Maximilian served for 30 days. Maximilian also helped construct Fort Sanford as part of his duties, *Piute County News*, August 5, 1938.

5. U.S. 1870 Census, Beaver City, Beaver County, Utah Territory. The census also shows a Lydia who was older than Butch. Lydia was a Gillies relative who was living with the family at the time.

6. John D. Lee Pardon Petition, 1877. Utah State Historical Society.

7. Brooks, *John Doyle Lee*, 365.

8. *Piute County News*, August 5, 1938.

9. Betenson, *Butch Cassidy, My Brother*, 33.

10. Betenson, *Butch Cassidy, My Brother*, 22.

11. Betenson, *Butch Cassidy, My Brother*, 33. There is also a story the cabin had been built on land where a young boy had been killed by Indians. Reports identify the boy as Charles Van Vleet and that the Van Vleet and James families had built the cabin and later traded property with the Parkers in Beaver. This history comes from Kerry Ross Boren.

12. Betenson, *Butch Cassidy, My Brother*, 34.

13. Betenson, *Butch Cassidy, My Brother*, 33.

14. Betenson, *Butch Cassidy, My Brother*, 34.

15. Betenson, "My Brother, Butch Cassidy," 23.

16. Betenson, "My Brother, Butch Cassidy," 24.

17. Betenson, Bill, "Lula Parker Betenson."

18. Betenson, Bill, "Alias Tom Ricketts."

19. Prison Files of Butch Cassidy and Dan Parker.

20. Betenson, *Butch Cassidy, My Brother*, 36.

21. Betenson, "My Brother, Butch Cassidy," 25.

22. Siringo, *A Cowboy Detective*, 351.

23. *Cheyenne Daily Leader*, April 18, 1891.

24. Betenson, *Butch Cassidy, My Brother*, 40.

25. *Salt Lake Tribune*, May 14, 1898. Pat Ryan said that Butch worked for him around 1890 which would have been after he left home in 1884 and had robbed the Telluride bank.

26. Betenson, "My Brother, Butch Cassidy," 23.

27. *Salt Lake Tribune*, Monday May 14, 1898.

28. *Eastern Utah Advocate*, Price, Utah, May 19, 1898; Rancher Pat Ryan made this claim in a newspaper interview with the *Salt Lake Tribune* in May of 1898 after it was thought Butch had been killed by a posse near Price, Utah.

29. Betenson, *Butch Cassidy, My Brother,* 40.

30. 1880 Census for Iron County, Utah, Panguitch Precinct, Sevier Valley. Charles Kelly interview with Joe Meeks, 1934, and correspondence with Robert Proctor on June 23, 2014.

31. *The People of the Territory of Utah v. James Marshall,* Second District Court, Beaver, Utah, December 8, 1885.

32. Letter from Jane Crook (descendant of Marshall), quoting Josie Bassett, June 10, 1998.

33. J.S. Hoy manuscript, 649-650. Also information in letter from Jane Crook to author, June 10, 1998. FamilySearch.org lists a death date of 1887 in Brown's Hole, Utah.

34. Recollections of David D. Bullock in "Our Pioneer Heritage," Vol 18, 234.

Chapter 4: Leaving Home (pages 35–39)

1. Beckstead, James H., "A War with Outlaws," 15. Jim reviewed the records in both Garfield and Piute county courthouses and found nothing to support Butch being involved in any type of grand larceny offense.

2. Pearl Baker letter dated August 23, 1973, The Larry Pointer Collection, American Heritage Center, Laramie, Wyoming. Wallace Ott of Tropic also claims that, much like Matt Warner, Butch got in a fight at a dance and thought he had killed a fellow and had to leave home as a result. He hid out near Red Canyon near Bryce Canyon and later went to Telluride.

3. Betenson, *Butch Cassidy, My Brother,* 53.

4. Betenson, *Butch Cassidy, My Brother,* 42-48.

5. Dunham, *Flaming Gorge Country,* 221.

6. *Wyoming State Journal,* May 7, 1942.

7. Conversation with Lyn Stoll in 2008. Lyn's great-grandfather George Stoll and great uncle Will Stoll homesteaded in Burntfork and knew Butch personally.

8. A copy of the petition was supplied by Jim Blake of Meeteetse, Wyoming.

9. It was rumored that Butch worked for the N Bar (Newman Brothers) near Miles City, Montana.

10. Pointer, *In Search of Butch Cassidy,* 48-49.

11. It is likely that Butch was in Brown's Park later in 1889 after the Telluride Bank Robbery. Ann Bassett was writing this history in 1952, nearly sixty years later. Ann contradicts herself as she later wrote of a lavish Thanksgiving dinner that Butch attended in Brown's Park.

12. *Colorado Magazine,* July 1952, 228-230.

13. *Colorado Magazine,* July 1952, 225.

14. Betenson, Bill, "Alias Tom Ricketts."

15. Tanner, *The Far Country,* 158-159.

16. *Rawlins Republican,* February 14, 1890; *Cheyenne Daily Sun,* February 13, 1890.

17. Baker, *The Wild Bunch at Robbers Roost,* 134-137.

262 Notes to Chapter Five

Chapter 5: TELLURIDE (PAGES 40–49)

1. Betenson, *Butch Cassidy, My Brother*, 53-54.

2. Betenson, *Butch Cassidy, My Brother*, 53-54. The Montrose jail is still standing in 2014 and is located behind Ace Hardware.

3. Warner, *The Last of the Bandit Riders*, 106.

4. Warner, *The Last of the Bandit Riders*, 106-107.

5. Warner, *The Last of the Bandit Riders*, 107.

6. Warner, *The Last of the Bandit Riders*, 105-110.

7. Warner, M. Lane, *Grass Valley, 1873-1976: A History of Antimony and Her People*, 6-8; Warner, Matt, *The Last of the Bandit Riders*, 105-110.

8. McCarty, *Tom McCarty's Own Story*, 54.

9. Rambler (Monte Morland), "The Telluride Bank Holdup," *Shenandoah Tribune* (no date), supplied by Howard E. Greager in Norwood, Colorado, Sept. 24, 1998.

10. Warner, *The Last of the Bandit Riders*, 117.

11. McCarty, *Tom McCarty's Own Story*, 28.

12. Greager, *Posey's Spurs*, 115. The nickname "Butch" could have started about this time.

13. Greager, *In the Company of Cowboys*, 36. Miller, "It All Began With Telluride." Miller says Cassidy worked for Adsit two different times, first in the summer of 1887 and the second in the spring of 1889.

14. Reyher, Ken, *High Country Cowboys*, 73.

15. *Dolores Star*, February 11, 1938. It has been written that Adsit shipped out so many cattle that Otto Mears gave him a lifetime gold and silver railroad pass valid on any of the Mears rail lines.

16. Conversations with Colin Taylor on March 7-8, 2009.

17. Greager, *In the Company of Cowboys*, 36.

18. *Dolores Star*, February 11, 1938.

19. Greager, *In the Company of Cowboys*, 36.

20. Greager, *In the Company of Cowboys*, 36.

21. *Rocky Mountain News* reported $20,750 (June 26, 1889).

22. Miller, "It All Began With Telluride."

23. McCarty, *Tom McCarty's Own Story*, 28.

24. Warner, *The Last of the Bandit Riders*, 121-122.

25. McCarty, *Tom McCarty's Own Story*, 28.

26. Tom McCarty indicated in his autobiography that one of their horses came up lame about five miles outside of town, and they traded horses with a man with a wagon as he was coming to town. He was none too happy until they paid him well.

27. *Dolores Star*, February 11, 1938.

28. Rambler (Monte Morland), "The Telluride Bank Holdup," *Shenandoah Tribune* (no date).

29. Tom McCarty told a wild story that when they reached the top of Keystone Hill they found an Indian pony, tied a dry branch to his tail, and sent him down the

trail toward the posse. The sound of the pony sounded like an army of men and sent the posse into a stampede.

30. According to Tom McCarty, the boys had to break into a miner's cabin for food and that is when they divided up the money in case they got separated.

31. Denison, *Telluride: Tales of Two Early Pioneers*, 39.

32. Miller, "It All Began With Telluride."

33. *Salt Lake Herald*, September 13, 1896.

34. Rambler (Monte Morland), "The Telluride Bank Holdup," *Shenandoah Tribune*. Howard Greager said that Rambler's real name was "Monte Morland." Interestingly Matt Warner said that relays of horses were not used, but most other sources indicate that they were indeed used and likely ensured their success. Tom McCarty indicated that "two of my partners" implying that several individuals had participated in the bank robbery, likely as relay holders, etc. Tom further says, the two partners used their share to purchase horses which they drove to Wyoming to a shipping point on the UP railroad. Then they went to some eastern state, where they sold out at a fair figure.

35. It is highly unlikely that Butch ran into his uncle Dan Gillies as Dan didn't move from Circleville to the Green River area until 1900 over ten years later. Lula even mentions Dan working at the post office in Circleville in 1890.

36. Warner, *The Last of the Bandit Riders*, 124-144.

37. Conversations with family members; and Kelly, *Outlaw Trail*, 32. Kelly mentions that a similar incident occurred between Butch and Dan. However, I doubt that this occurred, based on information from family members. Kelly said this occurred after the Telluride Bank Robbery after Dan was arrested and released. Dan was never arrested for the Telluride Bank Robbery.

38. There were two Arthur Parkers. The oldest was Maximilian's brother who was lost on the plains as a boy and later killed on his way to California. The younger Arthur was Butch's younger brother, and he died in Telluride.

39. *The Southern Utonian*, October 28, 1890; Betenson, *Butch Cassidy, My Brother*.

40. Lacy, *Last of the Bandit Riders—Revisited*. I've found no supporting documents for Lacy's claims that Arthur was involved in the robbery.

41. *Southern Utonian*, October 28, 1890.

42. Betenson, *Butch Cassidy, My Brother*, 56.

CHAPTER 6: DIXON TO RAWLINS STAGE ROBBERY (PAGES 50–59)

1. *Laramie Daily Boomerang*, December 23, 1889. The newspaper reported the stage was held up about 4 o'clock in the afternoon.

2. *Cheyenne Daily Sun*, April 18, 1891, reported the robbers wore pieces of buffalo hide for half-masks.

3. *U. S. v. William Brown and Dan Parker.*

4. *Cheyenne Daily Sun*, April 18, 1891, reported the two were told to walk one hundred yards from the stage.

5. *U.S. v. Brown and Parker.*

6. *Craig Pantograph,* April 30, 1891. Ironically, Mr. Elliot was quoted as saying after Brown and Parker were convicted, "they will now have a chance to work for Uncle Sam in the U.S. pen at Detroit, Michigan"; The *Cheyenne Daily Sun,* April 18, 1891, reported that Brown invited Elliot to come and see the fun of the robbery.

7. *U.S. v. Brown and Parker.*

8. *Cheyenne Daily Sun,* April 18, 1891.

9. *U.S. v. Brown and Parker.*

10. *Cheyenne Daily Sun,* April 18, 1891.

11. *Cheyenne Daily Leader,* Saturday, April 18, 1891. The paper reported that Coon mentioned, "one of the men was laughing all the time he and his partner were holding up the stage and seemed to think it was a great joke when he did not want them to go through his pockets." This was likely Brown as he was the one who searched the passengers. It was reported that the younger bandit was, "considerably excited and quite nervous" during the robbery.

12. *U.S. v. Brown and Parker.*

13. *U.S. v. Brown and Parker.* Three checks were recovered and used as evidence in the trial. During the trial, W.E. French from Vernal testified that he was shown several of the checks by a Mrs. Wilson in Vernal who ran a boarding house and had found them in William Brown's personal belongings.

14. *Craig Pantograph,* April 30, 1891. The *Rawlins Republican* reported that "all registered packages, of which there were eleven" were stolen, which resulted in "about $400 in currency and $500 worth of checks." In the Postal File, the postal inspector reported that "the amount of loss is not believed to be in excess of two or three hundred dollars."

15. The check was written for $30 on December 17, 1889, to D.C. Jones from N. Reader also by A. R. Reader. Check used as Exhibit B in the court case.

16. *Carbon County Journal,* December 28, 1889. The article names Allen as "Tex Allan of Savery"; *Laramie Daily Boomerang,* December 23, 1889, reported that Allen had a sack of gold amounting to $480, and he threw it into the sagebrush when the stage first stopped and later returned in the night to recover it. It was further reported Brown took the pocketbook containing $150, but handed back $25 to Allen.

17. U.S. Postal File of Daniel Parker.

18. U.S. Postal File of Daniel Parker; *Meeker Herald,* January 4, 1890; *U.S. v. Brown and Parker*; and *Laramie Daily Boomerang,* December 28, 1889. The Laramie paper reported that "Carr went as soon as possible to the scene of the robbery, but the robbers had two or three days' start and trail was pretty old."

19. *Rawlins Republican,* February 14, 1890.

20. The letter surfaced in the 1980s and is connected to the forger and murderer Mark Hofmann, calling into question its authenticity. However, it is still a very interesting letter. The original is reportedly held privately in California (Craig Fouts).

21. The 1880 Census shows a Lorenzo Watson living in Parowan, Utah. He was a polygamist with two wives and five children. On the 1900 Census, his wives and

children are shown without Lorenzo who might have been in hiding for being a polygamist or serving time in prison for cohabitation.

22. Butch's Horse Creek Ranch was nearly seventy-five miles from Lander. If the letter is authentic, then Butch was not at his ranch when he wrote it. Eighteen miles from Lander would have put him near Fort Washakie or maybe near his friend Emory Burnaugh's ranch or possibly Mail Camp.

23. If in fact, the letter is a Mark Hofmann forgery, Mark was smart to write it in pencil as it is more difficult to age verify pencil than ink.

24. Betenson, Bill, "Alias Tom Ricketts," 8.

25. U.S. Deputy Marshal Bush used many aliases himself. He is most often referred to as Joseph "Joe" R. Bush. He testified at Dan's trial as "George R. Bush." A Wyoming newspaper stated, "R. Clarke Thornhill, familiarly known as 'Joe Bush'" and another reported, "Joe Thornhill commonly known as Joe Bush."

26. *U.S. v. Brown and Parker*. Bush testified that Dan corrected him during the arrest saying the marshal didn't want him for horse theft, but for robbing a stage.

27. *U.S. v. Brown and Parker*.

28. U.S. Postal File. In the "Report of Arrest for Dan Parker," the date of the arrest was initially written as Sept. 4, 1890, but was later crossed out and replaced with August 28, 1890.

29. *Salt Lake Tribune*, October 7, 1890.

30. *Cheyenne Daily Leader*, April 18, 1891.

31. Dan Parker Pardon File. The *Denver News*, September 26, 1890, confirms Annie's statement about Dan being held in Salt Lake City. Wyoming's statehood seemed to complicate the prosecution of Dan. The paper said Dan was incarcerated in Salt Lake City because of Wyoming's transition to statehood: "there are no officials in Wyoming to prosecute the robber." This was later worked out, and he was transferred to Wyoming. A telegram in the postal file says Dan is: "In custody at Salt Lake Utah US Atty and marshal of Wyoming claim atty General has construed the law that they are not officers advise me what to do prisoner cannot be held in Utah must be examined in Wyoming cannot have Examination without Marshal and Attn."

32. Frye, "Butch Cassidy At The Pen," July 13, 2007.

33. Dan Parker's Wyoming Penitentiary records; The *Cheyenne Daily Sun* April 7, 1891, indicated that Parker and Brown were held in the Laramie County Jail (Cheyenne).

34. *U.S. v. Brown and Parker*; U.S. Postal File.

35. *Laramie Daily Boomerang*, December 28, 1889.

36. *Laramie Daily Boomerang*, January 22, 1891. The paper reported that Brown was wanted for other crimes committed in Arizona and New Mexico; *Lander Clipper*, February 11, 1891, reported that an accomplice of Brown's, McGee, stated that Brown admitted that besides robbing a stage he had also robbed and burned a store. Brown and his accomplice plotted to rob the Lander stage until they were frightened off. They had also planned systematic raids of horses in the area. The postal file also confirms these claims by McGee. McGee further claimed that Brown also bragged about a recent killing of a man in Colorado. Also, Brown must have given

a bad impression at his trial because the prosecutor later wrote that Brown, "was a man whose character was that of a desperado, and I can very well understand how a young man of Parker's age could commit a crime of this character while in the companionship of Brown, which by himself would ordinarily not have been committed." The postal file also mentions that the postal officials thought "Brown was the leader of the gang of desperadoes who held up and robbed, of $6,000, paymaster Wham of the U.S. Army in Arizona."

37. *Cheyenne Daily Leader*, April 19, 1891.

38. *U.S. v. Brown and Parker*, Postal File.

39. *Laramie Daily Boomerang*, January 22, 1891.

40. *U.S. v. Brown and Parker*.

41. Dan Parker's Wyoming Penitentiary File.

42. *Cheyenne Daily Sun*, April 10, 1891.

43. *Cheyenne Daily Sun*, April 15, 1891.

44. *U.S. v. Brown and Parker*. Fowler later became Attorney General for Wyoming. Van Devanter later became an Associate Justice of the U.S. Supreme Court.

45. *Cheyenne Daily Sun*, April 18, 1891, gives a full listing of the jury. Reportedly there were two W.A. Richards in Cheyenne at this time.

46. An interesting note in the postal file states, "Carr has a recent letter from Bush who repeats his former statements as to being able to 'produce' the witnesses to identify 'Parker.'"

47. Dan Parker Pardon File; *Cheyenne Daily Leader*, September 22, 1891. Joe Bush received $1000 for the capture of Dan Parker from Jeff Carr on behalf of Chief Post Office Inspector J.D. King. The postal file also confirms that Bush received the $1,000. This is interesting because, even though he took credit for Dan's arrest, there is evidence that shows Bush didn't actually capture Dan.

48. Dan Parker Pardon File.

49. *Cheyenne Daily Sun*, April 18, 1891.

50. *U.S. v. Brown and Parker*.

51. Dan Parker Pardon File.

52. Also in the Postal File, Fred Elliot, who was the freighter during the robbery and later became Deputy Marshal at Craig and Hayden, failed to identify Parker, but claimed he could identify Brown.

53. *U.S. v. Brown and Parker*.

54. *Cheyenne Daily Leader*, April 18, 1891.

55. *Cheyenne Daily Leader*, April 19, 1891.

56. *Meeker Herald*, April 26, 1890, and May 3, 1890. The articles describe a daring daylight robbery "and the operators are supposed to be the same parties who successfully held up the Rawlins stage. They rode up on horses, hitched them out front, one bandit covered the clerk with a rifle while the other relieved the cash drawer of $800. They escaped before an alarm could be given." Another article ran a week

later about the robbery and mentioned the discovery of an outlaw cave on Vermillion Creek near Brown's Park where numerous stolen articles were found.

57. J.S. Hoy unpublished manuscript, 220-222. Hoy said that Dan later visited Vernal and reported that Brown and Potter were "wrangling over an affair of honor among thieves." Potter was never seen again after that and it was supposed that he was killed by Brown and his body thrown into the Green River.

58. *Cheyenne Daily Leader*, April 19, 1891; *The Southern Utonian*, April 28, 1891.

59. *Southern Utonian*, April 28, 1891.

60. *Cheyenne Daily Sun*, April 19, 1891.

61. Dan Parker Pardon File; *Newcastle Journal*, May 1, 1891.

62. *U.S. v. Brown and Parker*.

63. *Cheyenne Daily Leader*, April 19, 1891.

64. Dan Parker Pardon File.

65. *U.S. v. Brown and Parker*.

66. Letter from Elnora Frye, February 28, 1995. Elnora further states, "The prison in Laramie had always been a federal institution, until that precise year. At the time they (Brown and Parker) were brought to trial in the federal court at Cheyenne, in April, 1891, the penitentiary was in the process of being transferred to the state of Wyoming, the state officials taking full charge of it on July 1. Because of that, the United States Marshal on orders from the Department of Justice, were to send the prisoners to the Detroit House of Corrections.

67. *U.S. v. Brown and Parker*.

68. *Rawlins Daily Journal*, October 1, 1891. Bush received $1,000 even though he did not capture Dan.

69. *Cheyenne Sun*, November 20, 1891.

Chapter 7: Wyoming Years (pages 60–69)

1. McCarty, *Tom McCarty's Own Story*, 29.

2. Betenson, *Butch Cassidy, My Brother*, 68.

3. The *Colorado Magazine*, July 1952, 228-230.

4. McClure, *The Bassett Women*, 57.

5. The *Worland Grit* refers to George Parker formerly of Owl Creek, Wyoming, indicating that Butch had also used the name Parker. March 3, 1910.

6. Betenson, *Butch Cassidy, My Brother*, 69.

7. Burton, *Mystery in History*, 87.

8. Information from the Rock Springs City Museum and the Schnauber family. I met with the grandchildren of Otto Schnauber in 2004 and they indicated that Butch had worked for their grandfather. They said that Butch had visited their grandfather in the early 1930s in Rock Springs. Otto also ran his own meat market, "Sweetwater Provision and Supply," on K Street in 1898. Some say this is where Butch worked.

9. Burton, *Mystery in History*, 105.

10. Burton, *Mystery in History*, 7.

11. Burton, *Mystery in History*, 7.

12. Warner, *Last of the Bandit Riders*, 109-110.

13. Betenson, *Butch Cassidy, My Brother*, 69.

14. After Butch's release from prison in 1896, he became known as "Butch" Cassidy in newspaper reports of his crimes.

15. Betenson, *Butch Cassidy, My Brother*, 74.

16. Conduit, Thelma Gatchell, *Annals of Wyoming*, April 1962.

17. Information supplied by Colin Taylor via e-mail on January 26, 2009.

18. Conversations with Colin Taylor and review of the homestead application. Karen Kithas, the current ranch owner, provided a copy of the original homestead application. Also a letter from Bill Jones dated March 8, 1976, confirms "Brown Parker" was no relation to Butch Cassidy. Brown Parker was described as "a remittance man from the east. He was a Harvard or Yale man, but delighted in being ungrammatical and a bit crude."

19. Condit, Thelma Gatchell, *Annals of Wyoming*, April 1957.

20. Allison, *Dubois Area History*, F49; Tax Records, Fremont County. Some argue that Butch never owned a ranch near Dubois, however, tax records indicate otherwise. The strongest case that Butch and Hainer owned land outside of Dubois on Horse Creek is the 1890 delinquent tax records for Cassidy and Hainer. According to the *Wyoming State Journal*, April 12, 1892, Hainer and Cassidy came to the area about two years earlier with a "considerable amount of money" and fine horses. They established a ranch on Horse Creek and spent their money freely, going through "ten thousand dollars" the first year.

21. Letter from Judge Jesse Knight to Governor Richards, dated September 28, 1895.

22. Bechdolt, *Tales of the Old-Timers*, 308; Allison, *Dubois Area History*, F49; Cassidy and Hainer moved into a cabin constructed by Hughie Yeoman and Charlie Peterson.

23. Allison, *Dubois Area History*, T53.

24. Will Simpson letter to Harry Logue, February 4, 1937. American Heritage Center, Laramie, Wyoming.

25. Pointer, *In Search of Butch Cassidy*, 57.

26. Allison, *Dubois Area History*, F49. Allison indicates that Amoretti purchased the ranch in 1900. Fremont County tax assessment roll indicate the ranch and improvements were sold to E. Amoretti, Jr., in 1890 (courtesy of Tom Bell, Lander). However delinquent tax records for 1894–1895 show they owned the land past 1890. Researchers Mike Bell and Pat Schroeder concluded the two only stayed in a cabin which was located on the Jack Wiggin's Rocking Chair ranch, south of the EA Ranch.

27. *Rock Springs Rocket*, October 25, 1929.

28. Betenson, *Butch Cassidy, My Brother*, 70. This was confirmed by Preston's friend, Finley P. Gridley, manager of a UP Coal mine in Rock Springs, in Kelly's, *Outlaw Trail*,

237. Patterson, Richard, "Douglas Preston: Butch Cassidy's Lawyer. *WOLA Journal*, Spring 1999.

29. Allison, *Dubois Area History*, F49.

30. Allison, *Dubois Area History*, F49.

31. Bechdolt, *Tales of the Old-Timers*, 309.

32. Allison, *Dubois Area History*, F147.

33. The Embar Ranch was originally started by J.K. Moore. Jakey Fork was named after J.K. Moore.

34. *Cheyenne Daily Leader*, January 20, 1883. The Embar Cattle Ranch was originally founded by James K. Moore in 1878. Moore sold the ranch to Captain Torrey in 1881. The *Laramie Boomerang*, March 10, 1892 explains the formation of the new company under J.L. Torrey. Also Bell, "Butch Cassidy's Big Horn Basin Bunch." Jay L. Torrey obtained the title "judge" from his days as a lawyer in Missouri and later was called "Colonel" from his time in the military.

35. *Natrona Tribune*, August 10, 1893. Joe moved back to Nebraska after he was released from prison and got married and raised a family. The 1910 Census shows him married with five children living in Holt County, Nebraska.

36. Allison, Mary, *Dubois Area History*, F49.

37. Letter dated July 25, 1954, from Harvey J. Shoe to Miss Homsher, Wyoming State Archives.

38. *New York Times*, April 29, 1898.

39. Dullenty, "Farm Boy," 6. *Fremont Clipper*, January 27, 1893. Fremont County Jail Records shows they were received on January 26 and released two days later.

40. Case Number 166, *State of Wyoming v. George Cassidy and Albert Hainer*, Third District Court, Fremont County, Lander, Wyoming.

41. Conversation with Larry Pointer on August 11, 2007.

42. *Wyoming State Journal*, Lander, October 24, 1961.

43. *Wyoming State Journal*, Lander, October 24, 1961.

44. Pointer, Larry, *In Search of Butch Cassidy*, 58.

45. Information from Larry Pointer on March 18, 2010.

46. Betenson, *Butch Cassidy, My Brother*, 87.

47. Pointer, Larry, *In Search of Butch Cassidy*, 58-59.

48. Bell, "Butch Cassidy's Big Horn Basin Bunch."

49. *Fremont Clipper*, October 4, 1895.

50. Don Cooper wrote in an e-mail on May 17, 2009, "Rose Williams moved to Arland in approximately 1886 and built a very nice cabin and started a house of ill repute. Rose was well known as a madame in Lander prior to this and she recruited a few of the finer ladies of the evening and set up a real nice respite for the local cowhands and travelers on the Billings–Lander Stage road. When Meeteetse was established, Rose moved her "house" out of Arland and down the creek to a point just north of the new town and operated out of there for a while later." In May

1887, Al Durant's wife was working for madam Rose Williams in Arland which led to a gunfight in which Durant was killed by a man named Meakin who had been with Durant's wife. Durant had threatened Rose also.

51. Christian Heiden interview with Jack Plane on December 25, 1937, in the Labor Broadcast, from Kelly's, *Outlaw Trail*, 54-55.

52. Greene, A.F.C. "Butch Cassidy in Fremont County."

53. *Lander Clipper,* August 15, 1890; *Wyoming State Journal,* April 6, 1950.

54. Betenson, *Butch Cassidy, My Brother*; National Register of Historic Places, Quien Sabe Ranch.

CHAPTER 8: ARRESTS AND TRIALS (PAGES 70–83)

1. Leonard Short owned Mail Camp until 1891; Henry Holland owned it in 1894. See *Fremont Clipper* September 7, 1894.

2. Case Number 144, *Wyoming v. Cassidy and Hainer.* Researcher Pat Schroeder of Wyoming says that Billy Nutcher was a friend and partner to Butch. Schroeder and Mike Bell believe the sale of the horses occurred at the Blondie/Pardee Ranch and then Butch went to Mail Camp to have the horses re-shod.

3. Case Number 144, *Wyoming v. Cassidy and Hainer.*

4. Case Number 144, *Wyoming v. Cassidy and Hainer.*

5. Otto Franc's full name was Count Otto Franc von Lichtenstein, and he was a member of a German royal family. He and his brothers first came to New York and were made wealthy from the banana importing business. There were reports that when Butch got out of prison Otto Franc had him blacklisted. He also accused Butch of stealing fifty of his horses. One report indicates Butch drove a herd of Franc's horses to Brown's Park for his friends.

6. "Cusack Relates Tales of Early Pioneer Days" *Wyoming Newspaper*, February 5, 1937. According to Franc's diaries he became JP in the late 1890s and was likely not JP when he filed the charges against Butch. He likely did this because he was a friend of Richard Ashworth's and a concerned large rancher attempting to rid the area of settlers and "rustlers." John D. McCullough was also Justice of the Peace in Fremont County at this time.

7. Case Number 144, *Wyoming v. Cassidy and Hainer*; Betenson, *Butch Cassidy, My Brother*, 91; Larry Pointer stated it occurred in late August 1892.

8. *Helena Independent*, August 11, 1889.

9. Platts, *The Cunningham Ranch Incident of 1892.*

10. Chapman owned the Two Dot ranch which is located north of present day Cody, Wyoming. According to Colin Taylor, Chapman raised horses north of Cody on Chapman Bench (named for him) and further north. Eventually, Chapman was influential around Red Lodge, Montana, in the banking business. He completed the sale of his ranch in 1903.

11. Platts, Doris B., *The Cunningham Ranch Incident of 1892*, 24-119.

12. Case Number 144, *Wyoming v. Cassidy and Hainer*; Betenson, *Butch Cassidy, My Brother*, 91; Larry Pointer states it occurred in late August of 1892.

13. Pointer, *In Search of Butch Cassidy*, 72.

14. *Wyoming State Journal*, March 25, 1937, and November 10, 1938.

15. Putnam, *History of Auburn, Wyoming;* (interview with) Pearl Sreed, June 10, 1948. The history indicates that Cassidy and Hainer were passing through the valley and were caught in a snowstorm and forced to spend the winter. The Lander cut-off did pass through Auburn. Tom McCarty married Auburn resident Sally (Sara) Lehmberg.

16. Hugh Morgan may have been Matt Warner's father-in-law. There is disagreement over whether Rosa's last name was Rumel or Morgan. *Star Valley and its Communities* (p. 104) states that McCarty married Sara Lehmberg and Warner married Rose Morgan.

17. *Star Valley and its Communities*, Chapter 8; *History of Auburn* by Ila Wilkes states that the outlaws were caught in a snowstorm and forced to spend the winter in Auburn. George Davis had plenty of hay that year and fed their horses.

18. Will Simpson has Cassidy and Hainer being captured on Ham's Fork, but if this is the case why would they have been brought to Auburn when several larger towns (such as Kemmerer or Evanston) were closer, and the county jail was in Evanston?

19. Some writers have mistakenly said that Auburn was located in Lincoln County and Deputy Sheriff Bob Calverly was outside his jurisdiction. Lincoln County was established in 1911. Uinta County was one of the five original counties in Wyoming, established in 1869.

20. Otto Franc journal, Dec. 26, 1891.

21. *Livingston Enterprise*, January 23, 1892.

22. *Red Lodge Picket*, January 30, 1892. Brothers Andrew and Henry Chapman were no relation to John Chapman until they later became brothers-in-law.

23. *Idaho Falls Times*, February 4, 1892.

24. Platts, Doris B., *The Cunningham Ranch Incident of 1892*, 64; In Case Number 144, it stated that John W. Chapman trailed the stolen horses to Uinta County; Putnam, "History of Auburn, Wyoming"; The *Daily Independent*, April 25, 1892, named posse participants as W.J. Anderson of Helena, Sim Roberts of Big Timber, and Albert Cook of Melville, MT. The newspaper account indicated that the two bandits had stolen seven head of horses from the Greybull Cattle Company and a stallion from Thomas Kent in Montana and then fled to Wyoming. The horses were reported as recovered after the capture. Platts names the posse as Calverly, Chapman, Cook, Anderson, Roberts and two others whom she guesses may have been Dave Stewart and Speed Stagner. Stagner, who lived in the Mail Camp area, knew Cassidy, and his daughter dated Cassidy and later married Cassidy's friend Emory Burnaugh.

25. Platts, Doris B., *The Cunningham Ranch Incident of 1892*, 52-54.

26. Calverly was originally from Missouri and had been orphaned at age ten. He made his way to Texas and got into cattle and horse herding. He had traveled extensively through Texas, Montana, Indian Territory, Arizona, New Mexico and Nebraska. He had hunted Buffalo in Montana for two years and then moved to Fort Bridger, Wyoming, where he was in charge of the cattle ranch for Judge Carter. He later

worked at the asylum in Evanston and then as city marshal of Evanston. He was chosen as deputy sheriff under Ward due to his strict and able service as marshal; Hamblin, *"Bridger Valley A Guide to the Past,"* 183-184.

27. Some accounts report Sheriff John Ward and Deputy Bob Calverly located and arrested Cassidy and Hainer. Court records mention Calverly and Chapman. A group led by Chapman was in the area and killed two rustlers at the Cunningham ranch less than two weeks later. Some reports say Davis's daughter Kate helped the posse locate the outlaws, but there is no record that Davis had a daughter named Kate.

28. *Wyoming State Tribune*, June 16, 1939; *Wyoming State Tribune*, April 12, 1892, states that Hainer and Cassidy were arrested on April 8. 1892.

29. George Davis had built the post office and store and later sold it to H. H. Harrison.

30. It was also reported that Butch asked to see a warrant for his arrest. The officers responded that they did not need a warrant to arrest him.

31. *Salt Lake Herald,* September 13, 1896; *Wyoming State Tribune*, June 16, 1939.

32. *Fremont Clipper*, April 15, 1892.

33. *Daily Independent*, April 25, 1892.

34. Letter from Will Simpson to Charles Kelly, dated May 5, 1939.

35. According to Will Simpson, Bob Calverly hit Butch over the head with his Colt .45 (Letter to Charles Kelly from Will Simpson, May 5, 1939).

36. Putnam, *History of Auburn, Wyoming.*

37. *Daily Independent*, April 25, 1892.

38. Taylor, "The Birth of the Horseback Outlaw."

39. *Fremont Clipper*, April 22, 1892.

40. *Fremont Clipper*, May 22, 1892, 2. The settlers met together on May 13, 1892, and George Sliney was elected chairman with committee members being Ed Cusack, Benj. Hanson, M. Brown, J.D. McCulloch, and S.D. Close.

41. *The Daily Independent*, April 25, 1892; *Billings Gazette*, April 21, 1892.

42. Putnam, *History of Auburn, Wyoming;* interview with Pearl Sreed, June 10, 1948; reportedly Butch and Hainer later returned to Auburn for their possessions and told the townspeople of the trials.

43. Jail Record of Uinta County, Wyoming; Kennington, *A History of Star Valley*, 105-107.

44. Jail Record of Uinta County, Wyoming; Platts, *The Cunningham Ranch Incident of 1892*, 90; Fremont County Jail Register indicates that John Bliss later escaped jail in Lander after being transferred there; On page 64, Platts indicates that Jack Bliss had stolen 150 horses from Speed Stagner. Bliss was later killed by his former partner Slick Nard.

45. Fremont County, Wyoming Jail Register ("Register for Sheriff 1884-1933").

46. Bell, "Butch Cassidy's Big Horn Basin Bunch," 12; *The Fremont Clipper*, November 16, 1894, and *Noble & Lane v. W.H. Nutcher.*

47. Bell, "The Friends and Enemies of the Notorious Nutcher Brothers."

48. *Wyoming Newspaper*, Feb. 5, 1937, "Cusack Relates Tales of Early Pioneer Days"; Fremont County Justice of the Peace Record Book.

49. Conversation with Pat Schroeder.

50. Larry Pointer Collection, American Heritage Center, University of Wyoming.

51. *Fremont Clipper*, June 23, 1893.

52. Betenson, *Butch Cassidy, My Brother*, 92.

53. Bell, "Butch Cassidy's Big Horn Basin Bunch."

54. Fremont County Justice of the Peace Record Book; Jakie Snyder filed charges against Noble and Lane on January 9, 1894, and Cassidy acted as surety. Snyder later dropped the charges.

55. Bell, "Butch Cassidy's Big Horn Basin Bunch."

56. Simpson's witnesses included David Stewart, Otto Franc, John Chapman, David Blanchard, James Thomas, Richard Ashworth, Frank McNally, Henry Sherard, Robert Calverly, Charles Green, George Dause, and Rouch who was the clerk at the Indian Agency. Preston's four witnesses included E.C. Burnaugh, Jack Price, Eli Signor, and James Heeman.

57. In A.F.C. Green's manuscript on Butch Cassidy, he tells of a story that Butch's defense team planned to present a phony bill of sale signed by a known horse dealer from Nebraska, but he was brought in by the prosecution at the last minute. This is also retold in Bechdolt, *Tales of the Old-Timers*.

58. The *Cheyenne Daily Leader* August 8, 1894, reported that Al Hainer and prisoner Frank Bryant "assaulted and terribly beat" fellow prisoner Joe Baldwin, using a board and a chair, while in the county jail in Lander. Apparently a prostitute, Devonia Durant, supplied whiskey to the men who were drunk during the beating. Hainer reportedly also horsewhipped an Indian who had testified against him.

59. Kelly, Charles, *The Outlaw Trail*, 58-59.

60. Kelly, Charles, *The Outlaw Trail*, 58.

61. *Saratoga Sun,* November 14, 1895. Warrants were issued and Hainer was arrested in Thermopolis while Snyder was arrested in Johnson County. The preliminary examination was waived, and they were held on $500 bonds each which they failed to meet. They were then brought to Lander; Fremont County Justice of the Peace Record Book.

62. Fremont County, Wyoming Jail Register ("Register for Sheriff 1884-1933").

63. Lacy, "Revealing Letter of Outlaw Butch Cassidy" *Old West*, Winter 1984.

64. *Wyoming Derrick*, Casper, Wyoming, January 25, 1900.

65. *The Wyoming State Journal*, May 7, 1942.

66. *The Worland Grit*, November 25, 1909.

67. Fremont County, Wyoming Jail Register (Register for Sheriff 1884-1933).

68. Researcher James O. Miller indicated that Judge Knight told Butch that if he was to be retried he would be given a stiffer sentence.

69. Judge Jesse Knight, Judge Third Judicial District of Wyoming, letter to Governor Wm. A. Richards, September 28, 1895.

CHAPTER 9: BIG HOUSE ACROSS THE RIVER (PAGES 84–92)

1. Green, "Butch Cassidy in Fremont County"; Patterson, "Why Didn't Butch Run"; Bechdolt, *Tales of the Old-Timers.*

2. The *Laramie Boomerang,* July 19, 1894, reported six prisoners traveled with Cassidy. They named Frank Bryant as the sixth, but prison records do not show him listed. Bryant had been sentenced to three years for assault with intent to commit murder. Wheaton had an eight-year sentence for manslaughter; Gilchrist and Nicols had three-year sentences for horse stealing. Charley Brown was in for three years for horse stealing (He was reportedly a friend of Butch's from Dubois.); Winkle had a two year sentence for killing Otto Franc's bull to feed his starving family.

3. *Laramie Boomerang,* July 19, 1894. Harry Logue said he and Charlie Stough took Cassidy to the pen (*Wyoming State Journal,* January 28, 1938). It is possible Stough used both Boedeker and Logue as deputies to help transport the six prisoners.

4. Pointer interview with Hank Boedeker, Jr., Dubois, Wyoming, March 14, 1973.

5. Pointer interview with Elmer Stagner, August 12, 1972.

6. *Laramie Boomerang,* July 19, 1894.

7. Huett, "'Butch Cassidy slept here', the Wyoming State Penitentiary could boast."

8. Frye, "Butch Cassidy At the Pen."

9. Stoner, "My Father was a Train Robber."

10. McInnes, "With the Instinct of the Natural Detective: The Story of Slick Nard."

11. Frye, *Atlas of Wyoming Outlaws at the Territorial Penitentiary*; "Butch Cassidy at the Pen," July 13, 2007.

12. *Fremont Clipper,* November 1, 1895.

13. Letter to the Editor, from Elnora Frye, *WOLA Journal,* Spring-Summer 1991.

14. Frye, "Butch Cassidy at the Pen."

15. Frye, *Atlas of Wyoming Outlaws at the Territorial Penitentiary,* 158.

16. John Dwight Woodruff served as a Wyoming state senator. He was the original settler and owner of the Embar ranch in 1871. Later he sold out to Jay L. Torrey's brother, R.A. Torrey. Judge J.L. Torrey purchased the Embar from his brother in 1882. Woodruff brought the first cattle into Owl Creek in 1879 (Walker, *Stories of Early Days in Wyoming*).

17. Judge Jesse Knight, Judge Third Judicial District of Wyoming, letter to Governor Wm. A. Richards, September 28, 1895.

18. Judge Jesse Knight, Judge Third Judicial District of Wyoming, letter to Governor Wm A. Richards, September 28, 1895.

19. *Wyoming State Journal,* Lander, Wyoming, date unknown.

20. Frye, "Butch Cassidy at the Pen."

21. The *Wyoming Tribune* on January 21, 1896, reported that "George Cassidy" had been granted a pardon the previous day by the governor after serving time for horse stealing. The paper indicated that he had six months left on his sentence. The petition signed by leading citizens including the judge who had overseen his case was mentioned along with Cassidy's plans to return to Lander for business.

22. Governor Richards letter to Hon. J.L. Torrey, Washington D. C., March 16, 1896.

23. Frye, "Butch Cassidy at the Pen." Frye names the prisoner as Thomas Morrison.

24. Frye, "Butch Cassidy at the Pen."

CHAPTER 10: DETROIT HOUSE OF CORRECTIONS (PAGES 93–98)

1. Betenson, Bill, "Alias Tom Ricketts."

2. *Superintendent's Report 33, Annual Report of the Officers of the Detroit House of Correction to the Common Council of the City of Detroit for the year 1894*, 8, 30.

3. William Brown's medical records from the St. Elizabeth's Hospital of the Insane.

4. Betenson, Bill, "Alias Tom Ricketts."

5. Dan Parker Pardon file.

6. Dan Parker Pardon file.

7. Dan Parker Pardon file.

8. Dan Parker Pardon file.

9. Dan Parker Pardon file.

10. Dan Parker Pardon file.

11. Dan Parker Pardon file.

12. Dan Parker Pardon file.

13. Dan Parker Pardon file.

14. *The Standard*, Ogden, Utah, September 6, 1901.

CHAPTER 11: MONTPELIER BANK ROBBERY (PAGES 99–106)

1. Lander, Wyoming newspaper, July 24, 1896.

2. Pointer, *In Search of Butch Cassidy*, 97-98. Pointer indicates in *Bandit Invincible* that someone swore out a warrant for Butch upon his release from prison for stealing fifty horses some five years previous.

3. Warner, *Last of the Bandit Riders*, 296.

4. Murdock, *The Educated Outlaw*, 9.

5. Conflicting accounts are told of the gunfight. Matt recounts that he was ambushed, but other sources indicate the two men who were shot were in a tent with one sleeping when the outlaws appeared at their camp. Bell, "Campfire Shootout."

6. Original Arrest Warrant is owned by Brent Ashworth. The document shows Matt Warner, William Wall, and E.B. Coleman as being charged with first degree murder on May 26, 1896.

7. Warner, *Last of the Bandit Riders*, 303.

8. Kelly, *Outlaw Trail*; Skovil, "A Sheriff Outsmarts the Wild Bunch," 57.

9. Warner, *Last of the Bandit Riders*, 304-305.

10. Warner, *Last of the Bandit Riders*, 306. Bob Swift was the go-between for Cassidy and Warner: *Salt Lake Herald*, September 13, 1896.

11. DeJournette, *One Hundred Years of Brown's Park and Diamond Mountain*, 274.

12. Warner, *Last of the Bandit Riders*, 162. *Salt Lake Herald*, Sept. 10 and 13, 1896.

13. Wilde, *Treasured Tidbits of Time*, 224.

14. Lester, *From Rags to Riches*, 48; Tippets, *Piedmont Uinta County, Wyoming Ghost Town*; *Salt Lake Herald*, Sept. 14, 1896.

15. Patterson, "Douglas Preston: Butch Cassidy's Lawyer."

16. Kelly, *The Outlaw Trail*, 95.

17. Trial deposition, *State of Idaho v. Henry Meeks, George Cassidy, John Doe, whose real name is unknown*.

18. Newspapers of the time indicated attorney Douglas Preston was paid directly from the Montpelier bank loot. Jack Meeks indicated that they met Douglas Preston near Rock Springs to pay him for Matt's defense.

19. Rose Warner suffered from cancer in her leg that eventually took her life.

20. Lacy, *Last of the Bandit Riders...Revisited*, 119.

21. *Salt Lake Herald*, September 9, 1896.

22. *Salt Lake Herald*, September 9, 1896; *Ogden Standard Examiner*, September 10, 1896; Lester, *From Rags to Riches*, 48-49.

23. Letter to J.H. Ward, Sheriff, from Heber M. Wells, April 21, 1898.

24. Siringo, *A Cowboy Detective*, 347.

25. *Salt Lake Tribune*, September 18, 1896.

26. Trial deposition, *State of Idaho v. Henry Meeks, George Cassidy, John Doe, whose real name is unknown*; *Salt Lake Herald, June 17, 1897*.

27. Hayden, "Butch Cassidy and the Great Montpelier Bank Robbery," 6; Interview with Jack Meeks in 2003. According to the Meeks family, there was no justice in Bub's sentence. He was given thirty-five years for holding horses, and Matt Warner was given five years for killing two people.

28. Betenson, "Bub Meeks."

29. *Laramie Weekly Boomerang*, June 24, 1897.

30. *Wyoming State Journal*, October 24, 1961. The article further stated that she never saw Cassidy again, which was likely not true because the Burnaugh family claimed they hid Butch and a least four others after the Wilcox train robbery in 1899.

31. The *Vernal Express* indicated the visit was in August 1896.

32. The 1880 Census shows Allen and Matilda Davis having four children at the time. Maude was born in 1875.

33. Crouse and Overholt were partners at the time. Crouse had built a home behind the saloon. He later sold out to Overholt and moved back to Brown's Park.

34. Burton, "Sheriff John Theodore Pope," 8-9.

35. McClure, *The Bassett Women*, 58-60.

36. *Salt Lake Tribune*, January 21, 1897.

CHAPTER 12: CASTLE GATE ROBBERY (PAGES 107–116)

1. *Green River Journal*, July 21, 1955. Pearl Baker said "they had a nice camp, with tents in the Upper Pasture of Horseshoe. There were a couple of women in the camp and one of them was Lay's wife."

2. Baker, *The Wild Bunch At Robbers Roost*, 216.

3. Pearl Baker names Etta as being there in the later edition (1971) of her book, *Wild Bunch at Robbers Roost*, 173. Baker mentions other possibilities as Sadie Moran, Rose Maguire, or Nancy Ingalls.

4. Frandsen, "The Castle Gate Payroll Robbery."

5. Murdock, *The Educated Outlaw*, 28.

6. Warner, *Last of the Bandit Riders*, 140-141.

7. Murdock, *The Educated Outlaw*, 28.

8. *Salt Lake Tribune*, April 22, 1897.

9. Stewart, *Tales From Indian Country*, 177.

10. Jackson, *Butch Cassidy, Matt Warner and the Unknown Outlaw*, 124.

11. E-mail conversation with Joel Frandsen on July 25, 2007.

12. Stewart, *Tales From Indian Country*, 223.

13. Frandsen, "The Castle Gate Payroll Robbery."

14. E-mail conversation with Joel Frandsen on July 25, 2007.

15. Charles Kelly calls the Dutchman "Neibauer." Joel Frandsen refers to him as "Heibaurer."

16. Stewart, *Tales From Indian Country*, 177; Frandsen, "The Castle Gate Payroll Robbery."

17. Joel Frandsen's presentation on the Castle Gate Payroll Robbery at the WOLA convention in Cheyenne, Wyoming on July 14, 2007.

18. Joel Frandsen's presentation on July 14, 2007.

19. *Eastern Utah Advocate*, April 22, 1897.

20. Frandsen, Joel, "The Castle Gate Payroll Robbery."

21. The newspaper accounts agree that one bag of gold held $7,000, but differ on the rest. The local paper, the *Eastern Utah Advocate,* reported four sacks (one with $7,000 in gold, two sacks of silver—one with $1,000 and one with $860—and a fourth sack containing a $1,000 in rolls and checks). The *Salt Lake Tribune* reported three sacks (one with $7,000 in gold, one with $1,000 in gold, and a third with $800 of silver).

22. *Eastern Utah Advocate*, April 22, 1897.

23. Kelly, *The Outlaw Trail*, 136.

24. Frandsen, Joel, "The Castle Gate Payroll Robbery."

25. *The Salt Lake Tribune*, April 22, 1897.

26. Stewart, *Tales From Indian Country*, 181.

27. *The Utah Journal*, April 24, 1897.

28. Jackson, *Butch Cassidy, Matt Warner and the Unknown Outlaw*, 132; Stewart, *Tales from Indian Country*, indicates that the loot was taken by Walker to his cabin up Green River at the mouth of Chandler Canyon and then to Brown's Park where it was divided.

29. Frandsen, "The Castle Gate Payroll Robbery."

30. Conversations with Butch and Jeanie Jensen on August 27, 2010. Jeanie Jensen is the great granddaughter of Jim McPherson. The Jensens run the Tavaputs Ranch near McPherson's original Florence Creek Ranch in the Book Cliffs.

31. Frandsen, "The Castle Gate Payroll Robbery"; according to Harvey Murdock they covered their horses' feet with leather to deter tracking.

32. Frandsen, "The Castle Gate Payroll Robbery."

33. According to Harvey Murdock, Butch and Elzy had split at this point, with Butch going to Robbers Roost and Lay going to Torrey.

34. Kelly, *The Outlaw Trail*, 139.

35. *Eastern Utah Advocate*, April 22, 1897.

36. *Eastern Utah Advocate*, April 22, 1897.

37. *Eastern Utah Advocate*, April 22, 1897.

38. *Salt Lake Tribune*, March 16, 1898.

39. *Eastern Utah Advocate*, April 29, 1897.

40. *Eastern Utah Advocate*, May 6, 1897.

41. *Salt Lake Tribune*, May 24, 1897.

42. Pointer, *In Search of Butch Cassidy*, 121.

43. Interview with Zane Hilman on October 13, 2009, in Sheridan, Wyoming.

44. According to Zane Hilman, his dad, Fred, was born in 1884.

45. Interview with Zane Hilman on October 13, 2009.

46. *Rawlins Republican*, July 18, 1897.

47. *Rawlins Republican*, July 30, 1897, and *Wyoming Press*, August 7, 1897.

48. Pointer, *In Search of Butch Cassidy*, 130.

49. Kelly, *The Outlaw Trail*, 160. Kelly also tells of a mock trial prosecuting an attending local doctor that was done for fun. Butch supposedly acted as the prosecuting attorney while Lay was the defense attorney.

50. Hilman said the gun was burned up in a house fire, but he kept the metal remains.

51. Interview with Zane Hilman on October 13, 2009.

CHAPTER 13: WS RANCH AND WILCOX TRAIN ROBBERY (PAGES 117–129)

1. *Salt Lake Tribune*, March 16, 1898; *Eastern Utah Advocate*, March 10, 1898.

2. *American Eagle Newspaper*, April 16, 1898; *Davis County Clipper*, April 15, 1898.

3. *Deseret News*, June 29, 1900; The *Wyoming Daily Press*, May 5, 1898, indicated that Idaho had joined the conference of governors. The papers stated Butch had five hundred men at his disposal. The image of Butch that accompanied the article looked nothing like Butch. It further claimed Butch had killed a rival when he had tried to bushwhack him on an earlier occasion.

4. Sheriff William Preece letter to Utah Governor Heber M. Wells, April 3, 1898, Utah.

5. *American Eagle Newspaper*, May 8, 1897.

6. It was stated Joe Walker was killed on Friday the 13th by a posse of thirteen men who had chased them for thirteen days.

7. Frandsen, "The Burial of Joe Walker and Butch Cassidy."

8. Some reports called him John Herron.

9. *Salt Lake Tribune*, May 14, 1898.

10. Bristow, "A Rude Awakening."

11. *Salt Lake Tribune*, June 5, 1898. The letter is suspect as it is signed "Butch Casity" and there are misspellings throughout. Other known letters from Butch show he signed his named consistently as "Cassidy" and that his spelling was acceptable.

12. *Wyoming Press*, August 13, 1898.

13. Butch and Elzy could have gone south sometime earlier, after the Castle Gate robbery. French has them arriving much later, however, French's dates are almost always in question. The *Sheridan Post,* April 28, 1898, reported that Butch was in New Mexico at this time. Author Jeffrey Burton says it was "Some time in the autumn of 1898" in his article "Suddenly in a Secluded and Rugged Place...." *In Deadliest Outlaws*, p. 152, he states they "arrived in the Southwest, along the Arizona/New Mexico border lands in November or December, 1898, as best can be determined."

14. Burton, *The Deadliest Outlaws*, 143-144.

15. Murdock, *The Educated Outlaw*, 36.

16. Siringo, *A Cowboy Detective*, 379.

17. Burton, *The Deadliest Outlaws*, 143-144.

18. Burton, *The Deadliest Outlaws*, 143.

19. French, *Recollections of a Western Ranchman*, 258.

20. French, *Recollections of a Western Ranchman*, 258-259.

21. French, *Recollections of a Western Ranchman*, 259.

22. French, *Recollections of a Western Ranchman*, 260.

23. *Salt Lake Tribune*, June 3, 1899.

24. Taylor, "Wilcox."

25. *Salt Lake Tribune*, June 3, 1899.

26. The *Salt Lake Tribune* reported four men jumped aboard.

27. *Salt Lake Tribune*, June 3, 1899. The Tribune reported that the bandits broke the seal to the mail car with dynamite when the clerks refused to open up.

28. *Salt Lake Tribune*, June 3, 1899.

29. Researched by Ed Wren of Rawlins, Wyoming. This is also confirmed by Kelly in *The Outlaw Trail*, 241, and by Finley P. Gridley, manager of the U.P. Coal mines in Rock Springs, who both say it was no coincidence that Preston was a passenger that night.

30. *Salt Lake Tribune*, June 3, 1899. Another report within the same paper said that no one was allowed to go back until they finally let a brakeman go back to warn the train to stop before the damaged bridge.

31. *Salt Lake Tribune*, June 3, 1899, described a piece of gunny sack over the face of the leader as a disguise; Jim Miller says that they wore white napkin bandannas from a Harvey House restaurant.

32. Taylor, "Wilcox."

33. Taylor, "Wilcox"; *Salt Lake Tribune*.

34. *Salt Lake Tribune*, June 3, 1899.

35. *Salt Lake Tribune*, June 3, 1899.

36. Ernst, "The Wilcox Train Robbery."

37. *Salt Lake Tribune*, June 3, 1899.

38. *The Wyoming Derrick*, June 8, 1899; the Roberts brothers were Harvey Logan and Harry Longabaugh.

39. Information from Larry Pointer, March 18, 2010.

40. *Salt Lake Tribune*, June 3, 1899.

41. Taylor, "Wilcox," 4-5.

42. Taylor, "Wilcox," 5.

43. Jones's testimony at Bob Lee's trial, Kindred, "The Wilcox Robbery: Who Did It?"

44. *Sun-Leader*, June 10, 1899; Kindred, "The Wilcox Robbery: Who Did It?"

45. Ernst, "The Wilcox Train Robbery."

46. *Salt Lake Tribune*, June 3, 1899.

47. Kindred, "The Wilcox Robbery: Who Did It?"

48. Kelly, *The Outlaw Trail*, 246.

49. Bechdolt, *Tales of the Old-Timers*, 330.

50. Pointer, *In Search of Butch Cassidy*, 153-154.

51. Headstone information for Lonie Logan, Kansas City, Missouri.

52. Kindred, "The Wilcox Robbery: Who Did It?"

53. Based on thoughts from Colin Taylor from his research on Kid Curry.

54. Kelly, *The Outlaw Trail*, 247-248; *Deseret News*, December 12, 1948; Ekker, "Charlie Gibbons."

55. Miller, "Did Butch Cassidy Plan the Wilcox Train Robbery."

CHAPTER 14: FOLSOM TRAIN ROBBERY (PAGES 130–137)

1. French said sometime in the fall, "Mac" quit the ranch to French's disappointment as he had taken a liking to him. However, if it was in the fall, it would have been after the Folsom robbery. French was often wrong with his timeframe and dates.

2. Burton, *The Deadliest Outlaws*, 144.

3. Alexander, *Lawmen, Outlaws and S.O.B.s*, Volume II, 86; Burton, *The Deadliest Outlaws*, 154. Most historians believe it was Will Carver, however historian Colin Taylor makes a convincing case that G.W. Franks was George West Musgrave.

4. I visited the Turkey Creek site with officials from the Philmont Boy Scout Ranch in 2009.

5. Burton, *The Deadliest Outlaws*, 158.

6. According to Harvey Lay Murdock, the posse was made up of nine or ten men. Their names included Wilson "Memphis" Elliot, Ed Farr, W.H. Reno, James H. Morgan, Henry M. Love, Perfecto Cordoba, Serna and Frank Smith. Harvey said

that Creighton Foraker was not physically present, although he was in charge of the posse. Stanley, *No Tears For Black Jack Ketchum*, 53.

7. Tanner, *New Mexico Prisoner #1348*. Other reports indicate that he died (Murdock, *The Educated Outlaw*, 40, 44).

8. Burton, *The Deadliest Outlaws*, 169. The ranch was owned by Henry Lambert, but occupied by Ed McBride and his wife. The building where Sam hid is still standing (2009) and used as a gift shop on a private resort.

9. Tanner, *New Mexico Prisoner #1348*; Murdock, *The Educated Outlaw*, 38, 51. Lay was shot twice; bullets entering and exiting created four holes. The prison record indicated he had a "bullet wound through top left shoulder, bullet marks on both loins, small scar on top of head."

10. Tanner, *New Mexico Prisoner #1348*. His correct height was measured at 5 foot, 9½ inches once he was in prison.

11. Tanner, *New Mexico Prisoner #1348*.

12. Burton, *The Deadliest Outlaws*, 190.

13. Siringo, *A Cowboy Detective*, 371.

14. Murdock, *The Educated Outlaw*, 49.

15. *Penitentiary Record Book of Convicts*, November 2, 1884 to April 4, 1904, 90; Murdock, *The Educated Outlaw*, 51.

16. Burton, *The Deadliest Outlaws*, 246. It is somewhat curious that the Pinkertons would send Frank Murray to the field to investigate. He was second in command at the Denver office and known to be in bad health.

17. French, *Recollections of a Western Ranchman*, 270-272.

18. Information from Larry Pointer, March 18, 2010. Another of the rodeo troupe, William Connell, was said to have met with Butch Cassidy in Argentina and the two traded pistols.

19. Burton, *The Deadliest Outlaws*, 238.

20. French, *Recollections of a Western Ranchman*, 273.

21. Burton, *The Deadliest Outlaws*, 238-239.

22. Burton, *The Deadliest Outlaws*, 246-7.

23. Siringo, *A Cowboy Detective*, 356.

24. French, *Recollections of a Western Ranchman*, 275.

25. Burton, *The Deadliest Outlaws*, 247. Arizona newspapers named the outlaws as Bill Smith, Bob Johnson, Wilson alias Smith, Kid Carver, and one unknown man.

26. Apache County Jail records in possession of the Sheriff's Office in St. Johns, Arizona.

27. *St. Johns Herald*, March 31, 1900; Burton, *The Deadliest Outlaws*, 249.

28. Apache County Jail Records, St. Johns, Arizona.

29. French, *Recollections of a Western Ranchman*, 276-277.

30. Apache County Jail Records, St. John's, Arizona.

31. Burton, *The Deadliest Outlaws*, 262.

32. Siringo, *A Cowboy Detective*, 367.

33. Murdock, *The Educated Outlaw*, 48-49.

34. Murdock, *The Educated Outlaw*, 60-61.

35. Murdock, *The Educated Outlaw*, 56-57.

36. Alexander, Lawmen, *Outlaws and S.O.B.s. Volume II*, 86; Tanner, *New Mexico Prisoner #1348*. Some reports give Elzy's release date as January 10, 1906. According to Tanners, Elzy was actually released on December 15, 1905, because of his work on the scenic road project between Santa Fe and Las Vegas which further reduced his sentence. It was also rumored that Butch gave attorney Douglas Preston $6,000 to spread around and help reduce Elzy's sentence; Murdock, *The Educated Outlaw*, 52. This clearly shows he was released on Dec. 15, 1905.

37. Murdock, *The Educated Outlaw*, 58-59. Harvey said Lay had carried the mail and payroll between the prison and town as part of his duties, showing his intentions of being a good citizen.

38. Tanner, *New Mexico Prisoner #1348*. The Tanners refer to a 1955 interview of Lewis Jones and John Allred.

39. Harvey Murdock says that Elzy actually buried the $70,000 booty near the Mexican border before he was captured.

40. Murdock, *The Educated Outlaw*, 65-66.

41. Murdock, *The Educated Outlaw*, 62-83.

CHAPTER 15: AMNESTY TALES (PAGES 138–141)

1. Warner, *Last of the Bandit Riders*, 320.

2. Governor Wells Correspondence. Utah State Archives and Utah State History, Salt Lake City, Utah.

3. Ernst, "The Montpelier Bank Robbery."

4. *Deseret Evening News*, June 29, 1900.

5. *Salt Lake Herald*, June 30, 1900; *Salt Lake Tribune*, June 30, 1900; *Salt Lake Tribune*, July 1, 1900.

6. *Salt Lake Herald*, June 30, 1900; *Salt Lake Tribune*, June 30, 1900; *Salt Lake Tribune*, July 1, 1900.

7. *Salt Lake Herald*, July 7, 1900.

8. *Deseret Evening News*, June 8, 1900; *Ogden Standard Examiner*, June 12, 1900.

9. *Salt Lake Herald*, June 1, 1900.

10. *Salt Lake Herald*, May 31, 1900 and June 4, 1900.

11. *Salt Lake Herald*, June 4, 1900.

12. *Salt Lake Herald*, June 4, 1900.

13. *Salt Lake Herald*, June 8, 1900.

14. Utah State Archives; also Wyoming Governor Richards Correspondence Letter, dated May 30, 1900 from W. S. Seavy, Denver Colorado. According to Richard Patterson, Seavey was an experienced lawman and had served eight years as the Chief of the Omaha Police Department and likely was reliable.

15. Lacy, "Revealing Letter of Outlaw Butch Cassidy". There is some question to the authenticity of this note.

CHAPTER 16: TIPTON TRAIN ROBBERY (PAGES 142–148)

1. Information from the Charter family, Jack Stroud, August 2008.

2. *Laramie Weekly Boomerang*, July 26, 1900.

3. Jack Ryan lived in Rawlins, Wyoming, at the time. Charlie Siringo, when he was undercover, became friends with Ryan and obtained information on Butch and the gang.

4. Jack Ryan later told Joker O'Melia, an Union Pacific Engineer, of this.

5. Information from the Charter family and research conducted by Colin Taylor in 2008.

6. Pinkerton Files, letter by J.H. Schumacher on the history of William Cruzan, File on William Cruzan. Also Harry Longabaugh file.

7. The Cruzan Rogues' Gallery and Siringo, *Cowboy Detective*.

8. Ernst, *Jack Ryan, Wild Bunch Friend or Pinkerton Informant?*

9. Pinkerton files; Siringo, *Cowboy Detective*; information from Jack Stroud.

10. Siringo, *Cowboy Detective*, 361.

11. *Salt Lake Herald*, August 30, 1900.

12. *Rawlins Republican*, September 1, 1900; Taylor, "Tipton Robbery."

13. *Rawlins Republican*, September 1, 1900.

14. The "through safe" was the safe that was going "through" to the final destination of the train. The expressman did not have the combination for the through safe. The other safe had contents to be delivered at local points and was usually referred to as the "local safe." The expressman had the combination to the local safe.

15. *Salt Lake Herald*, August 30, 1900.

16. *The Deseret News*, August 30, 1900.

17. E-mail from Colin Taylor, March 8, 2009, based on conversations with Jack Stroud. Stroud's grandfather remembered the forth outlaw as being called Billie.

18. *Rawlins Republican*, September 5, 1900.

19. Siringo, *Cowboy Detective*, 361; Pinkerton Files letter by Schumacher. It also mentions that Harvey Logan picked William Cruzan to replace Longabaugh who had gone to Nevada. Colin Taylor also confirmed the location of Ferguson's ranch, December 1, 2008.

20. Pinkerton Files, notes on James Ferguson.

21. Information supplied by Jack Stroud who is a grandson of Kid Charter.

22. *Rawlins Republican*, September 5, 1900.

23. *Rawlins Republican*, September 1, 1900.

24. Information from Jack Stroud, August 2008.

25. *Rawlins Republican*, December 12, 1900.

CHAPTER 17: WINNEMUCCA BANK ROBBERY (PAGES 149–160)

1. *Anaconda Standard*, July 10, 1910. Six days later, the *Salt Lake Telegram* also picked up the story and ran it (*Salt Lake Telegram*, July 16, 1910). The same basic article ran nearly two years later in the Buenos Aires newspaper, the *Standard*, April

17, 1912. There are numerous mistakes in the article calling into question its validity. One example is the spelling of Sundance's name as "Lonbagh" and "Lonbauch." The accompanying sketch of Sundance is actually Ben Kilpatrick. Further it confuses Carver as "Flatnose George" who was dead by 1900.

2. *Standard* (Buenos Aires), April 17, 1912; Bell, *Interview with the Sundance Kid*.

3. Discussions with Philip Homan 2013-2014; U.S. Census 1870 San Saba County, TX; Burton, *The Deadliest Outlaws*. Philip Homan, "Letter to the Editor," *WWHA Journal*, Dec. 2013; Ancestry.com, Kim Brackett.

4. *Anaconda Standard*, July 10, 1910. It is questionable that they would have sent Sundance ahead to do something that could easily have been done upon their arrival. The Buenos Aires version actually states that the Powder Springs hideout was in Nevada which is incorrect as it is located in Wyoming near the Colorado border. Discussions with Philip Homan, 2013-2014.

5. Homan, "The Sundance Kid Didn't Do It," *WWHA Journal, Oct. 2013;* U.S. Census 1900, Owyhee County, Idaho; Discussions with Philip Homan. The outlaws likely got horses from the Shoe Sole ranch in Rock Creek and could have also gotten horses from the Wilkins Ranch near Bruneau, ID.

6. *The Elmore Bulletin,* Sept. 6, 1900; Homan, "The Sundance Kid Didn't Do It"; Discussions with Philip Homan.

7. Discussions with Philip Homan, 2013-2014.

8. Brackett, *Chet's Reflections*; Discussions with Philip Homan, 2013-2014.

9. Homan, "The Sundance Kid Didn't Do It," 64; Homan, "Queen of Diamonds: Kittie Wilkins, Horse Queen of Idaho, and the Wilkins Horse Company" (presentation, WWHA Roundup, 2013).

10. Homan, "Powder Face: The Horse that Robbed the Winnemucca Bank" (presentation, WWHA Roundup, 2013). Discussions with Philip Homan, 2013-2014.

11. Vic Button, letter to Pearl Baker, Nov. 21, 1970; Kelly, *The Outlaw Trail*; Reynolds, "The Winnemucca Bank Robbery."

12. Button, "Butch Cassidy Gave Getaway Horse to 10-Year-Old." Button, recorded interview on May 26, 1974.

13. Kirby, "Lee Case Remembers The Great Winnemucca Raid."

14. Pinkerton Files, Criminal File on Butch Cassidy.

15. W. S. "Shorty" Johnson, the horse buyer, stood out as he was over seven feet tall and skinny as a rail.

16. *Silver State* newspaper, Sept. 19, 1900.

17. George S. Nixon founded the First National Bank of Winnemucca in 1886.

18. George S. Nixon letter to Mr. F.C. Gentach, Gen'l Supt., The Pacific Express Company, December 9, 1900.

19. *The Silver State*, Sept 19, 1900.

20. The leader may also have been Will Carver as he was described later by young Lee Case as being only 5 feet 7 inches tall, while the others were both described as being 5 feet 9 inches tall which more closely describes Butch and Sundance. This may explain why Nixon had a difficult time identifying the leader as Butch Cassidy.

21. Small hands was a known trait of Butch Cassidy. He was able to remove his hand-cuffs during his arrest in Wyoming in 1892 because of his small hands. His sister Lula also spoke of his "small gentleman hands" which was a common trait in the Parker family.

22. George S. Nixon letter to Mr. F.C. Gentach.

23. *Silver State*, Sept 19, 1900; George S. Nixon letter to Mr. F.C. Gentach.

24. *Silver State*, Sept 19, 1900; (Buenos Aires) *Standard*, April 17, 1912. According to Sundance's supposed version, both he and Butch dismounted and scooped up the gold, but had to leave five or six thousand in the street.

25. Reynolds, "The Winnemucca Bank Robbery," 96.

26. George S. Nixon letter to Mr. F.C. Gentach.

27. Today (2012) the Silve Ranch is known as the Petit Ranch.

28. *Silver State*, Sept 19, 1900.

29. Reynolds, "The Winnemucca Bank Robbery," 93-94.

30. *Silver State*, September 19 and 20, 1900, indicated the Winnemucca posse included an Indian tracker, while Reynolds, "The Winnemucca Bank Robbery," indicates the Golconda posse included two Indians.

31. *Silver State*, September 19 and 20, 1900.

32. Reynolds, "The Winnemucca Bank Robbery," 94.

33. *Silver Star*, September 20, 1900.

34. Vic Button letter to Pearl Baker, November 21, 1970. "Shorty" was the nickname of W.S. Johnson, the horse buyer in the bank when it was robbed; Kirby, "Lee Case Remembers the Great Winnemucca Raid."

35. Button, "Butch Cassidy Gave Getaway Horse to 10-Year-Old."

36. Hanks, *A Long Dust On The Desert*.

37. Reynolds, "The Winnemucca Bank Robbery," 95.

38. *Nevada News*, September 24, 1900; Discussions with Philip Homan, 2013-2014.

39. *Nevada News*, September 27, 1900.

40. Reynolds, "The Winnemucca Bank Robbery," 95.

41. *Silver Star*, September 20, 1900.

42. George S. Nixon letter to Mr. F.C. Gentach.

43. *The Deseret News*, September 20, 1900

44. Letter dated December 29, 1900, from Frank Murray to Hadsell; Ernst, "The Wilcox Train Robbery."

45. George S. Nixon letter to Mr. J.G. Fraser.

46. *Silver State*, Sept 19, 1900. Again, there is a chance that Will Carver was the one who held up Nixon with the knife. Some believe it was Jim Duncan.

47. The gun is now on display at the Little Snake River Valley Museum in Savery, Wyoming.

48. Gooldy, "Early Day History of Little Snake River Valley."

49. Ernst, *Will Carver, The Lovesick Outlaw*.

50. George S. Nixon letter to Fraser, February 21, 1901; *Laramie Semi Weekly Boomerang,* November 7, 1910, has a letter indicating that Tom Horn was working on the trail of the Winnemucca bank robbers. Apparently Horn and Nixon met and discussed the case.

51. Ernst, "George S. Nixon."

CHAPTER 18: FORT WORTH (PAGES 161–167)

1. Information from Jack Stroud in 2008. His great uncle Bert Charter and grandfather Kid Charter were present at the Brown's Park meeting.

2. Pinkerton Records, December. 5, 1901, from the Bob McCubbin Collection. According to the Pinkerton interview of Lillie May Hunt, she had met Carver and Logan at Fanny Porter's in San Antonio in October during the fair. She left with the two and Harvey's companion Maud Rogers (aka Annie Rogers or Maud Walker) and went to Maddox Flats in Fort Worth for five days, then to Houston for two days, and then back to Fort Worth. They also visited Denver and Shoshone, Idaho. Lillie Hunt (Callie Hunt/Lillie Davis) told the Pinkertons that she did not marry Will Carver for love, but to clear her name at home.

3. Ernst, "Will Carver, The Lovesick Outlaw"; Ernst, *Harvey Logan: Wildest of the Wild Bunch,* 43.

4. Pinkerton Records, December 5, 1901, Bob McCubbin Collection. Fanny described Harry as five feet ten inches tall and weighing 170 pounds, about thirty-five years old and dark complected.

5. Fort Worth 1899–1900 Directory. The directory shows seven Cassidys and three Cassidays listed.

6. Selcer, *Hell's Half Acre,* 255.

7. Selcer, *Hell's Half Acre,* 257.

8. Selcer, *Hell's Half Acre,* 256.

9. Selcer, "Last Word on the Famous Wild Bunch Photo," *Wild West,* December 2011.

10. Ernst, "Will Carver, The Lovesick Outlaw."

11. Selcer, "Last Word on the Famous Wild Bunch Photo."

12. Selcer, *Hell's Half Acre,* 260.

13. Selcer, "Last Word on the Famous Wild Bunch Photo."

14. Selcer, *Hell's Half Acre,* 256.

15. Butch Cassidy Letter to Matilda Davis, Aug. 2, 1902.

16. Selcer, "Last Word on the Famous Wild Bunch Photo."

17. Selcer, "Last Word on the Famous Wild Bunch Photo."

18. The date of first wanted poster was May 15, 1901. Ernst, *Harvey Logan: Wildest of the Wild Bunch,* 44-45.

19. Selcer, *Hell's Half Acre,* 263.

20. Although Spence identified the dead body in Glenwood Springs, Colorado, as the bandit Harvey Logan, the body was still buried without a name and controversy remains today on the final demise of Harvey Logan.

21. Vic Button recalled Butch, "sent more than one picture, as I remember one with an Indian also." These other photos have not surfaced. I.V. Button letter to Pearl Baker, December 28, 1970.

22. Selcer, *Hell's Half Acre*, 262; I.V. Button letter to Pearl Baker, December 28, 1970.

23. Ernst, *Harvey Logan: Wildest of the Wild Bunch*, 43; Annie Rogers used other aliases such as Maud Walker and Maud Rogers; Pinkerton report Dec. 5, 1901, from the Bob McCubbin Collection indicates that her real name was Boulah Phinburg.

24. Pinkerton Records on Winnemucca robbery, Dec. 4, 1901, from the Bob McCubbin Collection.

CHAPTER 19: NEW YORK CITY (PAGES 168–171)

1. Some historians refer to Etta Place as "Ethel" since she signed a hotel register as "Ethel Place," however, her real name remains unconfirmed.

2. Pinkerton Files, memo July 29, 1902; Kelly, *The Outlaw Trail*, 288; Pointer;, *In Search of Butch Cassidy*, 196; Kirby, *The Rise and Fall of the Sundance Kid*, 88.

3. Ernst, *Sundance, My Uncle*, 157-158.

4. Ernst, *Sundance, My Uncle*, 159.

5. Pinkerton Files, memo July 29, 1902.

6. Pinkerton Files, Harry Longabaugh Criminal File and J. McPharland, notes November 7, 1901, Denver, Colorado.

7. Pinkerton Files, letter from William A. Pinkerton to Robert A. Pinkerton, July 31, 1902; Pointer, *In Search of Butch Cassidy*, 195.

8. Pinkerton Files; Kelly, *The Outlaw Trail*, 288. Some confusion exists as to the location of the photograph as the Pinkertons had copies made and mounted on Bliss Bros., Buffalo, New York, cardstock.

9. Pinkerton Files, memo July 29, 1902.

10. Pinkerton Files.

11. Murphy, "When the Horn Silver Mine Crashed."

12. The Parker family received word that Butch had been involved in the train robbery on the Great Northern Railroad near Malta, Montana, July 3, 1901.

13. Pinkerton Files, memo July 29, 1902; Pointer, *In Search of Butch Cassidy*, 196.

14. Pinkerton Files, Butch Cassidy Criminal File.

15. Siringo, *A Cowboy Detective*, 370.

16. Siringo, *A Cowboy Detective*, 373.

CHAPTER 20: ARGENTINA (PAGES 172–188)

1. Pinkerton Files. It appears the trio were stowaways on the *Herminius*, a British cargo ship. However no ship or passenger record has been found.

2. Pinkerton Files; Kelly, *The Outlaw Trail*, 288.

3. Gavirati, *Buscados en la Patagonia*. Kirby, "Butch, Sundance, Etta Place Frolick in 'Fun City.'"

4. Pinkerton Files; Aguirre, *La Pandilla Salvaje.*

5. Pinkerton Files. The Pinkertons described the deposit as "Bank of England notes"; Gavirati, *Buscados en la Patagonia*, 55; Buck and Meadows, "Butch and Sundance Slept Here," 14; Kelly, *Outlaw Trail*, 288.

6. Gavirati, *Buscados en la Patagonia*, 56; Buck and Meadows, "Butch and Sundance Slept Here," 14.

7. Aguirre, *La Pandilla Salvaje.*

8. Aguirre, *La Pandilla Salvaje. National Geographic* magazine had run articles on the area in three issues: Nov. 1897, Feb. 1900 and Jan. 1901.

9. Unsigned and undated note. Pinkerton Files.

10. Aguirre, *La Pandilla Salvaje.*

11. Aguirre, *La Pandilla Salvaje.* Gardner was enamored by Etta and was later a frequent visitor.

12. Gavirati, "Back at the Ranch."

13. In 2007, I enjoyed fly fishing the Rio Blanco just yards from Butch's cabin.

14. Conversations with Raul Cea's daughter in Feb. 2007; Gavirati, *Buscados en la Patagonia*, 206.

15. Aguirre, *La Pandilla Salvaje.*

16. The immigrant was Primo Caprera who visited in 1904. Buck and Meadows, "Wild Bunch Dream Girl." Etta Place was reported to know the Spanish language much better than Butch or Sundance.

17. Gavirati, *Buscados en la Patagonia.* Information from Jose Cea.

18. Gavirati, "Back at the Ranch" and *Buscados en la Patagonia.*

19. Gavirati, *Buscados en la Patagonia.*

20. This same "JR" brand was used back in the Big Horn Basin in Wyoming by Englishman J. R. Kirby who sold cattle to Colonel J.L. Torrey who owned the Embar Cattle Ranch and was a nemeses of Cassidy (Burroughs, "Guardian of the Grassland," 150).

21. Information from Regi Hammond, Esquel, Argentina, and the museum located near Leleque, Argentina.

22. Gavirati, *Buscados en la Patagonia.*

23. Memo Dated July 29, 1902, Pinkerton Files; Ernst, "Wild Bunch Immigration Records."

24. Pinkerton Notes from the Bob McCubbin Collection.

25. Ernst, "Wild Bunch Immigration Records" spells the ship, "Hofiorhis." The Pinkertons had spelled it, "Harorius." Kirby spells it "Honorius."

26. Dimaio Notes, Pinkerton Files; Ernst, *Sundance, My Uncle*, 165-173.

27. Pinkerton Records.

28. Information from Regi Hammond, February 2007. Regi indicated they had settled on "625 hectors of government land" equaling about 1,500 acres. Pinkerton records indicate that Butch and Sundance were squatters and never owned the land. However, the mayor of Cholila said they had obtained proof that the trio were the

only owners of "titled" land in the valley. This was confirmed by the Cholila Valley cultural historian in Feb. 2007.

29. Gavirati, *Buscados en la Patagonia*.

30. Gavirati, "Back at the Ranch."

31. Gavirati, "Back at the Ranch" states that David Moore was a local boy, however he is a North American according to Gavirati's book, *Buscados en la Patagonia* and Larry Pointer's, "Rio Gallegos Revisited."

32. Buck and Meadows, "Neighbors on the Hot Seat."

33. The two men were likely Dan Gibbon's son, Mansel Gibbons and a Chilean, Wenceslao Solis (Gavirati).

34. The original letter is located at the Utah State Historical Society. It was donated by Harvey Murdock (grandson of Elzy Lay) in his mother's name (Marvel Murdock) in the 1970s.

35. Betenson, *Butch Cassidy, My Brother,* 162.

36. Dimaio Notes with George Newbery, Pinkerton Records.

37. *Wyoming Press*, November 29, 1902. The article indicated that Butch was living on a ranch in Idaho.

38. *Deseret News*, February 9, 1903, and *Salt Lake Herald*, February 10, 1903.

39. Conversations with Regi Hammond and local neighbors in February 2007.

40. Gavirati, *Buscados en la Patagonia*.

41. Gavirati, *Buscados en la Patagonia*. H.A. Place signed as a witness on November 1, 1901.

42. Gavirati, *Buscados en la Patagonia*.

43. 1911-1914 Argentine Police Report; Buck and Meadows, "Leaving Cholila" and "Neighbors on the Hot Seat."

44. Meadows, Anne, *Digging Up Butch and Sundance*, 9.

45. In Chapman's *Elks Magazine* April 1930 article on Butch Cassidy, he indicates that Butch told Seibert that "a former deputy sheriff from one of the Western states had located in the same region, and started ranching. He recognized Cassidy and Longabaugh, and no doubt with the intention of collecting the large rewards that were offered for their capture, informed the authorities."

46. Letter dated Feb. 14, 1903 from Robert A. Pinkerton to H.G. Burt of the Union Pacific Railroad, Pinkerton Files.

47. Dimaio Notes, Pinkerton Files.

48. Dimaio Notes, Appendix "A," Pinkerton Files.

49. Aguirre *La Pandilla Salvaje Butch Cassidy en la Patagonia*

50. Pinkerton Records from the Bob McCubbin collection.

51. Dimaio Notes, Appendix "A," Pinkerton Files.

52. The wanted poster was shown to me by a descendant of a former policeman and was actually offered to me as a gift. The wanted poster remains in Trevelin and can be seen on display at the tea shop.

53. Gavirati, *Buscados en la Patagonia*.

54. Letter dated July 1, 1903, from Robert A. Pinkerton to Francis J. Beasley, Chief of Police, Buenos Aires. Pinkerton Files.

55. Buck and Meadows, "Leaving Cholila."

56. Handwritten letter from J.P. Ryan to Dan Gibbons, Feb. 29, 1904, in Patagonia Police file. Buck and Meadows, "Leaving Cholila."

57. Buck and Meadows, "Leaving Cholila."

58. Gavirati, *Buscados en la Patagonia*.

59. Gavirati, *Buscados en la Patagonia* and "Back at the Ranch." According to Gavirati, the Cholila old timer recalled Sundance had played his guitar while the governor danced with Etta. However a newspaper reported Sundance was away and the governor played the guitar while Butch danced with a neighbor's daughter. Aguirre, *La Pandilla Salvaje*.

60. Gavirati, *Buscados en la Patagonia*.

61. E-mail from Marcelo Gavirati to author on Feb. 10, 2009.

62. Gavirati, "Back at the Ranch" and Larry Pointer, March 3, 2010. Aguirre, *La Pandilla Salvaje*. Wenceslao Solis testified that he had seen Grice in the home of Ryan and Place in Cholila.

63. Gavirati, *Buscados en la Patagonia*.

64. Pointer, Larry, "Birds of a Feather: Will Flock Together," 2010. "A Maze of Entanglements" and Larry Pointer, March 3, 2010. Pointer states, "There is serious question as to whether the bandit Robert Evans who appeared on the scene in 1907, after the departure of Ryan and Place was in fact the same man earlier called Emilio or Emil Hood."

65. Gavirati, *Buscados en la Patagonia*. Another report indicates that Sundance and Etta may have made another trip to the U.S., this time they visited the World's Fair in St Louis, but returned by late 1904, Gavirati, "Back at the Ranch"; Ernst, "Wild Bunch Immigration Records," Ernst indicates that the Pinkerton agents received reports that Sundance and Etta were in Fort Worth. The Longabaugh family also received an unsigned postcard from the St. Louis World's Fair that they believe came from Sundance.

66. Buck and Meadows, "Leaving Cholila."

CHAPTER 21: RIO GALLEGOS ROBBERY (PAGES 189–195)

1. Pointer, Larry, "Rio Gallegos Revisited" and "George West Musgrave." Pointer writes, "the leader [was] Brady, a loquacious hale-fellow-well-met. He was a North American, white but suntanned, somewhat husky, with a dark moustache, and no other remarkable features that stood out. The reticent Linden was his associate. He was tall and thin, with a skinny face, and his upper lip moved to reveal his teeth when he talked. Linden was of a ruddy complexion, and he wore a moustache, although a small one." The booty was reported to be $20,000 national money and 280 pounds sterling (Gavirati).

2. Aguirre, *La Pandilla Salvaje*. Relays of fresh horses were successfully used in the

outlaws' escape and the telegraph lines were cut. It is possible that Butch may have helped plan the robbery.

3. Gavirati, Marcello, *Buscados en la Patagonia* and Larry Pointer, "Rio Gallegos Revisited," 2010.

4. Buck and Meadows, "Leaving Cholila." Argentina Police file from 1911-1914 investigation conducted by Chubut Police Chief Leandro Navarro and Judge Luis Navarro Careaga.

5. Pointer, Larry, "Rio Gallegos Revisited."

6. Pointer, Larry, "Birds of a Feather: Will Flock Together."

7. Pointer, Larry, "Brady vs Musgrave"

8. Pointer, Larry, "Birds of a Feather: Will Flock Together." Wenceslao Solis who worked for Sundance in 1902, stated it had been seven years since he (Grice) had been in the house of Place and Ryan in Cholila (this according to author Osvaldo Aguirre).

9. Public records from Ancestry.com (Montana Death Index, 1900 U.S. Census, and New York Passenger lists). After 1917 better records were kept and show a Herbert Grice traveling twice in 1926 between Buenos Aires, Argentina, and New York City.

10. Aguirre, *La Pandilla Salvaje*, Chapter 6, "Brady and Linden."

11. Pointer, Larry, "Birds of a Feather: Will Flock Together" and correspondence March 24, 2010.

12. Gavirati, "Buscados en la Patagonia" and Larry Pointer, March 3, 2010.

13. Gavirati, "Back at the Ranch." *True West* (December 2002). One report indicates that they were gone by April 1 (Gavirati). A hideout was found east of Lake Cholila (Cea).

14. Conversations with Regi Hammond and local neighbors in February 2007. Regi also repeated a family story that while his grandparents were staying at Butch's ranch their dog dug up a human hand which was thought to be from a dead official. Also Aguirre, Chapter 6, indicates Butch and Sundance had taken horses from Jorge (George) Hammond.

15. Handwritten letter from J.P. Ryan to Richard Clarke, April 19, 1905, in Patagonia Police file. Buck and Meadows, "Leaving Cholila."

16. Buck and Meadows, "Leaving Cholila"; "Neighbors in the Hot Seat" states the value of the sale was 18,000 pesos. Italic text indicates that the company said they could only pay 18,000 pesos. Gavirati indicates that they went to Chile to negotiate directly with Thomas T. Austin representing the company.

17. Handwritten letter from J.P. Ryan to John C. Perry, May 1, 1905, in Patagonia Police file. Buck and Meadows, "Leaving Cholila."

18. Buck and Meadows, "Leaving Cholila"; "Neighbors on the Hot Seat."

19. Information from Regi Hammond in February 2007.

20. Buck and Meadows, "Leaving Cholila"; "Neighbors on the Hot Seat.'

21. Buck and Meadows, "Leaving Cholila." In a letter from H.A. Place to Dan Gibbons in Patagonia Police file. The original is lost, however, the Spanish translation was in the police file. Buck translated to English.

22. Gavirati, Marcello, *Buscados en la Patagonia.*

23. Ernst, "Ethel Place" and "Wild Bunch Immigration Records."

24. Buck and Meadows, "The Last Days of Butch and Sundance."

CHAPTER 22: BACK TO A LIFE OF CRIME (PAGES 196–205)

1. Later reports indicated that the four bandits were Butch, Sundance, and Etta and another unknown male. Arthur Chapman names the unknown fourth man as "Dey" from the United States (*Elks Magazine,* April 1930, 33) The Pinkertons suspected that the fourth man was Harvey Logan alias Kid Curry. Larry Pointer explains, "It was in later news stories, after the Pinkerton posters and photos had been distributed by Buenos Aires authorities following the robbery that testimonies surfaced from people who believed they had seen the robbers, either prior to the robbery, or along their supposed escape route. It was among these stories that versions of the presence of a woman came forward." One report even indicated that the three, Butch, Sundance, and Etta had been drinking whiskey moments before robbing the bank. Buck and Meadows in "What the Wild Bunch Did in South America" and the *Buenos Aires Herald*, December 20, 1905, gives the amount as 14,000 pesos.

2. Gavirati, *Buscadoes en la Patagonia.*

3. Buck and Meadows, "A Maze of Entanglements" and Gavirati, *Buscadoes en la Patagonia.* The newspaper reported one had given his name as Harry Longabaugh and had stayed twice in Rosario. Another James Ryan was known as a buyer of mules.

4. Gavirati, *Buscadoes en la Patagonia* and Larry Pointer, March 3, 2010. The posse included the chief, a sheriff, and four agents.

5. Larry Pointer e-mail, March 24, 2010, based on Osvaldo Aguirre's book.

6. Chapman, "'Butch' Cassidy," 33.

7. Buck and Meadows, "Merry Christmas from the Pinkertons." The newspaper *La Nacion* mistakenly identified Sundance as James Ryan and Cassidy as Harry Longbough.

8. Larry Pointer letter, March 18, 2010.

9. Gavirati, *Buscadoes en la Patagonia* and Aguirre, *La Pandilla Salvaje Butch Cassidy En La Patagonia.*

10. Larry Pointer e-mail, March 30, 2010. Hwa was described by Gavirati as knowing how to ride a horse and handle fire arms with precision; however, it is hard to believe that this behavior was ever demonstrated while being detained. Likely this was borrowed from the Pinkerton description of Etta Place.

11. *New York Herald*, September 23, 1906; *Salt Lake Herald* and *Ogden Standard Examiner* September 27, 1906, "Butch' Cassidy Alive Again," referencing the *New York Herald,* Sept 23, 1906, article.

12. Pinkerton files and e-mail from Dan Buck, February 13, 2009.

13. *New York Herald*, September 23, 1906.

14. Some reports have 1906 in the 1911-1914 Argentina Police File

15. Buck and Meadows, "Leaving Cholila" and "Neighbors on the Hot Seat."

16. Some articles indicated Sundance returned with Robert Evans. Cirilo Gibbons, who was a son of Dan Gibbons, later told investigators that Robert Evans had told him that he had used the alias Hood (Aguirre, 179-182).

17. Buck and Meadows, "Neighbors on the Hot Seat."

18. Buck and Meadows, "Leaving Cholila" and "Neighbors on the Hot Seat."

19. Buck and Meadows, "Leaving Cholila."

20. Buck and Meadows, "Leaving Cholila"; Cunningham, *Triggernometry*. This information surfaced in the discovery of the 1911 police judicial files.

21. Buck and Meadows, "Leaving Cholila" and "Neighbors on the Hot Seat."

22. Buck and Meadows, "Leaving Cholila" and "Neighbors on the Hot Seat."

23. Meadows, *Digging Up Butch and Sundance*, 93.

24. Chapman, "'Butch' Cassidy," 60.

25. Buck and Meadows, "The Last Days of Butch and Sundance."

26. Buck and Meadows, "The Last Days of Butch and Sundance."

27. Percy A. Seibert letter dated January 15, 1964.

28. Buck and Meadows, "The Last Days of Butch and Sundance."

29. Collector Brent Ashworth owns the original Percy Seibert Scrapbook and some of Butch's original letters from Bolivia. Ashworth shared the scrapbook and letters with me on February 7, 2009.

30. Original letter courtesy of Brent Ashworth, Provo, Utah.

31. Pointer, Larry, "The Robbery of Carlos Pero and the Aramayo Pack Train."

32. Researcher Jim Dullenty believes that the handwriting of the D.J. Myers letter does in fact match Butch's handwriting. In the letter, Myers mentions to Percy Seibert that he has recently returned from the interior where results were not as he had expected and wanted "light employment" due to his health which was not the best. Dullenty surmised this may have been due his being wounded during the gun battle in San Vicente (Dullenty, "Who Really Was William T. Phillips").

33. Original letter courtesy of Brent Ashworth, Provo, Utah.

34. Information found in Percy Seibert's scrapbook.

35. Chapman, "'Butch' Cassidy," 61.

36. Chapman, "'Butch' Cassidy," 60.

37. Percy A. Seibert Letter, January 15, 1964.

CHAPTER 23: ARAMAYO PAYROLL ROBBERY (PAGES 206–214)

1. Francis, "The End of an Outlaw." Several outlaws were in Bolivia at this time including, a man named "Dey," Jack McVey, Dick Clifford, Harry Nation, "Walters and Murray" and several unnamed outlaws.

2. Meadows, *Digging Up Butch and Sundance*, 228.

3. Meadows, *Digging Up Butch and Sundance*, 230-231.

4. Meadows, *Digging Up Butch and Sundance*, 231.

5. Meadows, *Digging Up Butch and Sundance*, 235-236.

6. Pointer, "The Robbery of Carlos Pero and the Aramayo Pack Train."

7. Meadows, *Digging Up Butch and Sundance* and Pointer, "The Robbery of Carlos Pero and the Aramayo Pack Train."

8. Meadows, *Digging Up Butch and Sundance*," 163.

9. Meadows, *Digging Up Butch and Sundance* and Larry Pointer, "The Robbery of Carlos Pero and the Aramayo Pack Train."

10. Francis, "End of an Outlaw."

11. Some researchers have determined that this was a simple mistake and this person was Harry Longabaugh, the Sundance Kid. Other researchers think Kid Curry wasn't killed in Parachute, Colorado, and did make his way to South America.

12. A.G. Francis is somewhat of a mystery. Researchers have found Walter Richardson Grant Francis, a mining superintendent, who was in the area at the same time.

13. Francis, "The End of an Outlaw."

14. Bingham, *Across South America*, 81. Bingham reported that in 1908 Tupiza only had two hotels and one was the headquarters of the Bolivian army stationed to guard that section of the frontier. The other, the Grand Hotel Terminus, was for travelers.

15. Buck and Meadows, "The Last Days of Butch and Sundance." According to Buck and Meadows, Francis moved his headquarters to Tomahuaico which was three miles south of Verdugo in late October 1908, about the time Butch and Sundance left for Tupiza.

16. Buck and Meadows, "The Last Days of Butch and Sundance." The outlaws surprised Pero's party at 9:30 A.M. and wielded brand new small caliber Mauser carbines with thick barrels. They were dressed in corduroy suits with bandannas masking their faces and their hat brims turned down so that only their eyes were visible.

17. Buck and Meadows, "The Last Days of Butch and Sundance" and "The Last Ride." According to Buck and Meadows's research, the manager was Carlos Pero with his young teenage son Mariano. One peon accompanied them with several mules.

18. Buck and Meadows, "The Last Days of Butch and Sundance" and "The Last Ride."

19. According to Buck and Meadows, the robbery didn't occur until the next day, November 4, 1908, as Pero's group stayed the night of November 3 in Salo.

20. Buck and Meadows, "The Last Ride."

21. Historian Dan Buck said, "You read Bolivian newspapers during that time and you'd think the country was in the middle of a crime wave. There were lots of holdups. There were bandits from America, Chile, Germany, New Zealand,—you name it." (*Chicago Tribune*, March 8, 1992)

22. There was also two rough looking Anglo-Saxon men whom American explorer Hiram Bingham met after the robbery.

23. Horan, *Pictorial History of the Wild West*, 239.

CHAPTER 24: SAN VICENTE (PAGES 215–229)

1. Pointer, "The Robbery of Carlos Pero and the Aramayo Pack Train."

2. The Corregidor was the elected town magistrate, mayor, and judge.

3. Meadows, *Digging Up Butch and Sundance* and Pointer, "The 1908 San Vicente Coroner's Inquest."

4. Pointer, "The 1908 San Vicente Coroner's Inquest."

5. Meadows, *Digging Up Butch and Sundance,* 269-271.

6. Bingham, *Across South America,* 81.

7. Bingham, *Across South America,* 81-82.

8. Bingham, *Across South America,* 92-93.

9. Meadows, *Digging Up Butch and Sundance*

10. Francis, "The End of an Outlaw."

11. McIntosh, "The Evolution of a Bandit"; the Harvey Logan alias "Kid Curry" photo was taken in Deadwood, South Dakota, October 2, 1897.

12. The outlaws typically only sent one person into town, while the other(s) waited outside for a signal that it was safe to enter.

13. The *Wyoming State Journal,* May 16, 1913. The death of Butch Cassidy was reported in several western newspaper including *Bill Barlow's Budget* (Douglas, Wyoming), May 29, 1913; *Casper Record,* May 20, 1913, and *Laramie Republican,* May 22, 1913.

14. Pinkerton Files, October 15, 1914, report and October 31, 1914, letter to Antofagasta, Chile Chief of Police.

15. Bechdolt, *Tales of Old-Timers,* 336-337.

16. *Standard,* Dec. 12, 1911 (Buenos Aires).

17. Chapman, "'Butch' Cassidy."

18. Betenson, *Butch Cassidy, My Brother.*

19. A new museum was established in San Vicente for the hundred-year anniversary of the deaths of the two bandits on November 7, 1908. Felix Charlar Miranda, a local San Vicente historian and Butch Cassidy expert, has devoted his life to scouring archives of the Aramayo mining company and attics looking for Butch and Sundance memorabilia. He was quoted as saying: "'I don't believe the story about them committing suicide,' he says, producing a file of documents and letters dating from 1908. 'They made off with 15,300 *bolivianos* (around US$1,900 at current exchange rates) from the Aramayo mining company, but the bodies were reported to have hardly any money on them. Plus Butch and Sundance used Colt 45s—that would blow someone's head clean off. But when the bodies were exhumed for identification, they were positively identified by their faces.'" He further said: "I believe a posse killed them, took the money, and made it look like suicide to avoid retribution."

20. Chapman, "'Butch' Cassidy," 33.

21. Pointer, "Dancing the Sundance Samba." Pointer refers to Ed Kirby research on Longabaugh.

22. Meadows, *Digging Up Butch and Sundance,* 302.

23. The *New York Times,* January 17, 1992, reported, "Dr. Snow has determined that one of the skulls he disinterred has entry and exit holes from a bullet that passed through the temples, and the other has a smashed forehead, consistent with the head-on impact of a projectile."

24. *Los Angeles Times*, May 24, 1992.

25. *Chicago Tribune*, March 8, 1992. Larry Pointer indicated that some media reports indicated that the team was ninety-nine per cent certain they had obtained Harry Longabaugh's remains.

26. Pointer letter to B. Bryon Price, Director of University of Oklahoma Press, August 2008. In the spring of 1992, WOLA reported, "The skulls of the two skeletons were complete and each had a bullet hole in it. Forensic specialists said the hole in one skull appeared to have resulted from a shot at close range and the other from a self-inflicted wound." (*WOLA* Vol 1, No. 4).

27. E-mail from Pointer, September 23, 2011.

CHAPTER 25: BACK HOME (PAGES 230–243)

1. Betenson, "Lula Parker Betenson," 5. Lula married Joseph Betenson on January 31, 1907.

2. Betenson, "Lula Parker Betenson," 4.

3. Betenson, *Butch Cassidy, My Brother*, 177.

4. Betenson, *Butch Cassidy, My Brother*, 177.

5. Betenson, *Butch Cassidy, My Brother*, 179.

6. Betenson, *Butch Cassidy, My Brother*, 179.

7. Betenson, *Butch Cassidy, My Brother*, 181.

8. Betenson, *Butch Cassidy, My Brother*, 182.

9. Betenson, *Butch Cassidy, My Brother*, 182.

10. Betenson, *Butch Cassidy, My Brother*, 182-183.

11. Betenson, *Butch Cassidy, My Brother*, 186-187.

12. Betenson, *Butch Cassidy, My Brother*, 184.

13. Percy Seibert provided key information to author Arthur Chapman in his April 1930 *Elks Magazine* article on the deaths of Butch and Sundance that identified Butch and Sundance as the two dead bandits.

14. I remember Mark talking about the experience. The experience was confirmed later by Mark's widow, Vivian, and Mark's brother, Scott, who was my grandfather. My brother Greg Betenson has also confirmed that he talked to Mark about seeing Butch in 1925. He said," I never knew Mark or Vivian to tell me anything but the truth. Never candy-coated something or tried to make up some story. They both told me he came back. Even after Mark died Vivian repeated the statement. I never had an instance to not trust them." Dan Buck has repeatly stated that Mark told researcher Roger McCord that Butch never came back, which is not consistent with what he told everyone else. Roger McCord is also the individual that stole South American documents related to Butch and Sundance, which makes him an un-trustworthy source.

15. Betenson, *Butch Cassidy, My Brother*, 182.

16. Betenson, *Butch Cassidy, My Brother*, 182.

17. Betenson, *Butch Cassidy, My Brother*, 182.

18. Betenson, *Butch Cassidy, My Brother*, 195.

19. Betenson, *Butch Cassidy, My Brother*, 196.

20. Murdock, *The Educated Outlaw*, 22.

21. E-mail from Harvey Murdock, September 24, 2011.

22. Burroughs, *Where the Old West Stayed Young*, 135.

23. Burt, *Powder River*, 328.

24. Boren, "Proof: Butch Cassidy Came Back."

25. Burroughs, *Where the Old West Stayed Young*, 135

26. Boren, "Proof: Butch Cassidy Came Back."

27. Zane Hilman interview, October 13, 2009, in Sheridan, Wyoming.

28. Rhoades, "Butch Cassidy Didn't Die in an Ambush in South America," Betenson, *Butch Cassidy, My Brother*, 204-205.

29. *Rawlins Daily Times*, December 9, 1967.

30. Ada Piper letter to Mrs. Blythe H. Teeple, February 6, 1963.

31. Interview, June 18, 2004, Rock Springs, Wyoming.

32. Ellnor was married to Dan's oldest son, Max.

33. *Billings Gazette*, December 6, 1970, "He Sang A Song To Her Baby" by Kathryn Wright.

34. Telephone interview of Ellnor Parker by Jim Dullenty, June 30, 1975.

35. Dullenty, "Dullenty Says Butch Cassidy Was William T. Phillips," 12. In Dullenty's 1991, "Who Really Was William T. Phillips," Dullenty says, "They [Max and Ellnor Parker] did not believe Butch used the name Phillips, but they said they 'knew' he had died in Spokane."

36. Interview of Wallace Ott, August 18, 2007, in Tropic, Utah.

37. Matt Warner letter to Charles Kelly, postmarked December 22, 1937, courtesy of Brent Ashworth.

38. Lacy, *Last of the Bandit Riders...Revisited*.

39. *Salt Lake Tribune*, October 10, 1993.

40. Agatha Nay interview in Circleville, Utah in 1998; *Deseret News*, April 16, 1998.

41. Burroughs, *Where the Old West Stayed Young*, 135.

42. Davidson, *Sometimes Cassidy*.

43. As mentioned earlier Billy Sawtelle went to Argentina in 1912 and based his conclusions on the deaths of Wilson and Evans, not Butch and Sundance.

44. Will Simpson letter to Harry Logue, February 4, 1937.

45. McPhee, John, *Rising from the Plains*, 115.

46. E-mail from Pointer, August 9, 2011, and *Deseret News*, August 17, 2011.

47. Allison, *Dubois Area History*, F49. Allison names Eugene Amoretti and Hank Boedeker.

48. Dullenty, The Cassidy Collection; *Wyoming State Tribune*, September 5, 1939, has information from Mart J. Christensen. He also names Leslie Reed, Harry Baldwin,

Bob Gaylord, and William Johnson. The article further states that Phillips was recognized by a scar that he had received during his arrest by Bob Calverly in 1892.
The Larry Pointer Collection lists 16 individuals who took Phillips for Cassidy.

49. *Wyoming State Journal*, January 28, 1937.

50. *Wyoming State Journal*, courtesy of Lander Pioneer Museum. No date, likely 1930s.
    Wyoming State Journal, January 28, 1937, has an article on Logue basically stating the
    same information. Logue does state that Cassidy was in Lander five years previous.

51. April 4, 1946 *Lander Newspaper* article, courtesy of the Pioneer Museum in Lan-
    der, Wyoming.

52. The *Wyoming State Journal*, May 21, 1942. "Regan says Phillips no Butch Cassidy."

53. The *Wyoming State Journal*, May 21, 1942. "Butcher Billy Jones…Knew Cassidy
    Well."

54. The original manuscript is owned by collector Brent Ashworth. The original
    manuscript typed on W.T. Phillips letterhead by Gertrude Phillips contains sig-
    nificantly more information than found in previously-known manuscripts.

55. Interview and email dated July 28, 2014, with Scott Patterson, the grandson of
    Reynolds. Patterson said that Reynolds first told his family of the trip after the New-
    man-Redford movie came out.

APPENDIX A: DAN PARKER (PAGES 244–249)

1. Baker, *The Wild Bunch at Robbers Roost*, 134; conversations with Dan Parker's
   granddaughter in 1996.

2. Mortensen, *Memories of Dan Parker*.

3. Conversations with Parker family members in 1996. One family member says Dan
   told her that he had lost his fingers while in prison.

4. Family records; *Iron County Record*, August 13, 1942.

5. Conversations with Dan Parker's daughter Beatrice in 1996.

6. Conversations with Dan Parker's daughter Beatrice in 1996. In 2008, descendants
   of Dan showed me the actual pardon signed by President McKinley.

7. Conversations with Dan Parker's daughter Beatrice in 1996.

8. Pinkerton Detective Agency file on Butch Cassidy, File #72, binder #7, Pinkerton Archives.

9. Family records.

10. Conversations with Dan Parker's daughter Beatrice; and family records.

11. Conversations with Barbara Carlson in 1996.

12. Conversations with Scott Parker Betenson in 1996.

13. Mortensen, *Memories of Dan Parker*.

14. Mortensen, *Memories of Dan Parker*.

15. Mortensen, *Memories of Dan Parker*.

16. Mortensen, *Memories of Dan Parker*.

17. Mortensen, *Memories of Dan Parker*.

18. Conversations with Scott Parker Betenson in 1996.

19. *Parowan Times*, January 6, 1926.

20. Conversations with Dan Parker's daughter Beatrice in 1996. Several *Parowan Times* from 1920-30 tell of Dan being home from Milford where he was working, including the October 9, 1931, issue.

21. Dullenty, *The Butch Cassidy Collection*, 77-82.

22. Conversations with Dan Parker's daughter Beatrice in 1996.

23. Mortensen, *Memories of Dan Parker*.

24. Conversations with family members in 1996.

25. Conversations with family members; *Parowan Times*, August 7, 1942; *Parowan Times*, August 14, 1942; *The Deseret News*, August 8, 1942.

26. Conversations with family members; *Parowan Times,* August 7, 1942; *Parowan Times*, August 14, 1942; *Deseret News*, August 8, 1942.

APPENDIX B: LULA PARKER BETENSON (PAGES 250–255)

1. Interview with Lula Parker Betenson by Dora Flack, October 31, 1974.

2. Family records.

3. Betenson and Flack, an unpublished manuscript on Butch Cassidy, 97.

4. Betenson and Flack, an unpublished manuscript on Butch Cassidy, 1.

5. Betenson and Flack, an unpublished manuscript on Butch Cassidy, 2.

6. Family records.

7. *Salt Lake Telegram*, April 22, 1962.

8. Betenson and Flack, an unpublished manuscript on Butch Cassidy, 4-5.

9. Betenson, *Butch Cassidy, My Brother*, dust jacket.

10. *Salt Lake Tribune*, April 22, 1962.

11. *Salt Lake Tribune*, April 22, 1962.

12. Betenson, *Butch Cassidy, My Brother*, 175.

13. Interview with Lula Parker Betenson by Dora Flack, October 31, 1974.

14. Lula Parker Betenson's funeral services program and the *Deseret News*, May 7-8, 1980.

15. Lula Parker Betenson's funeral services program.

Acknowledgments

A HEARTFELT THANKS GOES to the many friends and associates who have joined me on this amazing journey and to the wonderful people I've met along the way. My favorite part of being associated with the Butch Cassidy story is meeting and becoming friends with folks who have some tie to Butch—whether it is through special family connections or their love for the Old West.

Thanks to my wife, Liz; my kids, Chelsea, Will, Hayley, and Katie; my parents, Wade and JoAnn Betenson, who have always been supportive; and my siblings, Brenda, Nancy, and especially my brother, Greg. Nancy provided diligent assistance in editing.

Many older family members are now gone, but were a great support to me including my great-grandmother Lula Parker Betenson, great-uncle and -aunt Mark and Viv Betenson, who were second grandparents to me and my siblings; my grandparents, Scott and Mariam Betenson. Great-uncle John Betenson and great-aunt Barbara Carlson have always been generous in sharing their memories and artifacts with me.

Many friends have been selfless in helping and encouraging me. Colin Taylor is an incredible friend whose suggestions I especially value; Larry Pointer is a great and valued friend and resource; Jim and Norma Miller have been dear friends for years; Harvey Murdock shares a special kinship with me as we descend from two outlaws who were best friends. Also thanks to friends and outlaw researchers: Brent Ashworth, Joel Frandsen, Jack Stroud, Jerry Nickle, Ross Nickle, Steve Lacy, Pat Patterson, Elnora Frye, Pat Schroeder, the late Jim Beckstead, the late Dora Flack, Doris Burton, Dan Davidson, Norma Jackson, Don and Diane Cooper, Mary Stoner Hadley, Howard Greager, Earl Lanning, Joe Charter, Bob and Phyllis McKeen, Butch and Jeanie Jensen, Mike Rose, Karen Cotton, Mac Blewer, Donna and Paul Ernst,

Mike Bell, Debbie Allen, Roberta Vaughn, Mike and Joe Hickey, Gifford Hickey, Robert Proctor, Philip Homan, Max Lauridsen, Richard Fike, Randy and Becky Yard, Nancy Coggeshall, Kirk Smith, and Nancy Adams.

And special thanks to Nancy Curtis at High Plains Press for her incredible friendship and support (hard work) and for believing in this project from the start.

The staffs and employees of many libraries and museums around the world have gone out of their ways to help me, and I owe them all thanks.

Bibliography

BOOKS

Aguirre, Osvaldo, *La Pandilla Salvaje Butch Cassidy En La Patagonia*, (Grupo Editorial Norma: Buenos Aires, Argentina, 2004).

Alexander, Bob, *Lawmen, Outlaws and S.O.Bs. Volume II*, (High Lonesome Books: Silver City, NM, 2008).

Allison, Mary, *History of Dubois*, (Mary Allison Publisher: Dubois, WY, 1991).

Baker, Pearl, *Wild Bunch at Robbers Roost*, (Westernlore Press: Los Angeles, CA, 1965).

Bechdolt, Frederick R., *Tales of The Old-Timers*, (The Century Co: New York City, NY, 1924).

Berrett, LaMar C., *Sacred Places: Iowa and Nebraska* (Deseret Book: Salt Lake City, UT, 2006).

Betenson, Lula Parker and Dora Flack, *Butch Cassidy, My Brother*, (Brigham Young University Press: Provo, UT, 1975).

Bingham, Hiram, *Across South America*, (Houghton Mifflin Company: Boston, 1911).

Brackett, Chet and Kim, *Chet's Reflections*, (Privately published, 2014)

Brooks, Juanita, *John Doyle Lee*, (Utah State University Press: Logan, Utah, 1992).

Burroughs, John Rolfe, *Guardian Of The Grasslands The First Hundred Years of the Wyoming Stock Growers Association*, (Pioneer Printing and Stationary: Cheyenne, WY, 1971).

Burroughs, John Rolfe, *Where The Old West Stayed Young*, (William Morrow and Company: New York City, NY, 1962).

Burt, Struthers, *Powder River, Let 'Er Buck*, (Farrar and Rinehart, Inc.: New York City, 1938).

Burton, Eva P. W., *Mystery in History, Legends of Current Creek Ranch of Sweetwater County of Wyoming* (Burton Books: Cheyenne, WY, 2005).

Burton, Jeffrey, *The Deadliest Outlaws: The Ketchum Gang and the Wild Bunch*, (University of North Texas Press, Denton, TX, 2009).

Burton, Jeffrey, *Dynamite and Sixshooter*, (Palomino Press, Santa Fe, NM, 1970).

Cunningham, Eugene, *Triggernometry*, (The Caxton Printers LTD: Caldwell, ID, 1941).

Daughters of the Utah Pioneers of Beaver County (DUP), *Monuments To Courage, A History of Beaver County* (Utah), (DUP: Beaver, UT 1948).

Davidson, Art and Jim Aston, *Sometimes Cassidy: The Real Butch Cassidy Story*, (Hawkes Publishing: Salt Lake City, UT, 1995).

DeJournette, Dick and Daun, *One Hundred Years of Brown's Park and Diamond Mountain*, (University of North Texas Press: Denton, TX, 2009).

Denison, L.A., *"Telluride: Tales of Two Early Pioneers,"* (Indesign Studios: Odessa, TX, no date).

Dullenty, James, *The Butch Cassidy Collection*, (Rocky Mountain House Press: Hamilton, MT, 1986).

Dunham, Dick and Vivian, *"Flaming Gorge Country,"* (Eastwood Printing and Publishing Company: Denver, CO, 1977).

Edgar, Bob and Jack Turnell, *Brand of a Legend*, (Stockade Publishing: Cody, WY 1978).

Ernst, Donna B., *Harvey Logan: Wildest of the Wild Bunch*, (Wild Bunch Press: Souderton, PA, 2003).

Ernst, Donna B., *Sundance, My Uncle*, (Creative Publishing Company: College Station, TX, 1992).

Ernest, Donna B., *The Sundance Kid, The Life of Harry Alonzo Longabaugh*, (University of Oklahoma Press: Norman, OK, 2009).

Farlow, Edward J., *Wind River Adventures My Life in Frontier Wyoming*, (High Plains Press: Glendo, WY, 1998).

French, Captain William, *Recollections of a Western Ranchman*, (High Lonesome Books: Silver City, NM, 1990).

Frye, Elnora L., *Atlas of Wyoming Outlaws at the Territorial Penitentiary*, (Jelm Mountain Publications: Laramie, WY, 1990).

Fuller, Rollo Lorin, *A History of Circleville, Utah*, (Privately printed, 2003).

Gavirati, Marcelo, *Buscados en la Patagonia*, Second Edition (La Bitacora Patagonia: Buenos Aires, Argentina, 2005) and Third Edition (2007).

Greager, Howard E., *In the Company of Cowboys*, (Vantage Press: New York, NY: 1990).

Greager, Howard E., *Posey's Spurs*, (Western Reflections: Ouray, CO, 1999).

Hafen, Leroy R. and Ann W., *Handcarts to Zion*, (The Arthur H. Clark Company: Glendale, CA, 1960).

Hamblin, Kathaleen Kennington, *Bridger Valley A Guide to the Past*, (Privately printed: Mountain View, WY, 1993).

Hanks, Edward M., *A Long Dust On The Desert*, (Western Printing and Publishing Co.: Sparks, NV, 1967).

Hansen, Margaret Brock, *Powder River Country: The Papers of J. Elmer Brock*, (Privately printed, Kaycee, WY, 1981).

Horan, James D., *Desperate Men*, (G.P. Putnam's Sons: New York City, 1949).

Horan, James D., *The Outlaws, The Authentic West*, (Crown Publishers, New York City, 1977).

Horan, James D. and Paul Sann, *Pictorial History of the Wild West*, (Crown Publishers, Inc: New York City, 1954).

Horan, James D., *The Wild Bunch*, (Signet Books: New York City, 1958).

Jackson, Norma, *Butch Cassidy, Matt Warner and the Unknown Outlaw*, (Jorlan Publishing, Inc.: np, 2007).

Judd, Camilla Woodbury, contributor; Kate B. Carter, editor, *Treasures of Pioneer History*, Volumes 2 and 5, (Daughters of the Utah Pioneers: Salt Lake City, UT, 1952–1956).

Kelly, Charles, *The Outlaw Trail: The Story of Butch Cassidy and the Wild Bunch*, (Devin-Adair Company: New York City, 1959).

Kelsey, Michael, R., *Hiking and Exploring Utah's Henry Mountains and Robbers Roost*, (Kelsey Publishing: Provo, UT, 1990).

Kennington, Forrest Weber and Kathaleen Kennington Hamblin, *A History of Star Valley Formerly Salt River Valley 1800-1900* (Valley Graphics: Salt Lake City, UT, 1989).

Kirby, Ed, *The Saga of Butch Cassidy and the Wild Bunch*, (Filter Press: Palmer, CO, 1977).

Kirby, Ed, *The Rise and Fall of the Sundance Kid*, (Western Publications: Iola, WI, 1983).

Lacy, Steve and Joyce Warner (updated from Matt Warner's original manuscript), *Last of the Bandit Riders…Revisited*, (Big Moon Traders: Salt Lake City, UT, 2000).

Larson, Andrew Karl, *The Red Hills of November*, (Deseret News Press: Salt Lake City, UT, 1957).

Lester, Margaret Moore, *From Rags to Riches A History of Hilliard And Bear River 1890-1990*, (1st Impressions: Evanston, WY, 1992).

McCarty, Tom, *Tom McCarty's Own Story*, (Rocky Mountain House Press: Hamilton, MT, 1985).

McClure, Grace, *The Bassett Women*, (Ohio University Press, Swallow: Athens, OH: 1985).

McPhee, John, *Rising from the Plains*, (Farrar, Straus and Giroux: New York City, 1986).

Meadows, Anne, *Digging Up Butch and Sundance*, (St. Martin's Press: New York City, 1994).

Murdock, Harvey Lay, *The Educated Outlaw, The Story of Elzy Lay of the Wild Bunch*, (Author House: Bloomington, IN, 2009).

Olsen, Andrew D., *The Price We Paid The Extraordinary Story of the Willie and Martin Handcart Pioneers*, (Deseret Books: Salt Lake City, UT, 2006).

Patterson, Richard M., *Butch Cassidy A Biography*, (University of Nebraska Press: Lincoln, NE, 1998).

PK, JT (John Tolliver McClammy), *A Story of his Adventures and his friendship with Pancho Villa*, (PKH Publishing LLC, 2010).

Platts, Doris B., *The Cunningham Ranch Incident of 1892*, (Privately printed, 1992).

Pointer, Larry, *In Search of Butch Cassidy*, (University of Oklahoma Press: Norman, OK, 1977).

Riverton Wyoming Stake (compiled and written by members of the LDS Church), *Remember: The Willie and Martin Handcart Companies and Their Rescuers—Past and Present*, (Privately printed: Riverton, WY, 1997).

Reyher, Ken, *High Country Cowboys A History of Ranching in Western Colorado*, (Western Reflections Publishing Company: Montrose, CO, 2002).

Ruskowsky, Nancy Heyl, *Two Dot Ranch, A Biography of Place*, (Pronghorn Press: Greybull, WY, 2008).

Selcer, Richard F., *Hell's Half Acre*, (Texas Christian University Press: Fort Worth, TX, 1991).

Silvey, Frank, *History and Settlement of Northern San Juan County*, (Times-Independent: Moab, UT, 1990).

Siringo, Charlie, *A Cowboy Detective*, (University of Nebraska Press: Lincoln, NE, 1988).

Skovlin, Jon M. and Donna McDaniel, *In Pursuit of The McCartys*, (Reflections Publishing Co: Cove, OR, 2001).

F. Stanley, *No Tears for Black Jack Ketchum*, (World Press, Inc.: Denver, CO, 1958).

Stewart, George Emery Jr., *Tales From Indian Country, Authentic Stories and Legends from the Great Uintah Basin*, (SunRise Publishing: Orem, UT, 1997).

Tanner, Faun McConkie, *The Far Country: A Regional History of Moab and La Sal, Utah*, (Olympus Publishing Company: Salt Lake City, Utah, 1976).

Tanner, Karen Holliday and John D. Tanner Jr., *The Bronco Bill Gang*, (University of Oklahoma Press: Norman, OK, 2011).

Tanner, Karen Holliday and John D. Tanner Jr., *Last of the Old-Time Outlaws: The George West Musgrave Story*, (University of Oklahoma Press: Norman, OK, 2002).

Tippets, Susan Thomas, *Piedmont Uinta County, Wyoming Ghost Town*, (Privately printed:, 1996).

Walker, Tacetta B. *Stories of Early Days in Wyoming: Big Horn Basin*, (Prairie Publishing: Casper, WY, 1936).

Warner, M. Lane, *Grass Valley, 1873-1976: A History of Antimony and Her People*, (American Press: Salt Lake City, UT, 1976).

Warner, Matt (as told to Murray E. King), *The Last of the Bandit Riders*, (The Caxton Printers LTD: Caldwell, ID, 1940).

West, Allgara, *A History of the Hub Auburn, Wyoming 1878–1998*, (Gateway Press, Inc.: Baltimore, MD, 1998).

Wilde, J. P., *Treasured Tidbits of Time: An Informal History of Mormon Conquest and Settlement of the Bear Lake Valley*, (Wilde: Montpelier, ID, 1977)

Wilkes, Ila, *Star Valley and its Communities*, (Star Valley Independent: Afton Wyoming, nd).

MANUSCRIPTS AND ARTICLES

Bassett, Ann, "'Queen Ann' of Brown's Park," *Colorado Magazine*, July 1952.

Beckstead, James H., *A War with Outlaws, The Saga of Utah's Robbers Roost Country*, unpublished manuscript, nd.

Bell, Bob Boze, "Campfire Shootout, Matt Warner and William Wall vs the Staunton Bros. and Dave Milton," *True West*, Sept. 2007.

Bell, Mike, "Incidents of Owl Creek, Butch Cassidy's Big Horn Basin Bunch, An Illustrated Narrative," Privately printed, 2011.

Bell, Mike, "Interview with the Sundance Kid," *WOLA Journal,* Summer 1995.

Bell, Mike, "The Friends and Enemies of the Notorious Nutcher Brothers," *WWHA Journal*, August 2010.

Bell, Mike with Pat Schroeder, "Butch Cassidy's Big Horn Basin Bunch," *WWHA Journal*, June 2011.

Betenson, Lula Parker and Pearl Baker, *"My Brother Butch Cassidy,"* unpublished manuscript, nd.

Betenson, Lula Parker and Pearl Baker, *"My Brother, Butch Cassidy"* unpublished manuscript, 1965.

Betenson, Bill, "Lula Parker Betenson" *Outlaw Trail Journal*, Winter 1995.

Betenson, Bill, "Alias 'Tom Ricketts,' The True Story of Butch Cassidy's Brother Dan Parker,*" Outlaw Trail Journal*, Winter 1996.

Betenson, Bill, "The Parkers—Handcart Pioneers," *Outlaw Trail Journal*, Summer 1998.

Betenson, Bill, "Bub Meeks: The Unfortunate Outlaw," *Outlaw Trail Journal*, Summer 2003.

Berk, Lee, "Butch Cassidy Didn't Do It," *Old West*, Fall 1983.

Boren, Kerry Ross, "Proof: Butch Cassidy Came Back," *Westerner*, May-June 1973.

Bristow, Allen P., "A Rude Awakening," *True West*, June 1996.

Buck, Daniel, "Butch Cassidy Sought Amnesty, Fact or Folklore?" *WWHA Journal*, Dec. 2012.

Buck, Daniel, and Anne Meadows, "Butch and Sundance Slept Here," *True West,* Sept. 1999.

Buck, Daniel, and Anne Meadows, "Neighbors on the Hot Seat: Revelations From the Long Lost Argentine Police File," *WOLA Journal*, Spring/Summer 1996.

Buck, Daniel, and Anne Meadows, "The Last Days of Butch and Sundance," *Wild West*, Feb. 1997.

Buck, Daniel, and Anne Meadows, "The Last Ride: Butch and Sundance Play Their Last Hand," *True West*, November/December 2002.

Buck, Daniel, and Anne Meadows, "Leaving Cholila," *True West*, January 1996.

Buck, Daniel, and Anne Meadows, "A Maze of Entanglements," *WOLA Journal*, Fall 1992.

Buck, Daniel, and Anne Meadows, "Merry Christmas from the Pinkertons," *WOLA Journal*, Spring 1992.

Buck, Daniel, and Anne Meadows, "What the Wild Bunch Did in South America," *WOLA Journal*, Spring-Summer 1991.

Buck, Daniel, and Anne Meadows, "Wild Bunch Dream Girl," *True West*, May 2002.

Bullock, David, "Recollections of David D. Bullock" in *Our Pioneer Heritage,* edited by Kate B. Carter, Vol 18.

Burton, Doris Karren, "Sheriff John Theodore Pope," *Outlaw Trail Journal*, Summer 1991.

Burton, Jeff, "'Suddenly In A Secluded and Rugged Place . . . ' The Territory of New Mexico versus William H. McGinnis: Cause No. 2419–Murder." *Brand Book*, April, July 1972.

Button, I. Victor, "Butch Cassidy Gave Getaway Horse to 10-Year-Old," *Newsletter of the National Association and Center for Outlaw and Lawman History*, Summer 1975.

Chapman, Arthur, "'Butch' Cassidy," *Elks Magazine*, April, 1930.

Conduit, Thelma Gatchell, *Annals of Wyoming*, April 1962.

Conduit, Thelma Gatchell, *Annals of Wyoming*, April 1957.

Dullenty, Jim, "Dullenty Says Butch Cassidy Was William T. Phillips," *Newsletter of the National Association And Center For Outlaw and Lawman History*, Summer 1976.

Dullenty, Jim, "The Farm Boy Who Became A Member of the Wild Bunch," *Quarterly of the National Association and Center For Outlaw and Lawman History*, Winter, 1986.

Dullenty, Jim, "Who Really Was William T. Phillips of Spokane—Outlaw or Imposter?" *WOLA Journal*, Fall-Winter, 1991.

Dullenty, Jim (WOLA Editor), "What Have They Found in San Vicente?" *WOLA Journal*, Spring 1992.

Ekker, Barbara B., "Charley Gibbons, Friend of the Wild Bunch," *Quarterly of the National Association and Center for Outlaw and Lawman History*, Autumn, 1977.

Ernst, Donna B., "Ethel Place—A Look at the Possibility She Came Home Alone," *WOLA Journal*, Spring 2007.

Ernst, Donna B., "George S. Nixon, More Than One Run-in with Outlaws," *WOLA Journal*, Summer 2001.

Ernst, Donna B., "Jack Ryan, Wild Bunch Friend or Pinkerton Informant?" *Wild West History Association Journal*, June 2009.

Ernst, Donna B., "Maddox Flats, Kendall C. Maddox, Proprietor," *WOLA Journal*, Winter 2007.

Ernst, Donna B., "Montpelier, Idaho, A Robbery For a Friend" *WOLA Journal*, Fall 2001.

Ernst, Donna B., "Will Carver, The Lovesick Outlaw," *WOLA Journal*, Summer 1995.

Ernst, Donna B., "The Wilcox Train Robbery," *Wild West*, June 1999.

Ernst, Donna B., "Wild Bunch Immigration Records," *Quarterly of the National Association For Outlaw and Lawman History*, April-June 2007.

Francis, A.G., "The End of an Outlaw," *Wide World Magazine*, May 1913.

Frandsen, Joel, "The Castle Gate Payroll Robbery," *WOLA Journal*, Winter 2007.

Frye, Elnora L. "Butch Cassidy At the Pen" given as a talk to WOLA on July 13, 2007, in Laramie, Wyoming, at the Wyoming Territorial Penitentiary.

Gavirati, Marcelo, "Back at the Ranch." *True West*, November/December 2002.

Griffiths, Jeanne M., *Life Sketch of Ann Hartley Parker*, unpublished manuscript, November 1995.

Gooldy, John F. "Early Day History of Little Snake River Valley," unpublished manuscript, American Heritage Center, University of Wyoming.

Greene, A.F. C. "Butch Cassidy in Fremont County," from Jim Dullenty's *Butch Cassidy Collection*.

Hamilton, Douglas, "In Pursuit of the Flying Dutchman," *Old West*, Summer 1990.

Homan, Philip, "The Sundance Kid Didn't Do It," Wild West History Association Journal, October 2013.

Hoy, Jesse.S., "The J. S. Hoy Manuscript," unpublished manuscript housed at the Colorado State University Library.

Huett, Wil, "'Butch Cassidy slept here,' the Wyoming State Penitentiary could boast," *Wild West*.

Johnson, LaMont, *Heavy Holstered Men in Back West to Home,* a ballad in *Brand Book,* Denver,1948.

Kindred, Wayne, "The Wilcox Robbery, Who Did It?" *WOLA Journal*, Spring 1999.

Kirby, Edward M., "Butch, Sundance, Etta Place Frolicked in 'Fun City' ...." *Newsletter of the National Association And Center For Outlaw and Lawman History*, Winter 1975-76.

Kirby, Edward M., "Lee Case Remembers The Great Winnemucca Raid," *Quarterly of the Outlaw and Lawman Association*, January 1981

Lacy, Steve and Jim Dullenty, "Revealing Letter of Outlaw Butch Cassidy" *Old West*, Winter 1984.

McInnes, Elmer D., "With the Instinct of the Natural Detective: The Story of Slick Nard," *Old West*, Spring, 1999.

McIntosh, John H., "The Evolution of a Bandit," *Wide World Magazine*, September 1910.

Miller, James O., "It All Began With Telluride," *WOLA Journal*, Fall 2004.

Mortensen, Vern C., *Memories of Dan Parker*, unpublished manuscript.

Murphy, Miriam B., "When the Horn Silver Mine Crashed," *History Blazer*, January 1996.

Patterson, Richard, "Butch Cassidy's Surrender Offer," *Wild West*, February 2006.

Patterson, Richard, "Butch Cassidy's 'Peaceful Years'—1889–1894," *True West*, October 1996.

Patterson, Richard, "The Double Life of Charlie Crouse," *WOLA Journal*, Winter 2004.

Patterson, Richard, "Why Didn't Butch Run?," *WOLA Journal*, Spring 2002.

Phillips, William T., *The Bandit Invincible: The Story of the Outlaw Butch Cassidy*, manuscript, unpublished in this 1930s form, held by Brent F. Ashworth.

Pointer, Larry, "Brady vs Musgrave," unpublished manuscript, 2010.

Pointer, Larry, "Birds of a Feather: Will Flock Together," unpublished manuscript, 2010.

Pointer, Larry, "Dancing the Sundance Samba," unpublished manuscript, 2010.

Pointer, Larry, "George West Musgrave," unpublished manuscript, 2010.

Pointer, Larry, "Grice Whom Nobody Could Catch," Privately Published, 2014.

Pointer, Larry, "The 1908 San Vicente Coroner's Inquest," unpublished manuscript, 2010.

Pointer, Larry, "The Robbery of Carlos Pero and the Aramayo Pack Train," unpublished manuscript, 2010.

Pointer, Larry, "Rio Gallegos Revisited," unpublished manuscript, 2010.

Putnam, Vira Greene, "History of Auburn, Wyoming," Re-typed 2006 by B. J. Nebeker.

Reynolds, Franklin, "The Winnemucca Bank Robbery," *Frontier Times*, 1938.

Rhoades, Gale, "Butch Cassidy Didn't Die in an Ambush in South America!" *The West*, January 1974.

Selcer, Richard and Donna Donnell, "Last Word on the Famous Wild Bunch Photo," *Wild West*, December 2011.

Stoner, Mary E., "My Father was a Train Robber," *True West*, August 1983.

Skovil, Jon, "A Sheriff Outsmarts the Wild Bunch," *Outlaw Trail Journal*, Summer 2008.

Tanner, Karen Holliday and John D., Jr., "New Mexico Prisoner #1348," *WOLA Journal*, Spring 2001.

Taylor, Colin, "The Birth of the Horseback Outlaw" unpublished manuscript, 2010.

Taylor, Colin, "Wilcox," unpublished manuscript, 2009.

Walters, Archie, "Journal of Archer Walters, Enroute from England to Utah, U.S.A., March 18, 1856 to September 5th, 1856" in *Utah Pioneer Biographies*.

NEWSPAPERS

Anaconda Standard, Butte, MT

American Eagle Newspaper, Murray, UT

Bill Barlow's Budget, Douglas, WY

Billings Gazette, Billings, MT

Carbon County Journal, Rawlins, WY

Casper Record, Casper, WY

Craig Pantograph, Craig, CO

Cheyenne Daily Leader, Cheyenne, WY

Cheyenne Sun, Cheyenne, WY

Cheyenne Daily Sun, Cheyenne, WY

Daily Independent, Helena, MT

Davis County Clipper, Bountiful, UT

Denver News, Denver, CO

Deseret News, Salt Lake City, UT

Dolores Star, Dolores, CO

Eastern UT Advocate, Price, UT

Fremont Clipper, Lander, WY

Helena Independent, Helena, MT

Iron County Record, Cedar City, UT

Parowan Times, Parowan, UT

Piute County News, Junction, UT

La Nacion (Argentina)

Lander Clipper, Lander, WY

Laramie Daily Boomerang, Laramie, WY

Laramie Weekly Boomerang, Laramie, WY

Laramie Republican, Laramie, WY

Meeker Herald, Meeker, CO

Natrona Tribune, Casper, WY

Nevada News, Winnemucca, NV

Newcastle Journal, Newcastle, WY

New York Herald, New York City

Ogden Standard Examiner, Odgen, UT

Rawlins Daily Journal, Rawlins, WY

Rawlins Daily Times, Rawlins, WY

Rawlins Republican, Rawlins, WY

Rocky Mountain News, Denver, CO

Shenandoah Tribune, np

Silver State, Winnemucca, NV

Salt Lake Herald, Salt Lake City, UT

Salt Lake Telegram, Salt Lake City, UT

Salt Lake Tribune, Salt Lake City, UT

Standard, Buenos Aires, Argentina

Southern Utonian, Beaver, UT

St. Johns Herald, St Johns, AZ

Sun-Leader, Cheyenne, WY

Vernal Express, Vernal, UT

Worland Grit, Worland, WY

Wyoming Derrick, Casper, WY

Wyoming Press, Evanston, WY

Wyoming State Journal, Lander, WY

MISCELLANEOUS

Apache County Jail Records, Apache County Sheriff's Office, St. Johns Arizona.

Betenson, Lula Parker recorded interview, November 29, 1979, Circleville, Utah.

Coroner's Inquest on Nathan D. Champion and Nicholas Ray (courtesy Colin Taylor)

Crook, Jane, letter (descendant of Jim Marshall) to author, June 10, 1998.

Family Group Sheet, Church of Jesus Christ of Latter Day Saints.

Fremont County, Wyoming Jail Register ("Register for Sheriff 1884-1933"), Fremont County Sheriff's Office, Lander, Wyoming.

Frye, Elnora, letter to author, February 28, 1995.

Homan, Philip A, discussions on Three Creek, Idaho, 2013–2014.

Homan, Phillip A., "Queen of Diamonds: Kittie Wilkins, Horse Queen of Idaho, and the Wilkins Horse Company" (Wild West History Association, Boise, ID, July 10-13, 2013; Idaho Humanities Council Speakers' Bureau Presentation).

Homan, Philip A. "Powder Face: The Horse that Robbed the Winnemucca Bank" (Wild West History Association, July 10-13, 2013; Idaho Humanities Council Speakers' Bureau Presentation).

McCubbin, Robert, Collection, includes Pinkerton Records and Numerous Historical Photographs, privately held.

Quien Sabe Ranch, National Register of Historic Places, National Park Service, March 11, 1991.

Superintendent's Report 33, Annual Report of the Officers of the Detroit House of Correction to the Common Council of the City of Detroit for the year 1894, (Detroit Free Press Printing Co: 1895).

"Trial Deposition of *State of Idaho v. Henry Meeks, George Cassidy, John Doe, whose real name in unknown.*

Uinta County, Wyoming Jail Record, Uinta County Sheriff's Office, Evanston, Wyoming.

U.S. and U.K. Census Information.

Washington, Utah, Cemetery information.

MUSEUMS AND LIBRARIES

American Heritage Center, University of Wyoming.

    Larry Pointer Collection, Vic Button letter to Pearl Baker, dated November 21, 1970.

    Larry Pointer Collection, Vic Button letter to Pearl Baker, dated December 28, 1970.

    Larry Pointer Collection, Pearl Baker letter, dated August 23, 1973.

    Will Simpson Collection, Will Simpson letter to Harry Logue, February 4, 1937.

Brigham Young University Harold B. Lee Library, L. Tom Perry Special Collections, Provo, Utah.

Buffalo Bill Historical Center, Cody, Wyoming.

Carbon County Museum, Rawlins, Wyoming.

Church History and Art Museum, Salt Lake City, Utah.

Daughters of Utah Pioneers Museum, Beaver, Utah.

Daughters of Utah Pioneers Museum, Vernal, Utah.

Delta Historical Society, Delta, Colorado.

Fremont County Pioneer Museum, Lander, Wyoming.

Fort Bridger State Historical Site, Fort Bridger, Wyoming.

Hoofprints of the Past Museum, Kaycee, Wyoming.

Hot Springs County Museum, Thermopolis, Wyoming.

Idaho State Historical Society, Boise, Idaho.

Library of Congress, Washington D.C.

    Pinkerton Detective Agency Archives.

    Criminal File of George Parker, alias "Butch" Cassidy.

    Memo Dated July 29, 1902.

Little Snake River Museum, Savery, Wyoming.

Martin's Cove Visitor Center, Church of Jesus Christ of Latter Day Saints.

Meeteetse Museum, Meeteetse, Wyoming.

Museo Leleque, Argentina.

Museum of Northwest Colorado, Craig, Colorado.

    U.S. Postal File of Dan Parker

National Archives, Washington D.C. and Denver, Colorado.

    U.S. v. Brown and Parker.

    Pardon File of Dan Parker.

National Park Service, Department of Interior.

      National Register of Historic Places, Quien Sabe Ranch, March 11, 1991.

Nevada Historical Society, Reno, Nevada.

    George S. Nixon Files, George S. Nixon letter to F.C. Gentach.

    George S. Nixon letter to Mr. Fraser, dated February 21, 1901.

Old Idaho Penitentiary, Boise, ID.

Old Trail Town, Cody, WY.

Phillips County Museum, Salt Lake City, Utah.

Pioneer Memorial Museum, Salt Lake City, Utah.

Riverton Museum, Riverton, Wyoming.

Rock Springs Historical Museum, Rock Springs, Wyoming.

Sons of Utah Pioneers Library, Salt Lake City, Utah.

Sweetwater County Historical Museum, Green River, Wyoming.

Uintah County Regional History Center, Vernal, Utah.

University of Utah J. Willard Marriott Library, Special Collections, Salt Lake City, Utah.

    Will Simpson to Charles Kelly Letter, dated May 5, 1939.

Union Pacific Museum, Omaha, Nebraska.

Utah State Historical Society, Salt Lake City, Utah.

    Butch Cassidy Letter to Matilda Davis, Aug. 2, 1902, from Cholila, Argentina.

Utah State Archives, Salt Lake City, Utah.

    Letter from W. S. Seavy, Denver, Colorado to Governor Heber M. Wells of Utah, May 30, 1900.

Letter from Utah Governor Heber M. Wells to J.H. Ward, Sheriff , April 21, 1898.

Western Mining and Railroad Museum, Helper, Utah.

Wyoming State Archives, Cheyenne, Wyoming.

Case Number 144 and 166, *State of Wyoming v. George Cassidy and Albert Hainer*, Third District Court, Fremont County, Lander, Wyoming.

Justice of the Peace Record Book for Embar, Wyoming , February 1885 to July 1906.

Letter from Judge Jesse Knight to Governor Richards, September 28, 1895.

Letter from Judge Jesse Knight, Judge Third Judicial District of Wyoming to Governor Wm. A. Richards, September 28, 1895.

Letter from Governor Richards to Hon. J.L. Torrey, Washington D. C., March 16, 1896.

Letter from W. S. Seavy, Denver, Colorado, to Wyoming Governor Richards, May 30, 1900.

Letter from Harvey J. Shoe to Lola Homsher, July 25, 1954.

Dan Parker's Wyoming Penitentiary records.

Wyoming Territorial Prison State Historical Site, Laramie, Wyoming.

Index

316 ❖ Butch Cassidy, My Uncle

W. J. (BILL) BETENSON grew up hearing stories of his famous uncle Butch Cassidy and wanting to be a cowboy like his grandfather for whom he was named. Bill has a passion for Western Americana and family history. He enjoys traveling and researching places where Butch Cassidy spent time and "did time" over one hundred years ago. He especially appreciates the people he's met and the friendships he's made along the way.

Bill enjoys speaking and writing on Butch. He has published several articles and appeared in a number of TV documentaries on his great uncle.

With a degree in Mechanical Engineering from Brigham Young University, Bill has worked in the oil and gas industry for over twenty-five years, the last twenty in the natural gas pipeline industry.

Bill is married to the former Elizabeth Amott, and they have four children. He enjoys fly fishing and has fished from Alaska to Argentina.

Bill is always interested in additional information about Butch Cassidy. He can be reached at Bill.Betenson@gmail.com.

❖❖ NOTES ON THE PRODUCTION OF THE BOOK ❖❖

This book was originally simultaneously released in three editions.

A *limited edition* of only 960 copies was Smyth sewn
with headbands of green and gold, bound in Hunter Arrestox B,
embossed with gold satin foil, and wrapped in a full-color dustjacket.
Each copy is numbered and signed by the author.

A *deluxe boxed package* of only 40 copies was created.
The set included the text bound in green sonora goat Corona leather,
Smyth sewn, with marbled endpaper,
encased in a clamshell box custom-made by Bessenberg Bindery,
six color photographs, two documents, and other accoutrements.
Each copy is signed and numbered by the author.

The cover of *softcover trade edition* is ten-point stock,
printed in four colors, and coated with a scuff-free matte finish.

In 2014 and again in 2017, before reprinting only the *softcover trade
edition,* the text was updated slightly to include recently
discovered material.

The text of all editions is from the Adobe Garamond Family.
Display type is LHF Billhead 1890 and 1900,
with Fleurons and LHF Engraver's ornaments.

This book was originally printed by Thomson Shore on sixty-pound Joy
White an acid-free, recycled paper. The 2017 reprint edition is printed by
Versa Press on sixty-pound Versa Recycled White.